THE ROAD TO MAYERLING

Crown Prince Rudolph (in Hungarian hunting dress), aged thirty

THE ROAD TO MAYERLING

LIFE AND DEATH OF
CROWN PRINCE RUDOLPH
OF AUSTRIA

by

RICHARD BARKELEY

Frühgereift und zart und traurig . . .
HOFMANNSTHAL

(*Tender, wise beyond his years and sad*)

NEW YORK
ST MARTIN'S PRESS INC
1958

Copyright © Richard Barkeley 1958

MACMILLAN AND COMPANY LIMITED
London Bombay Calcutta Madras Melbourne

THE MACMILLAN COMPANY OF CANADA LIMITED
Toronto

ST MARTIN'S PRESS INC
New York

PRINTED IN GREAT BRITAIN

TO THE MEMORY OF MY FATHER
A LIFELONG LIBERAL
AND OF MY MOTHER
WHO FIRST SPOKE TO ME
OF MAYERLING

FOREWORD

THE mysterious circumstances of the death of the Austrian Crown Prince Rudolph on January 30th, 1889, at the hunting-lodge of Mayerling have never ceased to provoke speculation. Book, film and stage, and lately television, have dealt with his untimely end, but while concentrating attention on the manner and possible reason for his death, not sufficient consideration has been devoted to his life. Rudolph's death can only be satisfactorily explained if the whole of his life, and not only its last few weeks or months, is considered. The most talented Prince the House of Hapsburg had produced for centuries, a serious political thinker, a gifted writer — he did not die merely on account of an unhappy love affair, as has been so frequently asserted. His death was bound up with the fate of the Empire — the Empire which was not only the splendour of the Imperial Court and the gaiety of Vienna and Budapest, but also a heritage of increasingly intractable problems which he would have had to solve.

The usual conflict between monarch and heir was in this case enormously magnified by irreconcilable differences. Francis Joseph was as conservative as Rudolph was progressive, and while the Emperor was obstinately opposed to any change until it was forced upon him, the Crown Prince felt the urgent necessity of carrying out the most radical reforms while there was still time. He feared that the Empire would be destroyed while his father dissipated his energies with ridiculous details, studiously avoiding, or at least postponing, vital decisions.

Much has been written and still more said of Rudolph as a philanderer. Most of these reports are pure invention. There is no evidence to support them, and there are reasons which suggest that they were used to discredit his unorthodox political views. Admittedly he was not a model husband, but women were less important in his life than politics. In fact politics became too important. With rare prescience he divined that many of Austria's problems which could then be solved would be beyond solution by the time he became Emperor. Life grew unbearable when he saw how his father in his pedestrian way endangered the future of the Empire and of the Hapsburgs. The road to Mayerling started in the Imperial Palace in Vienna.

The problems which Rudolph felt so distressingly urgent had become even more so by the time his cousin, the Archduke Francis Ferdinand, was made heir apparent. He differed in almost every way from Rudolph, yet he too felt the inescapable necessity of a radically new orientation for Austria if the Empire was to survive. But Francis Joseph disregarded his ideas as he had disregarded Rudolph's. The Emperor's distrust of the heir increased when the latter married below his rank. In June 1914, at Sarajevo, Francis Ferdinand and his wife were killed by a young Serb student, a grim reminder of the many unsolved issues of the Empire.

The young Archduke Charles Francis Joseph was the new heir apparent, and succeeded the old Emperor in November 1916. The First World War, hastened, if not caused, by the tragedy of Sarajevo, had by then engulfed the world. The Emperor Charles tried unsuccessfully to end the fighting, but he was forced to resign after ruling for only two years. Had Austria's problems been solved in time, had Rudolph's ideas been realised, the Hapsburgs might have continued to rule. The loss of his throne was a deep grief to Charles, and he died at Funchal in Madeira, aged thirty-five, in 1922.

Three names are connected with the twilight of the Hapsburg dynasty : Mayerling, Sarajevo, Madeira. The present volume, *The Road to Mayerling*, tries to recreate the tragic life of Crown Prince Rudolph. The second volume, *Sarajevo and Madeira*, will seek to describe how Francis Ferdinand and Charles strove to save the Hapsburg Empire.

          *   *

         *

It is a great pleasure to thank all those whose help has made this book possible. First, my humble thanks to Her Majesty the Queen for Her gracious permission to quote at length from unprinted sources in the Royal Archives, Windsor. With sincere gratitude I record my appreciation for the help and advice unstintingly given by Her Majesty's Librarian, Sir Owen Morshead, K.C.B., K.C.V.O., and his Deputy, Mr. R. C. Mackworth-Young.

I am equally indebted to the Vienna Staatsarchiv, whose Director-General, Herr Hofrat Rath, supported by his able and amiable staff, not only rendered all possible assistance but permitted me to discuss with him the many difficulties which arose when working in the Archives.

My thanks are also due to Dr. Albert Hollaender, Assistant Librarian (Archivist), Guildhall Library, London, who put at my disposal the proofs of his article on Rudolph published in the *Festschrift für Heinrich Benedikt* (Vienna, 1957), and who went over the evidence again and again with me.

My sincere thanks are due to Monsignore Giusti of the Archivo Secreto del Vaticano for the information he gave me, and to His Highness the Duke of Hohenberg, elder son of the late Archduke Francis Ferdinand of Hapsburg-Este, for permission to use his father's papers. I owe much to the efficient services of the staffs of the Reading Room of the British Museum, the Record Office, London, the London Library, and the Oesterreichische National-bibliothek, Vienna.

For the photographs I am indebted to the Oesterreichische Nationalbibliothek, Porträtsammlung, Vienna.

I cannot thank individually the many friends and colleagues who have helped me by encouragement and advice. I would, however, like to mention Dr. J. J. McCann, Wokingham, for his help with craniological problems, Mr. E. M. Eppel of London University for his advice on psychological questions, Mr. Hitchcock, Director of the British Council, Vienna, who put me in touch with many people, and Mr. John W. M. Smith of the Joint Services School for Linguists for his translation of Count Lamsdorff's Journal. The responsibility for any mistakes or mistranslations is entirely my own.

Finally I must mention my wife and her help. Her devotion has made this book possible.

R. B.

CONTENTS

xi

NOTE ON SOURCES AND BOOKS

ONLY a fraction of Crown Prince Rudolph's papers have been collected in the Vienna Staatsarchiv. When these are quoted no source is given. Unfortunately the most important papers, those concerned with his death, have not been found. They were probably destroyed by the Emperor's orders. Among the microfilms of German documents in the Public Record Office, London, are some interesting dispatches dealing with the Crown Prince's death, but valuable as they may be, they cannot be a substitute for the missing papers.

There are only few serious biographies of Rudolph. The first full life to be published was by Oscar Baron Mitis, the late Director of the Staatsarchiv, Vienna (German edition 1928, English edition n.d., both out of print). This biography is a careful study, fully documented, but a little out of date, as new material has been published since 1928. There are two further full biographies: Werner Richter, *Kronprinz Rudolf von Oesterreich* (Zürich, 1941), a fair study based upon the sources, but frequently irritating because it does not give in detail the origin of its quotations, and an account by Count Carl Lonyay, a relative of Rudolph's widow by her second marriage, *The Tragedy of Mayerling* (London, 1950). Lonyay 'used' Mitis to the full, but vented his spite by basing his malicious remarks on 'personal information', which cannot be verified.

While there are many books dealing with Rudolph's

death, there are few serious enough to be considered. The first to be published was *Die volle Wahrheit über den Tod des Kronprinzen Rudolf von Oesterreich*, by Ernst von Planitz, Berlin, 1st edition, 1889. In spite of its 46 editions it is available in very few libraries. It was motivated by its author's wish to establish the truth, but his material was at that time naturally inadequate. Another serious attempt to explain Rudolph's death was published in Italian, *La tragedia di Mayerling*, by G. A. Borghese, Milano, 1925 (German translation, Heidelberg, 1927). It too suffers from lack of sources. A better documented study by Professor V. Bibl, *Kronprinz Rudolf, die Tragödie eines sinkenden Reiches*, Leipzig and Budapest, 1939, is not free from prejudice, particularly against Emperor Francis Joseph. The latest publication, *Das Mayerling Original* (Vienna, 1955), contains part of the Vienna police file concerning the Crown Prince's death. This had been lost for a long time but was found in 1955. It has been embellished by an anonymous writer with a distasteful highly coloured narrative which detracts from the, at best, limited value of the information.

The serious biographers of Emperor Francis Joseph and Empress Elisabeth base their accounts mainly on Mitis, except Count Corti, who found some additional sources which, however, do not add materially to the known facts.

The author must finally state that he is fully aware of the fragmentary character of the evidence on which he has based his study. It was, however, imperative to him to establish as many of the facts as the evidence permitted.

ILLUSTRATIONS

Prelude

THE South Station in Vienna is not far from the Imperial Palace, yet it seemed a long way to Count Hoyos, the Court Chamberlain, speeding in a horse-drawn carriage on the grey morning of January 30th, 1889. When at last he reached his destination he hurried to the Emperor's Adjutant and asked him to prepare his master for grave news. The Adjutant declined — only the Empress could undertake the task of preparing her husband for the shock of the sudden death of their only son, the Crown Prince Rudolph. The Empress Elisabeth was told the news by her Court Marshal. Rarely given to tears, she now wept bitterly, for she had loved her son deeply ; he had been one of the few people who had understood her strange ways. Only when the Emperor Francis Joseph was about to enter her room did she stem the flow of tears. For a short time husband and wife were alone together : when the Emperor left he looked years older, his face was ashen and his gait stumbling.

When Rudolph had died in his little hunting lodge at Mayerling in the Vienna Woods a young girl, Mary Vetsera, had been with him, and she too was dead. This fact could not be withheld from the parents. Count Hoyos had been at Mayerling as the Crown Prince's guest for a day or two, and on that fateful Wednesday morning had been fetched from his lodgings by the Prince's valet when he found that his master did not answer his call and had locked his bedroom door. The first impression was that the girl had poisoned the Crown Prince and herself, and this Hoyos had reported to the Emperor.

Count Taaffe, the Austrian Minister President, advised the Emperor to withhold the truth from the public, so that the Imperial prestige should not be gravely affected ; consequently a bulletin was issued that the Archduke Rudolph, Crown Prince of Austria-Hungary, had died of a sudden stroke. Nobody believed this official version ; everybody knew that the Prince had lately been nervy and distracted, but had otherwise appeared to be in good health. Moreover, Mayerling, though isolated, is not far from Vienna, and rumours nearer to the truth than the official report were already being whispered by the gossip-loving Viennese.

Not until the following day did the Emperor learn the full truth — that his son had shot and killed first his mistress, Mary Vetsera, and then himself. He had left a number of farewell letters, but not one for his father, so deeply hurt in his grief for his son and heir, lost in what seemed an entirely senseless way. None of the letters contained a coherent explanation of what appeared to be an insoluble enigma. A fit of madness seemed the only explanation and, after a post-mortem, it was claimed that some pathological changes of the skull bones pointed in that direction.

Only now did the Emperor decide that 'he owed his peoples the truth' — but it was already too late ; the first senseless report of a stroke had been a clumsy evasion and nothing was now believed which came from official sources, particularly since the simultaneous death of Mary Vetsera was still stubbornly kept secret. Wild rumours that Rudolph had been murdered by his mistress or by some unsuccessful and jealous rival for the favour of some woman were eagerly told and retold. Since the Austrian newspapers were prevented by censorship from printing anything but the official version, a run on foreign papers set in, soon in turn to be forbidden by the authorities. More than 4500 foreign newspapers were confiscated within a few days. They had contained fantastic and contradictory statements based on hearsay and surmise. The true reason for his early death Rudolph had taken with him.

To Francis Joseph, his son had been both his pride and hope, and, although he had not allowed him any political influence, he had loved him in his shy and impersonal way. He had had confidence that with the fullness of time, when experience would have taught his son to shed his idealism, he would have made a good successor. But the Empress, in her grief, was haunted by the thought that Rudolph's apparent insanity might have been brought into the family through her.

According to court etiquette Francis Joseph, but not Elisabeth, attended the funeral. It was a difficult duty for the Emperor, and only by a supreme effort could he maintain his usual dignity. But when, against all custom, he followed Rudolph's body into the Capuchin vaults, the Hapsburg burial place, he broke down. The Empress went there a few days later, quite alone and at night, unknown to any of her entourage. Alone she went down into the vaults, and the monk who had handed her a lighted torch waited at the top of the stairs. He felt cold shudders down his spine as he heard her calling 'Rudolph ! Rudolph !' Only the echo replied. After a time she came up and in a troubled voice told the trembling monk — 'He does not answer'.

Elisabeth found it very difficult to accept the fact that

Rudolph was really dead, and on one occasion even wanted to go to his bedroom to make sure that he was not there. While Francis Joseph had his daily routine to get through and kept to his usual pace in his deep sense of duty, the Empress found time to dwell more on the unfathomable. Weeks later, as she watched the first young green leaves unfolding in the March sun, she said to her younger daughter : 'How could Rudolph go and leave spring behind ?' How could Rudolph go and leave so much behind ?

CHAPTER ONE

Troubled Childhood

I

RUDOLPH FRANCIS CHARLES JOSEPH of Hapsburg-Lorraine, Crown Prince of the Austrian Empire, was born on August 21st, 1858, in the Hofburg, the Vienna Imperial Palace. His father, Emperor Francis Joseph I, had just celebrated his twenty-eighth birthday, and his mother, Elisabeth, the beautiful Princess of the Bavarian house of Wittelsbach, was not yet twenty-one. Rudolph was the third child of his parents — the first two had been girls. So one can understand that they were overjoyed at the birth of a son who would perpetuate the line of the Hapsburgs, rulers over the Austrian lands for six centuries. When congratulated on his son's birth Francis Joseph wept with emotion. He found the baby 'not exactly beautiful, but well built and strong'. The child, soon after his birth, was appointed a colonel in the Imperial Austrian army, but, in spite of his father's verdict, he proved to be at first rather weak and required a great deal of care, particularly since his mother was not permitted to feed him herself. To her great regret it was impossible not only because of Court etiquette, but also for medical reasons.

This failure increased her desire to nurse him through his difficult first months, but she met with the resistance of the Emperor's mother, the Archduchess Sophie, whose strict rule dominated the Court of Vienna. By her orders

Elisabeth was for some years prevented from taking part in her children's upbringing. This enforced rôle of observer was hard for her to bear, particularly as her first daughter had died when only two years old. She was convinced this had been due to the Court physician's ignorance, which was probably the case. The new-born baby's weak state must have driven her frantic with anxiety, yet her mother-in-law was adamant, and much as the Emperor was in love with his beautiful wife, especially now after she had borne him a son, obedience to his mother was second nature to him, and her pernicious influence permeated the life of the family as much as that of the state. Thus Elisabeth found no help from her husband in her struggle for her proper share in the care of her tiny son. Sophie, at least for the present, had her way, and it was a Baroness Welden, 'Wowo' as the baby soon affectionately called her, who nursed him expertly through his early troubles ; throughout his life Rudolph remained fond of her.

A few days after his birth, the most famous German stage of the day, the Vienna Burgtheater, celebrated the event by a gala performance in which the Muse of History was shown sitting among the ruins of the past. With a golden stylo she wrote on a marble slab the date of the child's birth, and whilst writing said, 'Here are engraved the year and the day, but the rest of the tablet shall remain empty, for I must have room for his great deeds which, I foresee, will be recorded here'.

II

The nations of Austria attached great hopes to the young child who was to be their future Emperor. The name of

Hapsburg had not yet lost its attraction for most of the peoples of the Empire, whatever their language, and they expected the young Prince to make good the short-comings of his father, who had lost much of their good-will by the mistakes made in the ten years since his accession.

The Emperor, despite his youth and regardless of earlier promises, had not stopped the rot which had set in under his predecessors. Most of his early advisers had been ill chosen, and he had ruled as an autocrat. Economic con-ditions had deteriorated, foreign policy had been inept and Austria's international prestige was extremely low. His subjects were fully aware of this ; many, particularly in the Italian-speaking provinces, chafed under Austria's domina-tion. His ambitious mother, the Archduchess Sophie, directed his political attitude just as she dominated his family life, and her narrow, bigoted clericalism had in-fluenced the malleable youth in his choice of advisers. Nearly all were men entirely unaware of the strength of the forces which they tried to destroy. The revolutions of 1848–49, which had shaken the very foundations of the Empire more than those of any other country, had been suppressed with much bloodshed and — in Hungary — with Russian help. It had been Francis Joseph's task, while still hardly more than a boy, to establish internal peace after the revolutions, but he had meekly submitted to counsellors who, by their cruelty, particularly towards Hungary, had prevented any healing of wounds. By allowing these men free rein to vent their spirit of vindictiveness, and by his inability to show clemency, he had forfeited the hopes aroused by his succession. Dis-satisfaction and disloyalty continued to smoulder beneath the surface, ready to flare into open revolt at the first opportunity. Francis Joseph, before he had reached the age of twenty, had allowed more death warrants to be carried out in his name than probably any other nineteenth-century ruler of a civilised country throughout his life. Even the Tsar, who had helped to suppress the Hungarian revolution, had been shocked at such severity.

Neither the excitable Viennese nor his other subjects had forgotten the Emperor's earlier shortcomings and they were not yet reconciled to his rule. Thus they all fervently wished that the little boy, now reared under such difficulties, would one day re-establish the bonds of affection broken by his father's inexperienced stubbornness. They hoped that Rudolph would one day take over the heritage of the Empress Maria Theresa and her son Joseph II, who had a century or so earlier recreated popular affection for the Hapsburgs by their understanding of their peoples' needs.

When Francis Joseph had first brought the young Elisabeth as his bride to Vienna, her extraordinary beauty had captivated her new subjects' imagination and they had been prepared to forgive her husband much of the past. But she was extremely shy and reserved. The Viennese not unnaturally wished for opportunities of seeing their Empress, but she refused to appear frequently in public. Although they were well acquainted with her domestic difficulties and knew very well how her mother-in-law — 'evil Sophie' as they called her in their respectless way — turned the young wife's joys into gall and wormwood, they did not forgive this reticence. Now the Crown Prince was said to resemble his beautiful mother, and a new wave of affection for her, too, swept the city.

Empress Elisabeth

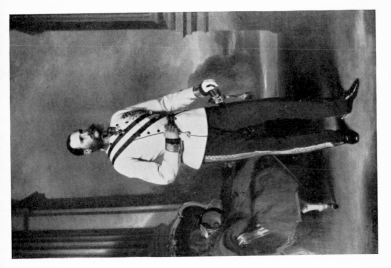

Emperor Francis Joseph

III

Francis Joseph was not immediately afforded much time to devote to his son. An extremely clumsy foreign policy had landed Austria in a war which she had to fight without an ally, with an incompetent Commander-in-Chief, and without any popular enthusiasm. The King of Sardinia, determined to unify Italy, wanted to incorporate the Italian-speaking provinces of the Austrian Empire, particularly Lombardy, and Napoleon III, Emperor of the French, gave him active support. The Austrian Commander-in-Chief, recommended by the Archduchess Sophie, had shown a complete lack of ability, and his army had been defeated. Now Francis Joseph, for the first and last time in his life, himself took command of his forces. He had not been trained for such a task and his presence in the field perplexed the military commanders. Too unimaginative to realise the consequences of the many death warrants he had signed in earlier years, now seeing before his eyes the dead and dying on the battlefield was a grave shock to him, and he sought to end the war sooner than the military situation required. He had to cede Lombardy, which rankled deeply. To have lost a flourishing, if rebellious, province, and to be defeated by an upstart, a scoundrel, as the Hapsburg considered the Bonaparte to be, caused the young Emperor to survey carefully the situation into which his policy had landed him. It brought home to him the fact that he had not been sufficiently trained for his office, and consequently he laid down rules for his son's education which even now, nearly a century later, seem sound and reasonable. Rudolph was to be well prepared for his task — better than his father had been.

To draw up a plan for the education of the Crown Prince of the multilingual Hapsburg Empire was no easy task. Apart from the necessity of mastering a number of indigenous languages he had to learn Latin, French and English. Other subjects, too, presented their difficulties : history had to be shown against a multinational background, and most important was the question of how much time was to be allotted to religious teaching, and how much it was to be allowed to overshadow the rest of the curriculum. Francis Joseph was a devout Catholic and had, moreover, by the Concordat of 1855 with the Holy See, handed over to the control of the Church all education in Austria. Yet in respect of his son's education he showed himself not so obedient to those principles which he considered so important for his peoples' spiritual welfare. 'He must not become a free-thinker, but he should be well acquainted with all the conditions and requirements of the modern times', a memorandum of the Emperor had stated.

IV

By the end of 1859, when in his second year, Rudolph already showed signs of a strong will ; if a wish was not immediately fulfilled only his mother or 'Wowo' could quieten him. Once, during a meal when he had no appetite, he was coaxed to eat by his uncle the Archduke Charles Ludwig. The boy very seriously asked to be left alone and told his uncle to go away. This the man took as an order from a higher ranking Archduke, and obeyed. The Emperor was overjoyed at any such sign of what he considered to be his son's individuality.

At the age of four Rudolph went with his father to

inspect the Military Academy at Wiener Neustadt, near Vienna. When the students gave the customary three cheers for the Emperor the little boy also waved his hat and shouted 'hurrah' — and Francis Joseph nearly cried with emotion and was for several minutes unable to speak. But the boy's ideal was his mother, she was so beautiful. Whenever he saw her in her ball dress he wanted so much to stay with her.

Rudolph's health caused much anxiety to his parents. In December 1863 he had typhoid fever, and again in the summer of 1864 he fell from a considerable height when climbing a tree and concussion was diagnosed. For months he remained sick, and after his recovery made full use of this accident to get out of any unpleasant task by pretending to have a headache.

In spite of his poor health he very early — when he was hardly four— showed sufficient intelligence to be given lessons in religious knowledge. His first tutor was one of the Court chaplains. Neither he, nor the Head Chaplain, who took over the lessons a few months later, could inspire in their pupil much enthusiasm for the subject.

The choice of his first governor was not a happy one. Count Gondrecourt took over the supervision of the Crown Prince's education when the boy was six. He was the Archduchess Sophie's protégé and she considered his apparent piety more important than his qualities as a governor. He lacked entirely any understanding for a child who was then described as being 'physically and spiritually more developed than children of his age, but very highly strung'.[1] He was a typical Colonel Chinstrap, and his methods might have been suitable for toughening a country yokel recruit, but were criminal for an overbred,

sensitive, precocious and excitable child. Yet Gondrecourt knew how to curry favour with bigoted women.
Obviously for the Archduchess Sophie's benefit he stated
in a memorandum: 'The highest duty of the governor is
to apply every means to secure that his disciple will never
waver in his religious belief'.[2]

Not only did he fail to achieve this aim of firmly establishing Rudolph's religious convictions, but he actually did
great and permanent harm to the child's personality. His
usual drill-ground methods were even intensified as he set
to work to 'educate' the supersensitive Prince. On one
occasion the Emperor, who always rose very early, looked
out into the courtyard one morning before settling down
to work. He had heard words of command, and, to his
painful surprise, discovered that his young son was being
drilled in the deep snow by lantern light.

It is not surprising that the delicate boy could not stand
such methods. In May 1865 he became seriously ill;
although the trouble was probably diphtheria the diagnosis
was not unanimous. People at the Court who did not
belong to the Archduchess Sophie's party maintained that
Gondrecourt's crude methods of strengthening the Crown
Prince's weak constitution were responsible. Elisabeth
from the beginning had had a poor opinion of his capability
as governor. She disliked his unimaginative approach and
like others saw in it the reason why Rudolph did not grow
stronger, but more and more nervous. Matters came to a
head when she learned a little later that the Count had
taken the boy to the Lainzer Tiergarten, a game park near
Vienna, had pushed him in, shouted 'A wild boar is coming', and himself slipped out leaving the frightened child
alone. Elisabeth complained to her husband, but Francis
Joseph was not yet certain that the governor, whom his

mother had so warmly recommended, was altogether
unsuitable, or had merely gone too far on this occasion.
Although the loss of the war in 1859 had shaken the
Emperor's faith in the wisdom of his mother's advice, he
was not yet prepared to disregard it entirely. But Elisabeth, fighting for her son's well-being, remained firm.
'Either Gondrecourt goes or I go', she told her husband,
and when he still wavered lest he should offend his mother,
she showed her determination in a letter: 'I wish to reserve
for myself unlimited authority in everything concerning
the children, the choice of their entourage, the place of
their residence, the complete direction of their education,
in one word, all this has to be decided by me alone until
the children become of age'.[3]

Only now, realising how determined his wife was in
this matter, did the Emperor give way and dismiss Gondrecourt. Rudolph was seven when the new governor,
Latour von Thurmberg, was appointed. Although he too
had been an officer in the Austrian army, he had also been
a civil administrator. He was — within the limits of his
time — an instinctive psychologist, an example of the best
type of Imperial servant which nineteenth-century Austria
had produced. Highly cultured, well read and with artistic
discernment, he was entirely devoted to Rudolph and
soon the boy was equally devoted to him. Between the
two developed a relationship more like that between two
friends than between master and pupil, a relationship
which lasted far beyond the time of stewardship.

Latour remained throughout his time of office on good
terms with both parents, and the mother, aware that her
son was now in good hands, made little use of the authority
over her children's education achieved by her ultimatum.
Francis Joseph, whatever the demands of his office, always

found the time needed to follow his son's education ; he conscientiously read all progress reports submitted by Latour and answered all his frequent memoranda promptly. He did not interfere in any way and only gave a decision when one was requested, but at all times Latour could be assured that the Emperor supported him. This was essential, as the various factions at the Court repeatedly tried to influence the Crown Prince's education. The Archduchess Sophie particularly took a long time to accept the new governor, if indeed she ever accepted him fully. As late as December 15th, 1868, Latour wrote to Francis Joseph : 'I go my straight way without regard for anyone. Thereby one does not become popular, but it is the only means of keeping one's independence at the Court.'

On another occasion he pointed in his criticism directly to female influences, stating in his memorandum that women had the peculiarity of expecting too much of any man who had succeeded in gaining their confidence. The Emperor must have been suffering, too, from attempts at interference, for although usually sparing in his comments, he noted in the margin, 'Quite right'.

V

Latour had not been in charge for a year when, in the summer of 1866, the war between Austria and Prussia was fought. Not only were Francis Joseph's hopes for the maintenance of autocratic government among the fatal casualties of the battle of Sadowa, but also the centuries-old Hapsburg dream of hegemony in Germany. Another fateful consequence was the new settlement between the Austrian and the Hungarian halves of the Empire, which contributed materially to its later difficulties and subsequent dissolution. The Emperor and Empress had had to remain in Vienna on account of the war, but Rudolph was in Ischl at the time, in the little alpine summer resort where his father loved to stay.

After hostilities had broken out and the Austrian troops had withdrawn, the boy wrote to his father: 'I am very sad that we had to withdraw, but I believe things will improve again. . . .' Two days later, after Austria had lost the decisive battle of Sadowa, Archduchess Sophie told Rudolph: 'A few words I am sending you, my beloved child, to tell you that your dear poor Papa is, thank God, at least physically well and that dear Mama remains at his side like his good angel'.[4] Rudolph had learned the news independently and he wrote: 'I am very sad that we have suffered such a heavy blow. I shall pray tonight that with the help of God we reconquer what we have lost.' A special prayer had been written which the Crown Prince had to learn by heart and which he had to say twice a day. It ran: 'Almighty God, Highest Lord of Heaven and earth, I implore Thee humbly, withdraw not Thy help from my fatherland Austria in this hour of danger; bless the arms of her warriors so that they will not be defeated in this fight for justice and honour, but by Thy grace obtain victory. . . .'

On a precocious child such events, brought near by his own and his parents' personal experiences, must have made a strong, even an indelible impression. He must have been aware that the journey to Budapest with his mother and sister so soon after the battle of Sadowa was an escape from the fast-approaching Prussian troops. The outcome of this war had such far-reaching effects for the Austrian Empire that it moved the centre of Austrian interest from West to East, and the boy's tutors could not have avoided referring to the new conditions in their lessons. Rudolph must also have seen for himself the effect of the reduced way of living in the Imperial household. A heavy indemnity had to be paid to Prussia, and among other economies made necessary by the reduction by 25 per cent in the allowances paid to the Imperial family, his mother, so fond of horses and of riding, had had to reduce her stock. The defeat of Austria made possible the foundation of the German Empire under Prussian leadership, and throughout his life the Crown Prince remained cool if not suspicious towards it. He rarely spoke of Germany but continued to refer to Prussia instead, and his strong dislike of its Emperors William I and William II was doubtlessly based on the events of 1866 which he had himself witnessed.

VI

Rudolph's education was from the start comprehensive. Altogether nearly fifty people took part and one marvels at the amount of knowledge which the boy, frequently ill, must have absorbed. The tutors were the first experts in their fields. Latour supervised their work very carefully, sending innumerable memoranda with his reports to the Emperor. Rudolph was extremely ambitious and few subjects caused him any difficulty. Fortunately he was still unaware of the complications which his education raised in a multilingual empire. Should it centre around German traditions, or should the Hungarian element be stressed? How far should the part played by the Slav nations then awakening to national consciousness be emphasised? Rudolph would have to learn at least some of the dozen languages in the dual monarchy ; in 1867 his father had been crowned King of Hungary, and Hungarian newspapers frequently demanded that this should be acknowledged in the Crown Prince's education. Fortunately, he possessed a marked gift in this direction, which he shared with his mother. She was as completely at ease with the Hungarian tongue as she was with her native German, and mother and son soon wrote their letters to each other in Hungarian. The boy also early acquired a fluency in Czech which enabled him later to address gatherings in that language with ease, and which greatly endeared him to the Czechs. Apart from the study of the languages, there were the problems inherent in the teaching of history, often contradictory, of the many nations which made up the Empire. Each tutor had to be a member of the nation whose language or history he taught, but too fervid nationalists were excluded, to prevent too biased an interpretation.

The languages and histories of the various nations created in the boy's mind a broad picture of a supra-national Empire, and he soon became conscious of his allegiance to a family of nations. As a boy he wrote patriotic poems filled with a puerile admiration for the Empire, but they do not yet show anything of the remarkable gift for self-expression which he possessed as a youth and a man. Francis Joseph, whose command of his mother tongue never exceeded that of a lower grade civil servant, could be well satisfied with his son's education in this respect. Well aware of his own shortcomings, he had stressed the importance of self-expression, and this was achieved, perhaps to a greater degree than he would have liked, had he known what revolutionary thoughts his son would soon be writing eloquently.

Rudolph learned easily and the acquisition of knowledge gave him great satisfaction. At nine years of age he was deeply hurt when one of his tutors told him that he could do better, and at the same time when Latour told the boy that his report was not good enough to be rewarded by permission to go shooting he replied : 'I am not learning for the sake of the reward. I am learning because it is my duty.' [5] Examinations were held after a course of study in a particular subject, and were always a special occasion. The Emperor and many courtiers were present while experts in the subject examined. Almost invariably Rudolph's knowledge was sound and creditable for any boy of his age ; his rank was never allowed to excuse poor performance. He was always very proud of these achievements and immediately told his grandmother of his successes so that she might praise him.

Yet in one direction the new educational régime was not such an unqualified success. The number of subjects was greater than could properly be demanded of any boy of Rudolph's age. Thus too much time had to be devoted to the acquisition of knowledge as such and not enough to the general development of his character. Latour was not blind to this. He noted, when the boy was ten, a certain tendency to insincerity and a readiness to forget unpleasant things too quickly. The boy also tried to avoid difficulties or to find the easiest way round those which had to be faced. Still more disturbing, Latour not infrequently caught him lying in order to gain praise. On one occasion he had been to a ballet performance with his governor, and told his grandmother later, to the old lady's delight but to his mentor's dismay, that he had been unable to look at the stage because the ladies on it had not been suitably dressed. This the Archduchess Sophie took to be a sign of inborn decency and piety, but Latour as the sign of a scheming character, as the boy had been enraptured with the performance.

According to his own statement, Latour thought it necessary to admonish the boy sharply whenever he showed these tendencies, and was gratified to find that they gradually disappeared. But was this really the case? Latour was doubtless the best man available for his office, but knowledge of psychology was limited in his day. We are left asking ourselves whether his methods of suppressing undesirable traits by punishment did not actually strengthen them, even though the boy would be careful to keep them below the surface.

When the Crown Prince reached the age of ten he was considered old enough to go to Confession for the first time, in accordance with the rules of the Catholic Church. This proved to be a terrifying experience for him. Latour wrote about it to the Emperor, 'With tears in his eyes because of the examination of conscience before the Confession he asked me to help him, since he was afraid he might overlook a sin'. The prayer which particularly excited him was taken from the general Prayer Book: 'O my God, I have provoked Thy vengeance, I am not worthy of being called Thy child any longer, I have deserved to be cast off for ever'. Latour continued: 'His sins and the words as he takes them are not in proper relationship — my heart was heavy, but I thought that I was not permitted any remark which might have changed the sense of those words, since he might in this case take the matter too easily, as in spite of his equally rich gifts of intelligence and a noble heart, a certain carelessness cannot be denied'.

The Court Chaplain, so the governor goes on, had promised to substitute another prayer, since 'the Crown

Prince takes everything so literally that the expressions are too pungent'.

But Latour was also worried by another matter. He had had to observe that Rudolph 'when tired does not say his evening prayers as he should ; he does not speak loudly enough, he, as it were, swallows his words, in short it seems that he wants to get it over'. The governor had so far not been strict in this matter 'as it might cause the Prince to consider praying as something distasteful'. He suggested that the father should talk to his son, 'but I request in all humility not to do so with severity, but with kindness . . . and in no circumstances in front of the Archduchess Gisela', Rudolph's elder sister.

Of Latour's numerous reports to the Emperor, none is so important. It is possible that much of Rudolph's later lack of religious feeling can be traced to the kind of religious education he was forced to endure and which was conspicuous by the entire absence of any psychological insight. Just as revealing is the reference that the boy should be admonished with kindness and not severity. If his governor thought it necessary to remind the father of this, it suggests that he had no great confidence in the Emperor's approach to his sensitive son.

Elisabeth had only a few years previously done everything within her power to secure the right to determine her son's education, but in 1868, when her youngest daughter Valerie was born, she was so much concerned with the care of the baby that no time remained to think of her son. Thus the governor had to take the place of both parents.

In many ways at this time Rudolph showed that he was much in need of a sense of security. One instance was pointed out by Latour in his letter — even a precocious child, secure in his parents' love, would not have felt the unfortunate words of the prayer to be such a threat as the Crown Prince had done. Moreover, Gondrecourt had already gravely disturbed the boy's emotional balance. It is not surprising that Rudolph early showed a morbid turn of mind.

Already at the age of six he learned that his father had had a sister who had died in childhood, and he had given his grandmother no peace until she had satisfied his curiosity by telling him all about it. He had listened attentively and then repeated, 'Thus she said the dear word "Mama" and then she died'.[6] Later, at the age of ten, walking with a member of his entourage, Count Palffy, in that part of the grounds of the Imperial Palace of Schönbrunn open to the public, they heard cries for help. On investigation they found a young man who had attempted suicide by drinking caustic soda solution. Although medical help was available almost immediately, it came too late. For days the Crown Prince discussed the incident, asking innumerable questions, how unhappy somebody must be before committing suicide, whether many people did it, what would happen after death ?

Children may frequently be morbid, but they rarely persist. That Rudolph was pondering so much on death, admittedly not all the time — a child has not sufficient power of concentration for that — suggests a great unhappiness at times which he did not even disclose to Latour. It may have had repercussions in his later life and one or the other trend may become intelligible when we bear in mind that there must have been early deep reasons for unhappiness.

They did not disturb his intellectual development. His thirst after knowledge seemed insatiable, although his tutors sometimes complained of a certain superficiality ; yet many children of high intelligence and quick perception — two undeniable gifts which the Crown Prince showed at an early age — can be at times considered superficial. Moreover, we may justifiably doubt the psychological training of most of his tutors who, as university teachers and civil servants, were not used to teaching children, and they may well have demanded more concentration than could be expected in a boy of his age ; they might have been misled by his highly developed intelligence. He early showed the true criteria of the enquiring mind. When for the first time he was told of the Revolutions of 1848–49 he questioned one of the witnesses of the events, his grandmother, and was not satisfied until she had told him all she knew about them.

Like both his parents he was exceedingly happy when he could be in the open air. At the age of six or seven his father had taken him on his first shooting excursions. Although he had learned to use a rifle, killing animals was neither then nor for some years later his main concern ; even at an early age observing nature was more important. While on the one hand he noted the habits of birds with infinite patience, yet he frequently killed small ones, particularly bullfinches, and had them cooked for his mid-morning lunch. He also liked to make drawings of himself as a keen hunter with shot birds, using coloured pencils freely to make the blood as realistic as possible.

Rudolph was a likeable child and, as with most children, very happy at times and very unhappy at others. His parents had rarely time to play or to talk with him. A sense of security, so important in a child's life, was provided only by his governor Latour, who must have been hampered in many ways by his pupil's rank. The boy may not have been conscious of anything lacking but nevertheless developed an emotional instability which would have disturbed a modern psychologist.

REFERENCES

1. Mitis, *Kronprinz Rudolph*, p. 1.
2. Mitis, *op. cit.* p. 12.
3. Egon Caesar, Conte Corti, Elisabeth '*Die seltsame Frau*' (Salzburg and Leipzig, 1935), p. 32.
4. Staatsarchiv, Vienna, and Corti, *Elisabeth*, p. 151.
5. Egon Caesar, Conte Corti, *Mensch und Herrscher* (*Franz Josef*, Vol. II) (Graz-Wien-Köln, 1954), p. 385.
6. Corti, *Franz Josef*, Vol. II, p. 325.

CHAPTER TWO

Turbulent Youth

I

The Emperor Francis Joseph may have been narrow-minded in many ways, but no prejudices of a political or religious nature were allowed to limit the breadth of his son's education. The tutors were chosen exclusively on the basis of their ability and were the best brains which Austria could produce. It was that short period of Austria's history when liberalism was the dominant force in the country. Brief as the period was, while it lasted all intellectuals were convinced that it would go on for ever. Reason and progress were the slogans of the day.

It was this spirit of the time which pervaded Rudolph's education. And just as the liberal intellectuals refused to take into account those political realities which in time would end the liberal interlude, so in the Crown Prince's education it was overlooked that knowledge by itself would not be enough, particularly when education was not to be continued beyond the age of eighteen, and was not to lead to a specialised training. In a relatively short time he was crammed with an enormous amount of knowledge, but little was done to help him to assimilate it. He had as a youth thirty to thirty-six hours of lessons a week to which was added the time for his riding, fencing and dancing instruction, military exercises, walks, besides

Rudolph
aged three

Rudolph
aged sixteen

his time for reading and homework. Yet he did well in nearly all his work, as his intelligence could cope easily with the supply of knowledge. He found history fascinating, also natural sciences, and he was an omnivorous reader. His facility for expressing himself in writing showed itself early ; already at the ages of fourteen and fifteen he filled page after page with his ideas, ideas which would have shocked his pious father and probably even his less conventional mother, had they been allowed to read them. Only Latour, who had succeeded in gaining the boy's unbounded confidence, was from time to time permitted a glance into Rudolph's strange world.

In December 1872, when a little over fourteen years old, he wrote : 'I am also convinced that mankind would have advanced much further without the terrible days of the Middle Ages. . . . The clergy, always hand in glove with the proud aristocracy, used their influence over the people and did not permit the development of any free ideas ; the Church chose ways dangerous for itself, for eventually the people would realise how they were treated and recognise the sacrilege of those indulgences and other means which the clergy had used to enrich themselves. . . .' But this was only the beginning of his revolutionary exuberance.

A year later, during the Christmas holidays of 1873, he dedicated to Latour a small notebook which he called 'Various Thoughts'. It contained his creed in such a frank manner that we can gauge how strong the bonds of confidence must have been between master and pupil. In this he stated : 'Thoughts of all kinds roam through my head ; all seems confused, all day long my brain boils and toils . . . all thoughts contradicting, sometimes serene and merry, sometimes raven black, crowded with frenzy, they struggle with one another and slowly truth develops from them. I always ponder : what will be the end ?

'Are we higher spirits, are we beasts ? Beasts, that is what we are. But do we descend from the apes, or have men always existed side by side with the apes as a special species of two-handed beings ?

'Often I ask myself : Are you already a madman or will you become one ? I realise that I shall never know all that I want to know, but one thing is certain : one must always strive, always endeavour to achieve more and always more, not titles and dignities nor riches. . . . No, I want knowledge.

'Love is certainly the most beautiful experience in the life of all organic beings ; it is an emotion which man still possesses, pure as in an animal ; when in love he is still at one with nature. . . .

'Kings and noblemen made laws to suit themselves, and among those many terrible devices of the Middle Ages was one according to which man could only marry within his own estate . . . so that man, the lord of creation could not, as every animal does, follow his heart, he had to submit to laws; the beast in the forest is freer. . . . In our own time when after the long dark night the bright sun of freedom and knowledge has risen and an entirely new epoch lies before our eyes, how can we keep up such conditions ? . . . The scion of the highest house will be able to follow his heart as a commoner or an animal. . . .

'The priests did most harm because they understood well how to make the people base and submissive by superstition and exaggerated piety, so that they, as well as the nobility, had an easy game, and could do with the poor people as they liked. . . .

'During the French Revolution the king, the nobility

and the clergy were punished for their own iniquities and for those of their forebears. The punishment was rough and bloody, but it was a necessary and salutary catastrophe.

'The government has changed and is a step nearer to the republic. Monarchy has lost its old power and clings to the trust and love of the people. . . . Monarchy is now a mighty ruin which may remain from today till tomorrow, but which will ultimately tumble. It has stood for centuries and as long as the people could be led blindly it was good, but now its task is over, all people are free and the next storm will bring the ruin tumbling down. . . .'

These few examples of the boy's thoughts show how much he differed from his conscientious, well meaning, but pedestrian father, who remained throughout his life bound by the tenets of the Catholic Church. Nor could there have been any influence on his mother's side to bring out such revolutionary outbursts. The Empress Elisabeth was constantly at war with that narrow Spanish etiquette which she found so stifling in the Austrian Court, but her letters show nothing of her son's rebelliousness nor of his gift of expression. Her only way of showing her opposition was by travelling and by her escape into the arts, while she remained basically a dutiful Catholic. Nor can we assume that the tutors, although certainly doing their utmost to develop the boy's intellect and natural gifts, would have gone so far in their time-bound praise of evolution and progress as to encourage revolutionary thinking. Much of it must be ascribed to the craving for revolt ever present in fermenting youth, but Rudolph certainly showed more than the usual amount of rebellious spirit. Some he may have inherited from earlier Hapsburgs, who had produced such rebels as Don Carlos and Joseph II.

In May 1872 his grandmother, the Archduchess Sophie, died. Here was another opportunity for the boy to probe into the secret of death which so fascinated him. Again and again he had to be told all details — how his mother, forgetting old feuds and her mother-in-law's persistent hostility, spent ten hours at the old lady's death-bed. The Crown Prince's uncanny preoccupation with the mystery of death returned to the surface again when in the summer of that year he sat beside Countess Festitics, his mother's new lady-in-waiting, while crossing the Attersee, that lovely deep alpine lake in Upper Austria. The serious expression on the lady's face intrigued the boy and he asked her to tell him her thoughts. Probably overwhelmed by the grandeur of the scene she told him that she had been thinking that a little boat was their only protection and that they were gliding over death. 'Gliding over death', the fourteen-year-old boy repeated, and then continued, 'how awe-inspiring that sounds. It makes one's blood run cold.' [1]

II

A year later the Crown Prince had to perform his first representative duties. He unveiled a memorial to the Empress Maria Theresa in Carinthia in July 1873 and his speech, which he composed himself, was justly praised. When, in the same year, the old Emperor William I of Germany visited Vienna, Rudolph received the victor of Sadowa at his father's side with accomplished grace. In the German Emperor's suite was Prince William of Prussia, later the Kaiser, a few months Rudolph's junior. Although it suited the political concepts of the leading statesmen to present the two young princes to the world as good friends, neither on this nor on later occasions did they really like one another, and in time definite enmity arose between them. Although Rudolph was naturally very polite to his father's guests, he had not forgotten 1866 and was still not willing to forget. He may have remembered the childish but well-meant poems which he had written after Austria's defeat in which he prophesied revenge.

Dressed in Russian uniform Rudolph was also present at the reception of Tsar Alexander II in Vienna. We do not know how far he enjoyed these ceremonies, but they must have been impressive for a boy of fifteen, in spite of his dislike of the policy which they represented.

The early 'seventies were important years in the development of Austria ; the relationship between the state and the Catholic Church had to be newly defined in the light of the now predominant liberal spirit. Education and public life in general were still governed by Francis Joseph's Concordat with the Holy See of 1855, considered by many to be a stranglehold, particularly in the field of education. The Emperor, though a devout Catholic, stood by the decisions of the new Austrian parliament to reduce Church influence both over schools and universities, and over public life in general. Marriage laws were reformed by the recognition of civil wedding ceremonies in certain cases, and citizens were given the freedom of choosing whether or not they wished to belong to a religious persuasion. It is, however, doubtful whether parliament in passing these reforms truly reflected public opinion ; the franchise was extremely limited, only those people being represented who paid more than a certain minimum in direct taxation. Liberalism was probably weaker than Liberals realised. But the sensitive boy had been steeped in this atmosphere, and unlike many Liberals who subsequently changed their allegiance, he stuck to his early convictions, which he expounded with vehemence throughout his brief life.

The mood of such early writings as 'Various Thoughts' was not just the passing phase of a boy in his puberty ; Rudolph's notebooks of 1875 and 1876 are full of ideas which show how he had been seized by the ideals of progress and enlightenment. In many ways he showed a better understanding of social questions than most contemporary Liberal politicians, nearly all of whom professed a liberalism which did not take into consideration important social problems brought about by the swift economic change. Growing industrialisation created great hardships : many small master craftsmen were uprooted and pauperised and wages paid to the workers were low. No social legislation of any kind had yet been passed to ease the severity caused by the transition from the old economy to the new. In the first stages of industrialisation a large part of the profits had to be used for the provision of new and improved machinery, yet ample profits remained to enable many industrialists to lead a life of luxury, and most Liberals considered this to be a natural state of affairs. The young Crown Prince never equated liberalism with a cheap 'enrichissez-vous'. His social conscience was too well developed to accept without question the tenets of economic liberalism, as is shown by the following extracts from his notebooks :

'Uplifting of the soul and progress will be difficult where economic inequality is so marked, that the many poor see in the few rich their enemies and the wasters of public property, to the extent that hatred for them and the struggle for their own survival becomes demoralising. Therefore we should, ideally, consider more or less equal wealth and prosperity a source of moral development. . . .

'Striving after perfection, after steadily increasing spiritual development, is a law of nature. . . .

'New ideas and principles emerged from the many corpses of the guillotines, and the nations of Europe arose from the period of revolutions and struggles for liberation rejuvenated, strengthened, ennobled and elevated. . . .

'Only during the upheavals of the last hundred years has man really become human. . . .

'There will always be wars until every race and nation has finished developing, until all unite and mankind has become one great family in which each strives and fights for a higher spiritual life for all. . . .'

He continued to progress in his studies, although the number of subjects increased year by year. Francis Joseph was well pleased with his son ; reports from all his tutors point out the great progress he was making. His German tutor noted, for instance, 'great elasticity of the mind, richness and vivacity of thought and perception, a command of the language . . . [and] a straightforward, expert style'.[2] But the Emperor would have been less pleased to know of the ideas to which Rudolph gave expression. It seems that in him the anti-clerical views of his great-great-uncle, the Emperor Joseph II, had been resuscitated ; the widespread hope that Rudolph might resemble that most beloved and unforgotten of his forebears had been well founded. This heritage, coupled with the handsomeness and sensitiveness inherited from his mother, made the Crown Prince the last and one of the finest flowers of the old Hapsburg tree, in spite of the fact that too much inbreeding had resulted in a supersensitivity.

There is little to show that the Crown Prince saw in

Francis Joseph anything but the Emperor. His filial affection was reserved for his mother — and Latour. Probably this was due to an aloofness in his father, who, in his early years, could unbend only towards his mother and his wife. As we have seen, he had not the gift of treating his son as a child ; his letters to him remain extremely formal and stilted. He saw him rarely, and they met in an informal atmosphere only when they went hunting together and at Christmas-time. When Francis Joseph dealt with such subjects as riding and marksmanship a slightly warmer tone crept in, but even then he always talked down to his son.

Thus Rudolph remained in many ways a stranger to his father. Even with his tutors he was not as frank as he was with Latour. Not before he was in his later teens did he show confidence in some of them, such as the biologist Brehm and the economist Menger. Thus his tutors' reports refer almost entirely to the progress made in their subjects, so that their opinions do not help us very much when we wish to ascertain how this character was developing. There is hardly a boy of sixteen or seventeen of whom one could not say that he was superficial or lacked methodical thinking or that his judgements were coloured by his overwhelming sentiments, as some of the tutors reported of Rudolph. It *may* have been an indication that, in spite of the increased accumulation of knowledge, his character had remained unchanged since his early boyhood, or the criticism might have meant that in spite of his intelligence he was rash and hasty in his judgements as gifted boys frequently are.

One can with some justification assume that, while showing great promise, he had not the strength of character that his high intelligence and his facility of expression led his tutors to expect. While this would have been quite natural it nevertheless concealed grave dangers. The Emperor had decided that his son's education was to end at the age of eighteen and that he was not to read science at a university, much as Rudolph desired to do this. He was well capable of attaining his degree and would have been forced to think and work more methodically than by private tuition. Most of the Hohenzollern princes attended university for a few terms, but this was not in the Haps-burg tradition. Thus at a very early age, with his educa-tion incomplete, not yet trained to systematic thinking, he would be subjected to a number of influences and to the many temptations of a high but empty position in a time when a young man, particularly of his rank, was expected to sow his wild oats. There were contradictory tendencies at the Court as well as in politics. Would he possess enough strength to follow the way which he had planned without being deflected or disturbed ? Would he persist in his early motto, 'I want to know ?'

III

The Crown Prince had had a late puberty and the facts of life were explained to him only when he was fourteen and a half years old. The first signs of his active interest in the opposite sex, though undated, would point to his sixteenth or seventeenth year, before his formal education was over. He was very handsome and women found his easy grace of manner and his charm attractive. A certain laxity of morals in aristocratic and Court circles was fashionable and although Austria was a Catholic country, rules of moral behaviour were not very strict in some of the wealthy circles of society. The Emperor's life was beyond reproach, but the same could not be said for many of the Archdukes.

Intellectually Rudolph towered above all the Court circles, with the possible exception of Archduke John Salvator. Would he follow the dictates of his intellect and keep aloof from their cheap pleasures ? Would he have sufficient moral strength ?

The kind of education which Francis Joseph had provided for his son was not received with unanimous approval ; it was so much wider in scope than that of the other Archdukes, and was considered too comprehensive and consequently suspect. There were few countries at that time where the aristocracy was further removed from the world of learning and research than Austria. The nobility, in those years when Rudolph grew to manhood, was strenuously defending its own position and that of the Church against the onslaught of the forces of progress, to which the Crown Prince belonged almost throughout his life. He was well aware of this hostility and was therefore usually careful to keep his thoughts to himself, but, typically boyish, he sometimes wanted to show off by shocking people, and then his views, added to the suspicions in which his tutors were held, caused many raised eyebrows and shrugged shoulders.

The Emperor's first Adjutant and friend, General Beck, later Chief of the Austrian General Staff, noted in his diary : 'I could not approve of the whole tendency of these studies, to introduce the Crown Prince to all branches of knowledge and of public life, to give him professors and tutors of the most liberal conviction and to let him, in accordance with the unfortunate Court regulation in existence, complete his studies in his twentieth year. The

young, over-excited mind of the Crown Prince, the
immaturity of his conceptions, the extravagance of his
undeniably high intelligence, cause me anxiety that he will
assimilate ideas and tendencies which would not correspond
to the conservative character of a future monarch.' [3]

Beck, whose misgivings were shared by others, made
them known to Latour, but the latter, conscious of the
Emperor's support in this matter, took no notice. The
boy continued to prepare himself for his future office, the
more earnestly the older he grew. In 1875 he wrote an
essay for one of his teachers on 'Vienna's position and our
future'. In it he already showed the two basic conceptions of his future political line, his opposition to Germany
('A cultured Danube state would form a fortunate counter-
weight to the German Empire, whose dissolution it would
expedite') and his sympathy for the Slav peoples ('The
future belongs to the Slavs, but Austria can preserve herself
if she conceives her task correctly and puts herself at the
helm of the Yugoslavs, and thus becomes a mighty
Danube Empire'). In both connections his views differed
considerably from those held by his father, and the stage
was already set for future conflicts. The essay, immature
as it was in some respects, showed an extremely high degree
of understanding for political problems.

In accordance with the Court statute, Rudolph's formal
education was declared complete when he came of age in
July 1877. His father wrote a warm letter of thanks to the
faithful Latour in which he said : 'You have splendidly
and in every respect justified the confidence placed in you
and you have truly deserved great merit of me and my
house. . . . You may look back with pride upon the fruits
which will secure for you my sincere gratitude and the
Crown Prince's unchangeable affection and attachment.'

The governor now retired and Rudolph was given his own Court, which was headed by a former naval officer, Count Bombelles. Rudolph was also granted a fixed allowance which, in accordance with the Emperor's customary generosity in financial matters, should amply supply all his needs.

Court circles now expected that he would lead the accepted life of a young Archduke. Beck wrote to his wife at this time : 'In Gödöllö [an Imperial hunting lodge in Hungary] I have studied the Crown Prince. . . . He has an effervescent mind and carries his heart on his sleeve and has not yet digested many of the liberal doctrines of some of his professors ; otherwise love will soon be his main occupation.' [4] Beck had no idea of what went on in the mind of the boy whose future preoccupation he thought he could so easily predict. He did not know that Rudolph had laid down as his creed, 'Man can find heaven on earth, not the worldly heaven of the pleasure seeking, but the heaven of the spiritual life of the world of thoughts, when through one's own expansion one can feel the progress of humanity in oneself'.

Although he had not been permitted to continue his studies at a university he was not unmindful of the advantages which his education had conferred on him. As late as 1882, when already a married man, he told a friend, 'If a terrible social catastrophe were to occur I fancy that I myself, having learned something, could earn a piece of bread by my pen, either in an office or in a similar way'.

The new way of life had its attractions. He could now drop those subjects which he had not liked and devote more time, as far as his new duties would permit, to the pursuits which most interested him. There would be travelling ; he would be able to see new countries and under less restricted conditions than before. Yet even with such agreeable prospects the break in his life and the loss of his faithful and devoted Latour were painful. The governor had always shown a tenderness and understanding, while his father had been the awe-inspiring Emperor. His mother, much as he admired her and much as he wished to be near her, spent less and less time with her family at ever-increasing intervals. Latour had held an important position in the boy's life, and, although they planned to meet frequently, Rudolph felt the loss very keenly. A few days after this break the new Court Marshal, Bombelles, wrote to Latour, whom he knew well : 'He lets no moment pass without mentioning you with the most grateful affection and recognising with enthusiastic appreciation the wise precaution, the devoted love, with which you have directed his youth. You will be glad, I am sure, that I can day by day count more on his confidence. The first step in this direction happened on the journey from Schönbrunn to Penzing [a near-by railway station]. I saw how he struggled with his tears and I said to him, "Have a good cry, you need not be ashamed of these tears". He cried, and we talked of you, and his heart opened to me and so it has remained. May God grant that it continues. He feels great longing for you.' And a fortnight later Bombelles again wrote to Latour : 'God help me that my advice be always the right one and that, should I err, no damage come of it'. Both letters would suggest that Bombelles felt the great responsibility which had devolved upon him, although his influence, owing to the changed circumstances, would never equal Latour's. There is nothing to suggest that he had evil intentions, as some biographers assert.

When Latour handed over his stewardship he also

presented the final accounts. From 1864 to 1877 Rudolph's education, tuition fees and books and stationery had amounted to over 150,000 florins (at the time £12,000) ; the boy's keep and other expenditure connected with his establishment had cost very little more than the education proper. Nothing had been spared. Francis Joseph, who was modest in his demands for himself, was certainly a generous father as far as money was concerned.

This was decidedly not enough. Rudolph would need a responsible, if limited field of activities, where he could show his capabilities and make at least some use of his training, and this was exactly what his father refused even to consider. He had no intention of parting with even the semblance of any of his duties : it did not occur to him that a proper field of activities for Rudolph would be the natural consequence of the training he had himself provided for him with such care. Military service could at best be no more than an extension of this training.

It was doubtful how long the Crown Prince, tempted by privileges not matched by responsibilities, would maintain the high standard he had set himself. Sooner or later conflict was inevitable.

REFERENCES

1. Corti, *Franz Josef*, Vol. II, p. 459.
2. Mitis, *op. cit.* p. 16.
3. Edmund von Glaise-Horstenau, *Franz Josefs Weggefährte* (Wien, 1930), pp. 230 f.
4. Glaise-Horstenau, *op. cit.* p. 231.

CHAPTER THREE

Testing Time

I

BEFORE Rudolph received the Imperial command to join a regiment as was planned, he was sent to Great Britain for two months to study political and economic conditions. There were several reasons for this visit. Parliamentary government in Austria had been established for only ten years, and was passing through a period of teething troubles. Francis Joseph, while still suspicious of the new institution which restricted his power, yet wanted his son to see and hear the Mother of Parliaments at work. Britain was the first economic power in the world, while in Austria industrialisation was only now getting into its stride. The severe crisis of 1873, which had followed the 'Black Friday' of the Vienna stock exchange, had retarded further industrialisation and aroused hostility towards it. Yet Austria had to become industrialised if she were to remain a great power. Great Britain was the obvious example, unique both in economic and political strength, and it was evident that a study tour there would greatly benefit the heir to the Austrian throne. Added to this the Empress, who had been to Britain for the first time in 1874, had been immediately attracted to the country and strongly advised her husband to send their son there.

Shortly after Christmas 1877 Rudolph travelled to

Britain with his mother. She went on to Nottingham-shire, while he remained in London before touring the country. He had to promise her that he would not ride to hounds as she intended doing, as he was not so good a horseman.

Only a small suite came with the Crown Prince, one adjutant and one tutor, Professor Menger, the celebrated economist and founder of the Austrian school of economic thought. Menger's impact on the youth must have been strong. He was certainly one of the tutors who impressed him most ; particularly in Britain, the country where the Liberalism which was Menger's creed had so visibly brought about a unique material advance, was this influence strongly felt. The British Parliament was experiencing one of its finest periods—the struggle between those two great protagonists, Lord Beaconsfield and Gladstone, had real significance at a time when party discipline had not yet stifled individual decision. To witness this form of political life must have been particularly stimulating to Austrians like Rudolph and Menger, and years later Rudolph's first impressions of British Parliamentarianism still coloured his political opinions.

To give the visit a less formal character, Rudolph did not stay at the Austrian Embassy but in a little hotel in Brook Street — now Claridge's. Nevertheless, as he was not incognito, he was received by the Queen, who was charmed by his easy grace. She wrote to the Prince of Wales from Osborne : 'The young C. Pce. left [word illegible] today and I am much pleased with him. He, as *all* Austrians, is most easy to get on with. I was sorry to clash with your invitations, but almost as soon as he arrived I invited him, anxious to shew all possible civility and respect to the Emp^r and Em^ess of Austria. He is very pleasing, but looks a little over grown and *not* very robust. . . .'¹ To which he replied : 'I am glad to hear that you were pleased with the Crown Prince Rudolph. I saw him yesterday on his return from Osborne — and he seemed much pleased with his visit — I thought him very pleasing. . . .'²

'The Queen is in love with the Crown Prince, but do not worry, she does not want to marry him',³ Princess Mary of Cambridge, jokingly told the Austrian Ambassador Count Beust. The Prince of Wales had already met Rudolph in Vienna in 1873 and had remarked to his mother that 'the young Crown Prince Rudolph [is] a very nice boy'.⁴ Now he was again impressed and asked his mother to confer on him the Order of the Garter. This the Queen declined, as she thought Rudolph too young for such a high honour. Garter or not, the two Princes discovered that they had many ideas and interests in common, and even at this early stage was founded that good relationship which, in spite of the seventeen years' difference in their ages, was to last till Rudolph's death. Both were interested in politics, and both were suspicious of Bismarck's Germany, though in 1878 Rudolph's attitude was based more on sentiment than judgement. The Prince of Wales gave a dinner in Rudolph's honour at which the other special guest was Lord Beaconsfield.

The Crown Prince did not limit his activities to Court functions ; he had come to learn. He paid several visits to the Houses of Parliament, one of them when Gladstone, then in opposition, was speaking on the Oriental question, in which the visitors on their part were even more interested than the Leader of the Opposition. Both Menger and the Crown Prince were so impressed by the British political system that while still in the United Kingdom they collaborated in writing a pamphlet, *The Austrian Aristocracy and its Constitutional Task*, which was published anonymously in Munich the same year. Already in his earlier essays Rudolph had been highly critical of the nobility as an institution. When he was fifteen or sixteen he had written : 'The Nobility's selfishness brought about the incessant struggles in the Middle Ages, the poverty of the people, the obstruction of all development. From that time onwards this estate had no task left ; on the contrary it became a curse to humanity. Today we can still see nations on which the last three centuries have left no trace and which have exchanged the highest principle, that of progress, for stability. (Poland, Hungary.)'

Impressed by the part played by the British aristocracy in political life, and probably influenced also by Menger's more moderate views, Rudolph now saw that the nobility still had a contribution to make, even in the modern state. In the pamphlet the interplay of government and opposition, or, of Conservatism and Liberalism, as it manifested itself in the British contemporary political scene, was recognised as an essential feature of modern parliamentary life. They conceived the task of the nobility as a rallying centre of conservative forces. It was the time when modern British Conservativism was revitalised by Disraeli's political acumen, by his appeal to the working class — 'discerning the conservative working man as the sculptor perceives the angel prisoned in a block of marble'.[5] They realised that the survival of aristocracy in other countries depended upon a similar infusion of new conceptions ; consequently since 'the constitution conveys on the [Austrian] nobility an eminently favoured position in our political life . . . the members of the aristocracy, who are called upon to take part in legislation, have not the right . . . to devote themselves entirely to the enjoyment of life. . . . Nothing is more certain in modern political life than that public forces can only maintain their positions for any length of time when their owners not only enjoy their privileges, but carry out their duties as well. . . .' [6]

Three years later, when the struggle of nationalities threatened the existence of the Austrian Empire, Rudolph, still very much influenced by what he had seen in Britain, suggested the merger of the Liberals within all the nations into a supranational Liberal Party, and a similar organisation of the Conservatives, so that in the Austrian parliament the basic political principles would be untrammelled by national differences in their fight for predominance.

A full programme had been worked out by Herr Scherzer, the Commercial Counsellor of the Austrian Embassy in London, who had been entrusted with the preparations for the visit. The Crown Prince was to see in Britain 'how the immensely increasing population of London was governed, fed and educated' and 'how a trade which reaches beyond the limits of the civilised world' was maintained ; he was to visit 'those industrial establishments which by trying to satisfy the needs of the masses form the main sources of national wealth'. [7]

Smithfield and Billingsgate markets were inspected ; the Bank of England, the Coal Exchange, and numerous factories and military establishments were visited. He went to the Midlands and the industrial North, to Scotland and Ireland, and in all the bigger towns not only were buildings of general interest inspected but municipal undertakings also carefully studied. In Dublin a grave *faux pas* was made. At the Viceroy's reception arm-chairs were provided for the Viceroy himself and the Lord Mayor of

Dublin, but none for Rudolph, who was annoyed when neither gentleman was prepared to forgo his privilege.[8] He was still more annoyed when the Lord Mayor of Dublin preceded him when going in for tea.

Shorter and longer stays at castles and country seats brought occasional rests and time to collate and compare impressions. With great interest Rudolph visited the Science Departments of the British Museum and was very gratified when the experts there paid well deserved compliments to his knowledge of their subjects.

The Crown Prince was greatly impressed by what he saw. From Chester he wrote to Latour, on January 27th : 'England has far exceeded my expectations ; so far I am greatly satisfied with my journey and really enthusiastic about England, without failing to recognise the grave and very obvious drawbacks of the country. Life here is magnificent and I strive to get to know as much as possible.'

Further industrialisation in Austria was inevitable, and the experience gained by the Crown Prince in Britain would be valuable. Local government too needed new impetus. The city of Vienna was then demolishing its old fortifications and building the famous Ringstrasse in their place and, as the population of the city grew apace by the influx of country people, new municipal enterprise was required to keep the city administration in step with this increased population and rebuilding.

When Rudolph left Britain in late February 1878 after his first visit, he became for the rest of his life an admirer of her institutions and her political system, and the establishment of a similar political system in Austria became one of his aims.

II

After his return he joined the army for his period of active service, his troop being not the Guards, but an ordinary infantry regiment, whose officers were almost exclusively of middle-class origin. The fact that the Emperor ordered Rudolph to serve with an ordinary regiment of the line suggests that he wanted his son to be a working soldier, and not merely a drawing-room officer. Thus the Crown Prince joined a body of men more important to the existence of the monarchy than any other. At the time when the disruptive forces of nationalism became stronger every day, and the existence of the multilingual Empire seemed an anachronism to an ever-increasing number of people, the army was soon to be the only institution which held it together.

The Austrian Empire had come into being in 1804, but consisted of countries most of which had belonged to the Hapsburgs for centuries. They had been acquired in a variety of ways, but less frequently by war than was the case with most other dynasties. '*Bella gerint alii, tu felix Austria nube!*' (Let others wage war, you, happy Austria, marry), had been said in the fifteenth century.

While feudalism was the ruling social force, the government of all these countries and provinces, extending from Central Europe deep into what was then semi-Asia, was possible, although never easy. A class of German-speaking, fairly efficient and honest officials had brought some kind of order into the administration. After the Napoleonic wars, ideas of nationalism began to spread. Economic development had already shaken the foundations of feudalism and had made it necessary in some districts to give the rudiments of education in the national tongues instead of in German. National aspirations, which were able to develop when feudal loyalties lost their power, loosened the cohesion between the various provinces and weakened allegiance to the throne, and the Hapsburg administration became precarious. This process was accelerated when the Emperor Francis resigned the dignity of Holy Roman Emperor in 1806. It had been a supra-national dignity which, though elective, had been held so frequently by members of the Hapsburg family for more than five centuries that it had greatly enhanced their prestige by its mystical lustre. The new crown which Francis had assumed in 1804, that of Emperor of Austria, lacked in its utilitarian novelty some of the supra-national universality of the Roman Crown.

There were dozens of languages and dialects spoken in the Empire and with the nations becoming increasingly self-conscious and articulate, their continued domination by a German merchant class and administration and a German or Germanised aristocracy became well nigh impossible. On the other hand, the Germans, having dominated the monarchy for so long, refused to accept the idea that nations, such as the Czechs or the Ruthenians, hitherto considered useful inferiors, should be their equals. Moreover the Germans were heavily outnumbered by the Slavs, and the loss of their administrative predominance would have meant being submerged and forced into an inferior position.

In 1866 Austria had had to renounce what little influence she had still retained in German affairs, and the Germans in Austria were cut off from their source of strength. For many reasons the Magyars had had to be given in Hungary a status equal to that which the Germans held in the

Austrian parts of the Empire. This gave them the right to suppress the national minorities within the Hungarian half of the Hapsburg possessions. Their equality transformed the Austrian Empire into Austria-Hungary and was constitutionally expressed by the 'Settlement of 1867' which virtually divided the Empire into two parts almost independent of each other. Francis Joseph was formally crowned King of Hungary in the same year. Both countries had only foreign affairs, foreign trade, and most units of the armed forces in common. Each was autonomous in raising its respective revenues. Each had its own Parliament, and a committee of members from both met annually to fix the proportion which each was to contribute to the common expenditure. Whenever an opportunity, arose the Magyars not only tried to strengthen the number of the units of their army at the expense of the joint forces, but also tried to reduce their contribution towards the over-all costs of affairs of the Monarchy.

Unchecked by outside forces, the Magyars now ruthlessly refused minority rights to the nations within their own territory. Although they themselves formed only a minority of the total population, they could do as they pleased, as they dominated a parliament which was entirely unrepresentative. The minorities — Slovaks, Romanians and the Yugoslavs (Serbs and Croats) — resented this unjust treatment and held the Emperor responsible for their suppression. One of these now suppressed nations — the Croats — had for centuries supplied the Hapsburgs with some of their finest soldiers, and in the Revolutions of 1848-49 their unswerving loyalty had saved the throne.

The Crown Prince would one day have to contend with these problems, as his whole future would depend on

his capacity to solve them. In spite of Magyar encroachments, most of the army was still untouched by constitutional changes. Its professional officers and N.C.O.s were
the only people in the Empire whose loyalty was un-
divided, and who were at home everywhere between the
Lake of Constance and the Russian plains of Galicia or the
coast of the Adriatic. They, whatever their background,
owed allegiance to no one but the Emperor ; they, whatever their mother-tongue, spoke uniformly that blend of
German and Slav words with Slav intonation which was
used on the drill square and the parade ground, and which,
after a few weeks of service, united the recruits of the
many lands and languages. They served faithfully for
little pay and, in the regiments of the line, with little
prestige. True, this army had been beaten in 1859 and
1866, but both men and officers had fought well, and their
defeat was exclusively due to poor leadership, obsolete
armament and bad organisation, and not to any lack of
gallantry.

It was a good object-lesson for Rudolph to be in the
36th Regiment of Infantry. Owing to his rank his military
promotion had been swift, but he had now to show his
prowess. The regiment was stationed at Prague, a beautiful
city, particularly attractive to a young man of romantic
disposition interested in history. He was soon under the
spell of its old squares, its quaint streets and its mellowed
buildings, many of which dated from earlier periods than
the Baroque so frequently found in Austria. Among them
was the old town hall, with its time-blackened walls and
its wondrous clock. He stayed at the Hradschin, the old
Royal Castle, high above the town. Here the Thirty
Years War had started with the defenestration of the
Imperial envoys. He was also captivated by tales about

another Rudolph Hapsburg, a German Emperor, who had
lived there in the sixteenth century. According to legend
this Rudolph had tried to find the philosopher's stone, and
the little houses of the alchemists still stood near the Castle.
He had also followed other mystical pursuits, aided by
the head of the Jewish community, the Rabbi Loew, who
was well versed in the mysteries of the Cabbala.

In the old synagogue the seat of the Rabbi Loew was
left permanently unoccupied, no matter how crowded the
synagogue might be on High Holidays : the Jews considered nobody worthy to fill his place. Around the
synagogue there was still the small Jewish graveyard which
had served as a burial ground for hundreds of years and
was still in use, one layer of dead buried upon another.
In the same way modern Prague was a new layer built on
an old foundation, and, repeating this pattern, the struggle
for national supremacy now being fought out between
Czechs and Germans was basically the old struggle, now
with nationalist and not religious slogans.

III

The Crown Prince, although he felt keenly the spirit of
the place working on his impressionable mind, did not
allow his romantic sentiments to interfere with his duties,
which he took very seriously. His regiment soon became
his real home. He was only twenty at this time and
strove his utmost to justify his rank of Colonel with all
its responsibilities. The officers of the regiment were
conscientious men, so that the atmosphere of respectability
and awareness of duty into which he had entered was a
good influence. He liked the camaraderie of the mess, the

life so far removed from the luxuries which few could afford, their plain but wholesome food made more palatable by an appetite sharpened by long hours spent in the fresh air. He was quickly learning to be a leader of men, one of the purposes of his service. He frequently wrote to his former governor Latour, and his letters show how seriously he took his duties. 'Work pleases me ; I have always been used to it and it does not matter to me if I am occupied from 6.30 A.M. to 6 P.M. with the exception of half an hour for luncheon.' And again : 'Thank God I do not feel within me the calling to repeat the so-called accustomed paths, the foolish everyday life of my relatives with their blinkers. . . . Today one must work to deserve to hold a high position; to remain in Vienna and to possess only a dignified attitude, and not to know people, how they are and what they feel, that does not fit into our century.'

After only six months of active service Rudolph delivered a lecture to his brother officers on the Battle of Spichern (1870) which was considered 'an achievement which would have done honour to an experienced officer'.[9] Less than a year after he had joined the service his commanding officer reported : 'I soon recognised that I had no ordinary person before me — his is a rich mind, impetuous and impulsive, with a warm heart and a noble character, developed far beyond his years. . . . It is a real pleasure to see how each seed planted in him soon bears fruit. . . . What he does is well considered . . . his calmness and objectivity are praiseworthy. . . . A factor almost equally valuable as the purely military one for H.I.H. is the contact with men. . . . His kind heart and his natural amiability will hardly ever permit an outrage. . . . I am convinced that H.I.H. will command a regiment so satisfactorily in every respect that there will be no need to make allowances. . . . He will play his part to the fullest satisfaction and — I can vouch for that — he never will seriously fail, for that he is too well educated, too reasonable, too able, too deliberate, too kindhearted. . . .'[10]

In 1879 Rudolph, with a youthful exaggerated sense of duty, refused to come to Vienna to enjoy the carnival season ; he liked dancing and parties, but now his military duties were first in his estimation. He informed his Court Marshal Bombelles : 'I shall not be in Vienna for the Court Ball. I told Papa that I would much rather stay at the place where my duties lie than amuse myself in Vienna. People will be surprised to see that I am really serving with body and soul and they will have no reason to say that I only like being in Vienna for amusement's sake.'

On August 18th of this year, on the Emperor's birthday, the usual promotions were made, and Rudolph was overjoyed at being appointed Colonel commanding the Imperial and Royal Infantry Regiment No. 36. After a year's service with the colours 'his most ardent wish had been fulfilled' he told Bombelles. He had many shooting companions among the nobility but he felt deeply hurt when he saw how the Bohemian aristocracy scorned the less affluent officers. 'I belong to the army with life and soul, every tactless remark against the officers' corps I consider my own affair. . . . The army needs real friends among the members of the Imperial family, men who feel, work, and live with it', he wrote about the attacks on the armed forces, very frequent at the time.

For a while life in Prague was agreeable and quiet. Rudolph's off-duty Sundays were used for shooting expeditions, a pastime which he increasingly enjoyed. The Archbishop of Prague had actually forbidden shooting on Sundays, and this led to several quarrels with the impetuous Crown Prince.

At this time, as later, many rumours were current in Vienna about Rudolph's love affairs. It was said that he was having a liaison with an actress and at the same time consorting with a married woman, the wife of an industrialist, but no evidence of loose living can be found. It seems unlikely that he could have found time for amorous adventures while he was so deeply engrossed in his military duties. This does not suggest that he was an ascetic, but had he transcended the admittedly wide limits set by the moral code of the time for young men of means, his commanding officer would not have failed to mention the fact in his reports. On the basis of the evidence Rudolph must have been fully occupied during his free time. He was prolific in his correspondence — he kept Latour well informed of his thoughts and movements — and he wrote a lengthy memorandum, of which unfortunately only a summary has been kept, on the position of the Slavs in Austria. He continued his studies by private tuition in Slavonic philology. The preparation of his lecture on the Battle of Spichern must have taken many hours, and so must his studies of tactics and strategy.

Only one story, which has been told again and again, will be retold here, as, unlike others, it bears the stamp of truth, and Rudolph himself later spoke of it to Dr. Benedikt, a nerve specialist whom he was then consulting. It has been recorded by the latter's daughter [11] and also by Berta Szeps, daughter of Rudolph's later friend and political adviser.[12] According to this story Rudolph, when on an official visit to the old ghetto of Prague, met a young Jewish girl of exquisite loveliness, and the two fell deeply in love. The girl's cautious parents, fearing that ill might befall their daughter from a friendship with a prince of the Imperial house, sent her away to the country. After a short time, driven by her longing to see the prince, the young woman returned secretly to Prague, but on the day of her arrival fell ill and died soon after without seeing Rudolph again. She was buried in the old Jewish cemetery in the centre of the city and Rudolph, unable to forget her, frequently visited her grave. The beauty of this girl is said to have haunted him all his life.

In the spring of 1879 he went on a long trip to Spain, hunting and sightseeing. Before leaving Prague he made his Will, possibly feeling morbid at the time, as he often did, both as a youth and a man. In this Will he called the 36th Infantry Regiment his real home. The testament gives a clear insight into the political convictions which he held throughout his life : 'Our time requires new views. Everywhere, particularly in Austria, reaction is the first step to perdition. Those who preach reaction are the most dangerous enemies. I have always fought them and I advise caution against them.' Well aware that he differed in his outlook from the rest of the family he added : 'My ways have differed from those of my relatives, but I have always been moved by the purest motives'. After this solemnity he added a gayer note : 'A last farewell kiss in thought to all the beautiful women of Vienna, whom I have loved so much'.

His warning against reaction was not without deeper significance ; the political scene in Austria was changing during the time he had spent in Prague and Spain. The Congress of Berlin in 1878 had given Austria the mandate to occupy Bosnia and Hercegovina, two Turkish provinces in the Balkans. After the loss of the Italian provinces of Lombardy and Venetia, Francis Joseph had here for the first time an opportunity to increase his Empire. The parliamentary majority in Austria, consisting of German Liberals, had turned down their own government's request for a grant of sixty million florins for the occupation costs. The government resigned and the brief period of Austrian Liberalism came to an end. In the new government the Ministry of the Interior was taken over by a friend of Francis Joseph, Count Taaffe, a man of Irish origin who had retained his claim to the Irish peerage. It was his intention to reconcile the German and Czech conservative elements so that an anti-Liberal government could count on a safe majority in parliament.

IV

Rudolph faced a complicated political situation on his return from Spain. He had never shared the narrow nationalism which so many members of the Liberal party considered an essential part of their creed, and unlike most of the German Liberals he had great sympathy for the Slavs. On the other hand Count Taaffe, in spite of his programme of reconciliation with the Czechs, stood for complete reaction, and it was only a question of time before he would be Minister President. The Crown Prince had no prejudice against the Czechs ; he spoke their language fluently and was for this, if for no other reason, well liked by them. But his feelings for the Czech nation were modified when he saw how readily some of their representatives supported the German reactionaries. It was a confusing situation which would have baffled more experienced students of politics than the young Crown Prince, whose ideal was to bring about a union between German and Czech progressive forces. Unfortunately the progressive forces in both nations were more aggressive in their nationalism than the Conservatives, and thus his was a hopeless and thankless task, yet necessary if the Monarchy was to survive and to become a progressive modern state.

Although the Crown Prince considered himself a Liberal, his views differed on several points from party-Liberalism. The Liberals, when in power, had forced a reduction in the army estimates — at a time of high political tension — an example of their lack of political experience, as Rudolph judged it. He had had ample opportunity of seeing the unifying force of the army in a country where so many disintegrating forces were at work, and was greatly annoyed at this political short-sightedness. He expressed this feeling in strong terms to Latour and even considered the possibility of a *coup d'état*, suggesting an unauthorised issue of bank-notes to cover the costs of the occupation of Bosnia, as Parliament showed itself so recalcitrant.

Now that the Crown Prince was in a position to consider politics seriously, his political creed, Liberalism, was declining. The economic crisis of 1873 had shown that many Liberal politicians had used their official positions to get rich quickly. Their greed and corruption brought discredit on their party — although doubtless any inexperienced party in an inexperienced parliament is more prone to fall victim to the bribes and perquisites which big business may offer. Rudolph rightly realised that at a certain stage of its economic development a state must be based on the power of the middle class. Only the Liberals enjoyed the confidence of the upper *bourgeoisie* and the progressive element of the aristocracy, and these

were the classes which would carry out further industrialisation. This strengthened his determination to remain a
Liberal although he was not blind to his party's shortcomings, economic or political.

It was not only these considerations which made the
Crown Prince faithful to Liberalism throughout his life.
Austria was in many ways a backward country : its
educational system was out-dated, many of its laws obsolete,
neither the individual nor the press free. Liberalism was
the only progressive force which could change all this.
But the Emperor had never cared for it and welcomed
its eclipse. He gave his full support to Taaffe, who aimed
at setting up a Conservative and anti-Liberal government.
Rudolph was deeply disturbed that his father should
follow reactionary advisers, but he was still young and
optimistic and hoped that when older and more experienced he would be able to influence the Emperor. In a
letter to Latour he said : 'In later years, when I shall have
obtained influence and experience, I shall dissuade the
Emperor from the ways which are now used in military
and political affairs, and which are wrong in my view, and
I shall help to create a new system. To do so I would move
to Vienna and gladly live there.'

Any intention of influencing his father meant speeding
the unavoidable conflict. Although Francis Joseph had
been Emperor with unlimited power at an age when
Rudolph was merely a Colonel, he was too unimaginative
to concede to his son any political influence. The Crown
Prince's intention of helping his father to create a new
political system was all the more likely to lead to a clash
as their relationship had never been one of mutual confidence. Rudolph rightly felt that time was not on
Austria's side ; the forces of disintegration were growing

stronger day by day.   He had set himself a difficult task ;
he had to consolidate his ideas quickly, to convince the
Emperor that 'reaction was the first step to perdition'.
There was no time to lose.

REFERENCES

1. Royal Archives, Windsor, Vic. Addl. MSS. A/2 33.
2. Royal Archives, B 55 2.
3. Mitis, *op. cit.* p. 39.
4. Sir Sidney Lee, *King Edward VII : a Biography* (London, 1925), Vol. I,
p. 355.
5. *The Times*, April 18th, 1883.
6. *Der oesterreichische Adel und sein constitutioneller Beruf.   Mahnruf an die
aristokratische Jugend.   Von einem Oesterreicher* (München, 1878), p. 45.
7. Mitis, *op. cit.* p. 36.
8. Mrs. George Cornwallis-West, *The Reminiscences of Lady Randolph
Churchill* (London, 1908), p. 78.
9. Mitis, *op. cit.* p. 64.
10. Mitis, *op. cit.* pp. 63 f.
11. Clotilde Benedikt, 'L' arciduca Rodolfo e la bella ebrea', *L' Epoca*,
August 21st, 1923.
12. Berta Szeps (Berta Szeps-Zuckerkandl), *My Life and History* (London,
1938), p. 19.

CHAPTER FOUR

Marriage

I

RUDOLPH confided his political thoughts and anxieties only to those close to him, but on occasion he would be carried away and would disclose his ideas about politics in conversation when he thought he sensed an interest. This was not always wise ; he assumed too often that the interest was in the subject, while in reality people wanted only to hear his views in order to be shocked by their radicalism. Many at the Court had frowned upon his comparatively liberal education, and they only waited for an opportunity to point out its evil consequences. Few realised how deeply rooted his convictions were ; his radicalism appeared to them an assumed air and he was consequently considered a 'talker' (ein Plauscher, as the Viennese called him). This was also the judgement of the former Austrian Ambassador in Paris, Hubner, who, after hearing his views on religion and the aristocracy, found him excitable and erratic in his behaviour and his opinions.[1]

But most people at the Court and elsewhere merely saw in the Crown Prince a handsome young Archduke who, they assumed, led the kind of life which young men of his position were accustomed and expected to lead.

Rudolph, in spite of his preoccupation with politics,

was full of the joy of life. His earlier morbidness seemed
to have vanished or to have been relegated to the background. 'If I could only live to be a hundred', he said to
his sister Valerie in November 1879. 'It is dreadful to
think that one has to die in the end.' [2]

He was handsome, and many girls and women found
him attractive and sought his favour. He once confided
in one of his mother's ladies-in-waiting, Countess Fes-
tetics, and she noted in her diary, 'How temptation
approaches such a young man . . .'.[3] While it is certain
that Rudolph's life was much less depraved than that of
many of his fellow Archdukes, there is just one letter
which might point to a suspicion by one of his former
adjutants, Walterskirchen, a reliable witness, not influenced by mere gossip. Rudolph had sent him his
photograph which was acknowledged in a letter. 'The
. . . portrait . . . cannot quite satisfy me ; I miss in it the
trait of spiritual freshness which used to please all of us. . . .
You have a beautiful, joyful youth behind you ; you need
not empty the cup of life greedily like one who had
thirsted for a long time. Enjoy life at a moderate pace.
It is your right. Do not let your joy of life turn to gall by
brooding speculations, whose traces I believe can be seen
in the eyes in your portrait. Your intelligence and your
striving after higher things guarantee that you will not
founder in the whirlpool of pleasure.' This letter, coming
from an older man may have been as much a warning
against the possible dangers of taking life too seriously as
against libertinism.

Although Francis Joseph was of the opinion that 'My
son's youth shall not be stolen as mine was',[4] he considered
it was time for Rudolph to marry. There were many
reasons for an early marriage. The Austrian Empire, in

spite of all its difficulties, was still a power in Europe, and naturally the heir to the throne was expected to marry young and have a family to ensure the succession. It was not easy to find a Catholic princess of suitable age and rank. Although Francis Joseph had himself married for love and had no intention of forcing his son into a marriage for reasons of state, he insisted on a consort of equal standing. This limited Rudolph's choice considerably. After declining a Princess from Saxony whom he found too fat, and the Infanta of Spain because she was too plain, the one remaining candidate was Stephanie, second daughter of King Leopold II of the Belgians and granddaughter of Queen Victoria's 'dear Uncle Leopold'. Her mother, Marie Henrietta, was a Hapsburg Princess of that branch of the family which lived in Hungary. Leopold II, as scheming as his father Leopold I, but less wise, welcomed the idea of his daughter becoming one day Empress of Austria; money he could make himself, but he could not command the awe which the Hapsburgs still inspired.

After due diplomatic reconnaissance by the Austrian Ambassador Count Chotek (later father-in-law to Archduke Francis Ferdinand), Rudolph went to Brussels in March 1880. A few weeks before, he had confided to Latour that the prospects of a new life seemed 'uncanny', but once in Brussels he was carried away by the show put up for his benefit by the wily king. Rudolph proposed marriage as quietly and as obediently as was expected of him, and, as was expected, he was readily accepted.

He was impressed to find himself for once the centre of attention at a Court, and his letters to Latour reflect an enthusiastic mood. On March 11th he wrote: 'I am intoxicated with happiness and contentment. The days pass all too quickly and I think anxiously of the moment when I shall have to leave. I have learned to love my parents-in-law very much. I am on a very good footing with the King, we talk a great deal together. He is one of the most intelligent, cleverest and wisest men, and one of the best orators I have ever seen ; one can learn a great deal from him.' Two days later he wrote : 'In Stephanie I have found a real angel, a faithful good being who loves me, a very clever, well educated and able companion for this life who will stand by my side well and successfully in all my difficult tasks. I am convinced that she will soon love her beautiful new country and as a good and faithful subject of her master and Emperor she will be an adornment to my dear Fatherland.'

Stephanie was not quite sixteen at the time, not fully developed, a rather colourless, overgrown schoolgirl, but apparently showing already a certain stubbornness. She was intellectually anything but her future husband's peer. Her education had been superficial and had not awakened her critical faculties ; she felt inferior to Rudolph, whose wide education and intellectual achievements had been talked of at many courts. She compensated this feeling of inferiority with a certain aggressiveness which would be difficult to bear by the highly strung bridegroom. Her gaucherie and poorly developed dress sense contrasted sharply with Rudolph's charming manners, his ease and grace. He was, perhaps then more than later, critical of religious dogmas, whereas Stephanie's education had been based strictly on the teachings of the Catholic Church, which she accepted without question. On the face of things the marriage seemed to have little prospect of success, but both were young and might still develop together if she were sufficiently free from prejudice and willing to learn.

It is strange that the Empress Elisabeth foresaw the possible evil consequences of the impending marriage. She was in England when, early one morning, the telegram announcing her son's engagement arrived. When reading it she turned so pale that her lady-in-waiting ventured to ask after its contents. When told she remarked, 'Thank God it is not a calamity'. 'Please God that it will not become one', was the Empress's reply.[5] In spite of these dark forebodings she hurried to Brussels to see her son while he was still there with his fiancée. Rudolph and Stephanie were at the station to welcome her and Rudolph was so deeply moved that, in spite of all etiquette he embraced and hugged his mother. It cannot have been an easy moment for Stephanie, seeing herself face to face with one of the most graceful women of the time, and it may well have served to increase her awkwardness. The Empress, though twenty-seven years older, was much more beautiful. Proudly the Crown Prince looked at his mother, and then his glance fell on his future bride, her bearing clumsy, her dress ill-chosen, her fresh complexion her only advantage.[6] It must have been a formidable ordeal for the young girl.

The Emperor was overjoyed that Rudolph, without giving trouble, had chosen a suitable Princess as his future wife, that he would settle down, and that in due time, it was to be hoped, an heir would be born to the ancient house of Hapsburg. The engagement was celebrated in Vienna with a reception of foreign diplomats ; when they congratulated the Emperor, he said: 'though he had done nothing to influence his son, the Prince's choice had given him the greatest possible pleasure, and appeared to be one that met with universal approval', the British Ambassador in Vienna, Sir Henry Elliot, reported.[7] When the Empress returned to Vienna from Brussels she was still uneasy in her mind. 'If it will only end well', she said to her husband, when he met her at the station. Francis Joseph was too unimaginative to share her premonition ; he tried to lift her spirits by saying, 'You worry too much, my Dear'.[8]

II

The Austrian peoples showed great pleasure at the news of the forthcoming marriage. Sir Henry Elliot reported : 'In all parts of the Empire the news has been received with the utmost satisfaction'.[9] The enthusiasm was especially marked in Bohemia, as was shown in its capital city, Prague, after Rudolph's return from Belgium. His well-known sympathies for the Czechs, his ability to speak their language, his intention to remain in Prague after his marriage, all contributed to a spontaneous welcome. Rudolph wrote to Latour : 'The patriotism here is colossal ; moreover everybody, nobility and all other classes of the population, is very devoted to me. . . . The effect of my short speech to the numerous representatives of the town of Prague left nothing to be desired. When I spoke in German of "my dear city of Prague" I was interrupted by loud *"slava"* calls [cheers] and when I continued in Czech about my further stay in Prague a real roar broke loose. Next day my words were posted at all street corners. Wherever I appear I am greeted by *"slava"* calls. . . . As a betrothed man Bohemia and Prague have received me most graciously and heartily, from the highest nobility to the poorest working class. I have never before to the same extent known the feeling of gratitude and love for the population which I have felt these days. And it is just the most ordinary gratitude when I say that, in whatever situation, I shall remain a true friend and champion of this beautiful good country. . . .'

He seemed to have grown more manly, more mature with his engagement. His elder sister Gisela was impressed by this and wrote to Latour: 'Admittedly Rudolph is still rather young, but I found him during his last visit more manly, quieter and firmer than a short time ago'.

In July 1880 he again went to Brussels to visit Stephanie and enjoyed the public appearances made necessary by his betrothal. He was probably more in love with love than with the girl, but he was in love with her too. Every letter he wrote to her during this time and in the following few years prove it. It may be that he thought Stephanie, still so young, would be willing to be guided by him to share his world, his hopes and his ambitions. This was bound to take time, as politics, his main preoccupation, had never interested her.

The girl was lonely. Her father was a poor family man ; his amorous adventures were so notorious that Queen Victoria, who had always considered his father, her uncle, her most confidential adviser, refused to have anything to do with him except when reasons of state demanded it. On one occasion the Queen of the Belgians had run away from her husband and returned only after her Father Confessor had reminded her of a Catholic wife's duties. Stephanie's elder sister, Louisa, was married, and her only brother dead. Thus Rudolph's attentions must have been very welcome to her, although she was probably too young and too immature to understand fully what was expected of her.

Rudolph too was lonely. His mind was too active to be entirely satisfied with regimental duties and the comrade-

Rudolph and Stephanie at the time of their engagement

ship of the mess. Latour was a good and fatherly friend
certainly, and Bombelles a faithful servant, but within the
family little real affection was shown to him. His father
may have been well meaning, but was narrow-minded and
unimaginative and was unable to show affection to anyone
but his wife and small children. His mother, for whom
Rudolph had the veneration of a mediaeval knight for
his lady, was away on her travels for most of the time.
His elder sister was happily married and had little time and
less interest in her brother, and his other sister, ten years
younger than himself, was still a little girl. He had no one
with whom to share his world of dreams, and it is understandable that he hoped that, by marrying a young,
apparently impressionable girl, he would have somebody
to listen to him when he outlined his plans for his own and
his country's future. The wedding was fixed for December 1880, but had to be postponed as the bride was still
not fully developed to womanhood. The Empress continued to feel uneasy, and Rudolph, noticing her strange
behaviour, commented on it to Latour.

He had now reached a critical stage in his development.
His training had been sufficiently thorough to enable him
to judge conditions for himself. He saw that Austria, in
spite of the cracks already appearing in her fabric, was
making a tremendous effort to assert her position both
culturally and economically. The University of Vienna
was leading Europe in medicine and economics ; the city
of Vienna, freed from the old fortifications — there was
no longer any danger from the Turks — was extending
her boundaries. New industries were growing, commerce
flourishing. He could see all this, but he had also to see
how the political scene had deteriorated ; how, after a
new Ministry under Taaffe had been appointed in June

1880, the last vestiges of Liberalism had been shed and a policy of undiluted reaction inaugurated. The remainder of his short life was dedicated to fighting his father's government. He feared that the reactionary policy would endanger Austria's very existence : he was convinced that it would stunt her growth at a time when other states such as France and Germany were making big strides in their development. Austria was now 'a state of ministerial, bureaucratic despotism under the guise of constitutionalism', as a member of parliament stated.[10] Censorship tried to suppress all opposition, and in 1880 alone 635 single editions of newspapers were confiscated by the police. Even election manifestos were censored.

The Crown Prince should stand outside politics — his position as heir to the throne and as an army officer demanded this. It would have been understandable had he washed his hands of all these problems and led the carefree life of most of the Archdukes with all its privileges, but his intelligence and training had combined to arouse in him not only an interest in politics but an intuitive feeling for it which his father entirely lacked. This awareness had been strengthened by his stay in Prague, the capital of a province whose loyalty to the Hapsburgs could be easily shaken by an unwise policy. Rudolph, by his attitude, had succeeded in increasing the prestige of the dynasty. Now he had to watch the effects of his father's government destroying the good-will he had created. He feared that the consequences were equally pernicious in other parts of the Empire.

To serve as an officer only could satisfy him no longer. He must act, warn public opinion, fight his father's government. Francis Joseph maintained that it was *his* policy which the Ministry was carrying out, but Rudolph, the

Emperor of tomorrow, was left entirely uninformed and had to learn of important political decisions no sooner than the man in the street. The Emperor, who had with great insight arranged that his son was given the best possible training as a future ruler, now expected him to be an idle onlooker. The Crown Prince would have to postpone the application of what he had learned until he became Emperor himself, no matter how many years would have to pass — and then, he feared, it might be too late. It was a time of flux, political development throughout Europe seemed strangely accelerated, and waiting passively seemed criminal, particularly now when he was about to be married, to take on the responsibility of perpetuating the Hapsburg line. Thus, regardless of his position, he entered whole-heartedly into politics and was deeply preoccupied during much of the period of his engagement.

For Stephanie this was unfortunate. She was not used to sharing a man's world, but that was precisely what Rudolph wanted of her. Would she be willing to learn and if so, would he find the right approach to lead her into his own realm ? The Empress Elisabeth's forebodings had some justification ; her son was a young man who took life seriously, who would not readily live his own life and let his wife live hers. Being in opposition to his father's policy, he would want his wife to show an interest in his plans, possibly even to help him in preparing them. A mother should have been aware of this. The Empress, unlike her husband, was imaginative, highly strung and subject to moods herself. She should have been easily capable of understanding Rudolph's nervousness. He was so much more her son than Francis Joseph's, and a marriage to a dull and spiritless girl would bring him the same frustration that she herself knew so well.

Had she but uttered a single word of warning against expecting too much of Stephanie at first and advised him to lead her slowly and patiently into his world, he, who so venerated his mother, would have heeded her words, and she might have saved her son and daughter-in-law much heartache and evil consequences, and herself the bitter regrets which never left her. But she could not talk, she was too shy. She shirked the issue and went to England to ride to the Combermere foxhounds in Cheshire. She returned to Vienna only a day or two before the wedding, and even then, so far as we know, remained silent.

III

Rudolph was romantic, Stephanie matter of fact. He was, though proud of his position, not intoxicated by it, but remained a human being interested in everything and everybody ; she was far too much aware of her position. Her mother, possibly by virtue of the undignified conditions in which she had been forced to live, did not possess sufficient insight to enlighten her daughter, to show her that her first duty would be to learn to understand her husband and to be his companion. Prospects were not promising when the Belgian Royal party were at last able to set out in May 1881 for the wedding in Vienna, the wedding which had already been twice postponed.

The Prince of Wales was fond of Rudolph and wished to attend his wedding. The Emperor thought this would be difficult, as the Imperial Palace in Vienna was crowded with the many Belgian wedding guests who had to be accommodated, but later changed his mind. The British Ambassador, Sir Henry Elliott, informed the Queen's private secretary on December 15th, 1880: 'The Emperor told me that he had been unable to resist the Prince of Wales's renewed proposal to be present at the marriage of the Crown Prince, but he begs as a favour, that [word illegible] mention of his having given his consent to it should be deferred as long as possible'.[11] *

Vienna was *en fête* for the wedding. There were two public festivals on the evening before the ceremony, one in the Prater, the old amusement park of the Viennese, the other in the park of the Imperial Palace of Schönbrunn. The Court set out for the Prater in 62 carriages, but they could not get through owing to the crowds. The great enthusiasm of the people on this occasion showed the high hopes they had in Rudolph. So much was wrong in Austria, so multifarious her problems, they felt that he was so sincere, his face so open and eager, that the expectations which they placed on his ability and good-will were understandably high. They wanted to honour their Crown Prince, to show him their appreciation and their love. No other member of the Imperial family, except Francis Joseph himself, had ever been given such a tremendous ovation on his wedding eve.

Rudolph had unmistakably the feeling of an anticlimax. Was it the waiting for the long-postponed wedding or was it the sudden realisation, now when it was too late, that Stephanie might after all not be the right choice? Or was it the shyness of a young man of twenty-two? On the wedding morning he was in a strange mood.

* Mitis in his biography is wrong when he states (p. 39) that Queen Victoria, annoyed by Rudolph's 'dissolute life' (English in the original) did not permit the Prince of Wales to attend the wedding. The same mistake occurs in Lee's *King Edward VII*, I, 574, from which Mitis probably took his information. According to Stephanie there was only one other foreign guest, Prince William of Prussia, later the Kaiser William II.

Countess Festitics wrote : 'When I came out of my room fully dressed, a footman ran past with Rudolph's fabulous bridal bouquet. I suddenly felt ice cold and when I took my train over my arm I heard the dear attractive voice of the Crown Prince — "Countess Mary, do not run away, wait a little". This I did and I was apprehensive, so serious, no, so nervous and despondent did he look. "I am pleased that we still meet as of old." He remained standing, as if he could not make up his mind to go through the door. I said, "the bouquet is waiting already". "Yes," he replied, "it was too heavy for me, it is all right." So speaking he made a movement with the hand to which I said nothing. I felt ill at ease, he noticed it and asked, "Are you in a hurry?" "Yes, your Imperial Highness, fairly so." "I am not," he said very seriously. "I have time." "Oh, your Highness," it slipped out, whereupon he extended his hand and said, "Goodbye, say something cheerful to me." The tears rolled down my cheeks and I said, "God bless you and be happy, dear, good Imperial Highness." "Thank you," and with a handshake he vanished behind the door of his apartment. That was the prelude to the wedding.'[12]

It is difficult to decide what caused Rudolph's change of mood after appearing so happy during the first months of his courtship. Stephanie possibly seemed now too sure of herself, not as malleable as she once appeared to be. On the previous day Countess Festitics, a keen observer, noted that the Princess was badly dressed, not pretty, looked 'not at all timid, very banal, so strangely drilled'.[13] It was too late for second thoughts and fate had to take its course.

The rings used in the wedding ceremony were those used by the Empress Maria Theresa and her husband Francis of Lorraine, one hundred and fifty years earlier.

Whether Rudolph would be as unfaithful as Francis had been, only the future could tell. Would Stephanie show the wisdom and shrewdness of Maria Theresa, who had made a success of her marriage in spite of all difficulties ?

The honeymoon was spent at Laxenburg, a castle a few miles outside Vienna, where the Emperor and Empress had themselves spent the first few days of their married life. The Princess described later how she and Rudolph drove there after the ceremony through the falling snow, on an extremely cold day for the time of the year. The young couple had nothing to say to each other ; Rudolph was more taciturn than usual — he was possibly shy and may have felt a little embarrassed by the situation. Stephanie describes how, when they arrived at the Castle, they found it lacking in amenities and comfort ; no fires had been lit and there was a musty smell everywhere. It was cold and depressing. There had been no loving touch, not even flowers to cheer them, and all preparations had obviously been left to an unimaginative staff. It is strange that the Empress, who knew from her own experience how cheerless and depressing the castle could be, had not herself insisted on suitable preparations being made for the young couple.

The Crown Prince, we are assured, did nothing to cheer his young wife, and, according to her memoirs, the way in which he approached her was crude and repulsive. This statement seems to suggest a lack of experience on his part which contradicts the stories about his numerous adventures with women. The absence of any real home atmosphere at the Belgian Court led to Stephanie's being sadly lacking in any preparation for married life. But this was a time when ignorance was equated with innocence, and many happy marriages must have begun in no better circumstances. Had all other factors been favourable the distressing initiation would soon have been forgotten.

Yet it could not have been as bad as Stephanie maintained. On the next morning both visited the local gamekeeper to arrange a shooting excursion for the following day. The keeper described how eager Stephanie was for her first shoot, and how happy they both appeared.[14]

REFERENCES

1. Corti, *Franz Josef*, Vol. II, p. 501.
2. Corti, *Elisabeth*, p. 311.
3. Corti, *Elisabeth*, p. 311.
4. *Erinnerungen und Gedanken des Botschafters Anton Graf Monts*, herausgegeben von K. F. Nowak und Friedrich Thimme (Berlin, 1932), p. 128.
5. Corti, *Elisabeth*, p. 316.
6. Corti, *Elisabeth*, p. 317.
7. P.R.O., London. F.O. 120/586.
8. Corti, *Elisabeth*, p. 317.
9. P.R.O., London. F.O. 120/587.
10. R. Charmatz, *Oesterreichs innere Geschichte, 1848–1895* (Leipzig, 1918), Vol. II, p. 45.
11. Royal Archives, Windsor, I, 53, 13.
12. Corti, *Franz Josef*, Vol. III, p. 15.
13. Corti, *Franz Josef*, Vol. III, p. 14.
14. Anon, *Kronprinz Rudolf als Forscher und Weidmann* (Vienna, n.d.), p. 37.

CHAPTER FIVE

Politics and Early Married Life

I

AFTER the brief honeymoon the young couple settled in Prague, where Rudolph resumed his military duties. Whatever had been his mood on his wedding day he was anxious that his marriage should be a success, yet he was not prepared to change the pattern of living he had followed as a bachelor. His military duties took up much of his time and he felt he could not pay less attention to his political studies and writings than before. Stephanie would need much of his company — she was young and inexperienced ; she had come into a new country, and her 'school-German' would not help her much to understand the Austrian dialect. Rudolph was too young and too preoccupied to realise her needs. If she did not show an interest in his political pursuits she would see little of him. This was not easy, as the intricacies of Austrian politics required a special knowledge far beyond her experience and training. To her husband politics was part and parcel of his everyday life, and now, with the prospect of perpetuating the Hapsburg line, this interest was intensified — he had to secure his country's future.

This future, as Rudolph saw it, was greatly endangered since Taaffe had been at the helm of the Austrian half of the dual monarchy. During the months preceding his wedding he had written frequently to Latour to give vent to his misgivings and to express his opposition to the growing tendency towards clericalism exhibited by the new government. In February 1881 he had written : 'I conceal neither the fact that I have no sympathy whatever for the influence of the Church on the state, nor that I detest all tendencies towards Church influence. I would much rather send my children to a school whose head-master is a Jew than to one whose headmaster is a clergy-man, a runaway protagonist of the "black" tendencies. The State has to treat all denominations equally ; a strengthening of the Catholic hierarchy has so far brought always evil consequences. We are approaching difficult times and the number of those still standing faithful to the banner of Liberalism is getting smaller and smaller.'

Such views, had they been known, would in the eyes of the Court and Austrian society have condemned Rudolph as an atheist. This was as bad as being an outlaw. As the Crown Prince frequently derived a certain satisfaction from shocking people by his remarks it may well be surmised that in Vienna, where mud-slinging had always been recognised as a political weapon, particularly against anyone of progressive opinions, he was maligned to dis-credit his political views.

Rudolph viewed the political situation with increasing alarm, as Taaffe had succeeded in combining the reactionary forces of Germans and Slavs in order to suppress Liberalism. The Crown Prince was both a Liberal and a friend of the Czechs. In his Slav memorandum he had said : 'the Slavs, to whatever nation they belong, have a mighty future, thanks to themselves, to their strength of character, and it would be madness in a state like Austria to make a policy which does not take full account of the Slavs', and he had recommended that the government should be based on Slav support more than had so far been the case, as German and Magyar preponderance had no factual reason. Now such a government existed, but it was based on the reactionary and not the progressive forces among the Slavs, as the Crown Prince had desired. In February 1881 in a letter to Latour he had defended the Czech people in spite of the readiness of some of their parliamentarians to assist Taaffe : 'I have much sympathy for the great Slav race and just for this reason I am so enraged with those feudal gentlemen who owe allegiance to no nation and who drag the Czech people down with them into the mud, to exploit them for the achievement of their reactionary and obscurantist aims. The Slavs are liberal and the day will come when they will thoroughly disown those gentlemen. . . .'

He continued to believe that a strong Slav influence on the Austrian government was necessary. In a note written much later than the Slav memorandum, but kept with the short summary of the latter, which was found among his papers, the Crown Prince had stated : 'The Danubian Empire must be extended to the [Aegean] Sea, to Salonika; that is only possible with Slav help. . . . Only by cultivating the Slavs can Russian influence be paralysed.'

II

Rudolph tried hard to establish contacts between German and Czech Liberals, particularly when he saw that the government was trying to revoke the Liberal Education Law passed a few years previously. He wrote to a former Liberal Minister, Chlumecky : 'Of all the sad experiences which we had to go through none has touched me so much as these attacks against enlightened education, to be pushed back into evil times I thought long past. As an Austrian I was proud of our so liberal, really modern institutions which we had acquired after a long struggle in the cultural field, and I am proud of the education for which I have to thank those teachers and scholars who belonged to this era. . . . I am filled with indignation and disgust at the present conditions. . . . How long will Slavs go on supporting such a reactionary policy? Is agreement between Liberal German and Liberal Slav elements an impossibility?'[1]

Rudolph was greatly dismayed when Chlumecky in his reply showed no enthusiasm for an alliance between German and Czech Liberals. 'An understanding between Liberal Germans and Slavs is indeed possible, even essential, but it becomes more and more remote. . . . It is only conceivable if and when political conditions permit the Germans to possess decisive influence, when therefore they and not the Slavs are the ones who concede something. . . .'

It was gravely disappointing that the Liberals, in order to strengthen their political position, failed to overcome national differences as readily as the reactionaries had done. The insistence on German preponderance, foolish though it may seem, finally broke the Austrian Empire. Rudolph did not realise that the German Liberals in Austria were unwilling to concede any diminution of the predominance which they claimed for the German nation ; that nationalism and Liberalism were but two facets of the same political idea at a certain stage of its development. His self-appointed task of creating the conditions for a government composed of Liberals and based on equal rights for all nations was made much more difficult, if not impossible, to achieve. But he refused to give up hope — yet.

While he was thus preoccupied with his politics, Stephanie felt neglected, but according to her own statement she did not try to share his interests — she was not even aware of them. In her memoirs she writes, 'The Crown Prince was much occupied with his military duties. He spent most of his days with the officers in the barracks, not as a rule returning . . . until three o'clock. After that he would go out shooting, take a ride or work with his officers. I scarcely saw him unless I accompanied him on an occasional shooting excursion.' [2] In Rudolph's letters, however, there is undeniable evidence of how much he wanted to be with Stephanie when, early in the summer of 1881, there were indications that she was pregnant.

He confided more in Latour in 1881 than at any other time since his majority, and in a letter dated July 9th he referred to the lack of understanding on the part of his parents and expressed great tenderness for his wife. 'As you know, Stephanie is pregnant. She is very young, has been used to the moderate and humid sea climate of Belgium and has now been transferred to a continental dry summer just when exposed to other changes as well. In Prague . . . the heat is so great that the staff officers send their families into the country. For Stephanie good air is now absolutely necessary. She looks already a bit poorly. I have repeatedly written to the Emperor, his reply is always the same — "Send her to the country". After two months of married life this is a hard sentence, but I would have swallowed it, though with bad grace. But for her the separation would be terrible . . . and might damage her health, and probably even more that of the child. If one wants healthy progeny, which reasons of state demand, everything must be done to achieve a favourable development of her condition, particularly the first time, without regard to personal considerations. But that may not be. She may not go to Ischl with its good air . . . because this could become a nuisance [to his parents]. So this young woman must remain in the hot unhealthy air of Prague.' He continued, that to go to Schönbrunn was forbidden by the Empress — one of the few instances when he is critical of his mother. Nor could he ask the Emperor's permission to go with Stephanie to the country as he would be considered 'lazy'.

This letter shows not only how unjustified Stephanie was in her strictures: 'The Crown Prince . . . cared for little outside his own pleasure and sport'.[3] This was a misstatement not only in the light of the letter quoted but also in the light of many of Rudolph's letters to Latour. In September, when he was about to attend military exercises, he wrote: 'Life here is so pleasant and quiet, and I have become so used to married life that I am really afraid of the eight days' separation'.

His undeniable domestic happiness and the increased concern for the future, which he felt when he thought his wife pregnant, made him more apprehensive than ever about the trend of political events. He felt the cohesion, even the very existence of the Austro-Hungarian monarchy — which he and probably his child were to rule one day — were threatened by Taaffe's growing influence. In an attempt to bring about a basic change in these gravely disturbing circumstances he summed up his views on the political situation in a memorandum of some twenty pages. He took great pains in marshalling his arguments and gave the task all his spare time for several months, completing it in November 1881.

The first copy he sent to Latour, and much more timidly than usual asked him to read it and judge 'how you like the matter and whether it might have a good or bad influence on the Emperor' if it were submitted to him.

The intention of presenting it to his father is clearly shown by its mild and temperate argument and diction, quite unlike the pungent and often violent style of his letters. In retrospect one may say that it was not only reasonable, but also that had the advice been tried it would probably have proved beneficial and might have delayed the disintegration of the dual monarchy for some time. He did not want to invite his father's opposition from the start by stating his case too strongly, but he stated it in unmistakable terms and suggested an alternative policy to the existing one which he considered so disastrous.

III

The Crown Prince began by indicting the Constitutional Party, the former Liberal government party. It was badly organised, lacked leadership and was incapable of forming or even consistently supporting a government. Nevertheless a number of its members in parliament were clever and patriotic. The party as a whole tried to support the government and to be in opposition at the same time. Cheap popularity was too often the motive force of their policy even when vital issues were at stake. Blissfully unaware that penetration into the Balkans was 'a vital need for Austria', the Constitutional Party had tried to prevent the occupation of Bosnia and Hercegovina by voting against the military grants required for this task.

The new government Taaffe tried to rule without this party, thus excluding the most important German elements. Taaffe could only obtain his majority by concessions to other national groups, frequently only by what amounted to outright corruption. The government's basic principle, decentralisation, was dangerous to the existence of the state, and just as dangerous was its leaning towards the Catholic Church.

Rudolph suggested that in the interest of Austria's future, decentralisation was not to be encouraged by new concessions to the Slav nations. On the other hand, government, with either the Constitutional Party alone or a coalition of German parties, was impossible. The only solution was to dissolve parliament and after elections to appoint a Ministry of progressive and understanding civil servants. These Ministers would be above party and would end the disgraceful quarrels in parliament. The new government should not encourage further decentralisation, but at the same time should be careful not to be too centralist, as in people's minds centralism too often stood for absolutism. It should avoid experiments of any kind. The budget should be balanced, if necessary by a new tax on movable property to extract a higher contribution from bankers and stock exchange jobbers. No clamour should be permitted to interfere with this.

The main task of this government was to be the education and reconciliation of the parties, so that eventually ideological differences would become more important than national diversity. What was elsewhere taken for granted had to be achieved in Austria by the government. The aim should be the encouragement of the growth of unified Liberal and Conservative parties combining the various nationalities — the two-party system as he had seen it at

work in Britain. Such a development was imperative ;
ordered administration was otherwise impossible, also the
Austrian half of the Empire would otherwise lose too much
prestige as compared with the more coherent Hungarian
half. The best guarantee of progress was firm belief in
Austria's future.

While Rudolph was convinced that a sufficiently chas-
tened and improved Liberal party would finally be able
to govern Austria, he had, probably under the impression
of the utterly undignified behaviour of parliament, become
so highly critical of this institution that he stated tersely,
'Where would a state come to if the last decisions in
foreign policy were not reserved for the Monarch and
his Ministers ?' This is one of the few passages in
Rudolph's writings where he questions the rights of
parliament.

Latour seemed to have been pleased with the document
and the Crown Prince was elated by his praise. He
answered in a long letter which must be quoted at length
because it shows better than any detailed description, not
only the views Rudolph held both about his parents'
attitude and Austrian politics, but also because it gives a
vivid picture of his domestic happiness which contrasts
sharply with the entirely distorted picture which Stephanie
presents in her memoirs. Rudolph wrote on December
2nd, 1881 : 'I was very pleased with your praise for my
simple effort and the way in which you accepted the whole
affair. It is not written for the sake of forming a *Fronde* or
even to earn praise or to make myself important, but solely
and exclusively out of conviction. I see the slippery slope
down which we slide ; I am very close to affairs but I
cannot do anything in any way, I must not even speak out
to express what I feel or believe. Our Emperor has no

friend, his whole character and his disposition do not permit it. He stands lonely on his eminence ; to his servants he talks of their duties, but a real conversation he studiously avoids. Thus he knows little of the thoughts and feelings of the people, of their views and opinions. Those who are in power now are the only people who have access to him and they naturally interpret matters in a way which is most convenient to them. He believes that we are living in one of the happiest periods of Austrian history, he is officially told so. In the newspapers he only reads the passages marked in red and so he is divorced from every human intercourse, from all impartial and really loyal advice.

'There was a time when the Empress frequently concerned herself with politics, whether with luck or not I will not discuss now. She also talked with the Emperor about serious things, motivated by views which were diametrically opposed to his. These times are past. The great lady no longer cares for anything but sport ; and so this access of outside opinions which were on the whole tinged with liberalism is now also closed. These convictions caused me, after mature consideration, to write this little political essay. When I intended to hand it over I was assailed by doubts and misgivings. Shall I, to whom there was never spoken a word of politics, to whom has never even been conceded the right of a personal opinion, not be considered presumptuous, and shall I not be taken as a *Frondeur* ? I am distrusted — I have noticed it for several months and latterly increasingly. . . . I have the reputation of being a Liberal, I have the closest associations with people who are not popular, even have a bad name. Three or four years ago the Emperor was already liberal to a certain degree and reconciled to the 19th century.

Now he is again as he was at the time of poor Grand-mama ; bigoted and harsh and distrustful ; matters can still go very far.

'God knows, I am not pushing, I do not want to play an important part, I have not the slightest intention of becoming a *Frondeur*. My views, my loyalty, my obedience, my good sense are greater than my vanity. If I wanted to play an evil, harmful part, if I wanted to become a rebel, I could do it in the most extensive, in the most far-reaching manner ; I am offered this part from all sides. From this essay there speaks no voice of revolt, of the tendency to play a part, but only the voice of distress, the voice of the adviser, in deepest incognito, so that matters can be changed and then the fruits enjoyed, and nobody shall know where the salutary change comes from. I want nothing, only a peaceful time, for myself a small military sphere of activity which leaves me also time for other studies and labours on which I am engaged.

'I have never been as happy as last summer, when, surrounded by blissful domesticity, I could devote my-self quietly to preliminary studies and to work on the *Orientreise* [title of a book which Rudolph had then written]. Now, if I am left in peace, I want to work on Spain.

'But now to the reason why I am writing to you today. Do you believe — you know our master very well indeed — that my essay will be taken amiss and interpreted as presumption, will be repulsed ? That, moreover, I could from this moment onwards be treated with distrust and met coldly and sternly and that this could be extended to my wife ? She is clever, very attentive and sensitive, full of ambition ; she is a granddaughter of Louis-Philippe and a Coburg ! I need not tell you more. I am very much in love with her and she is the only one who could tempt me to do many things. That is to be considered.

'Will the Emperor take my little work seriously or just glance through in the evening before retiring and lay it in a file, take the whole for the eccentricity of a dreamer who is not true to pattern ; as I often notice, he has become used to taking my whole way of living, thinking, and writing so. Will he show it to someone among his favourites, who would oppose it with the sacred fire of baseness ? Shall I let the Empress read it first ? She is an inactive, but thoroughly wise woman. Please do be good enough to answer these questions. I will wait for your opinion and act accordingly, or before that discuss it with you in Vienna.'

Historical opinion is divided as to Francis Joseph's merits as an Emperor. As a father, in his relationship to Rudolph, there can be only one verdict — he understood his son not in the slightest.

Rudolph's letter to Latour had to be quoted almost *in extenso* because it shows better than any other document the deep sincerity and the grave concern with which he approached political problems. His ideas may have been immature, he may have been imperfectly informed and his arguments not always valid, but his sincerity was beyond dispute. The memorandum and still more his letters to Latour in this connection show how deep his concern was. Had he been given a sphere of political duties, either instead of his army service or after a couple of years of service, a time of preparatory work and apprenticeship in the Foreign Ministry for example, he would have worked hard and conscientiously, and would have learned that politics is not so much the art of what is desirable as of what is possible. His tutors, most of them excellent, could not teach him what a year or two of regular work in a Ministry would have done.

It did not occur to Francis Joseph that his son was too ambitious, too intelligent to be satisfied with the accepted life of an Archduke. If the Emperor was blind in this respect there was no reason why his mother should be so. She had fought so hard for influence in Rudolph's education, and the fact that he was in his early twenties and now married should not have prevented her from exercising that influence she had fought for earlier. After twenty-five years of married life she should have known Francis Joseph well enough to realise that he would show no more imagination in dealing with his sensitive son than with the more usual pedestrian Archdukes. Liberally supplied with money, they were expected to lead an idle life relieved by a show of military and representative duties. If, as the evidence suggests, Elisabeth was afraid Rudolph's marriage would bring him unhappiness, as she did not consider clumsy Stephanie (*das Trampeltier*, as she called her) the right partner for her highly strung son, she must surely have known that a position which satisfied him and occupied his time fully would have been the best way of preventing what she feared. But she shirked the issue ; she did nothing, although she must have known that her husband could never say no to her requests. Nor did she talk to Rudolph ; again she must have been aware that a word from her would have helped him so much. He had to continue to lead a basically empty and, worse, frustrated life. He was far more intelligent than his father realised, and far more ambitious. His father's soulless routine and his mother's self-centred inertia drove the restless Crown Prince into many strange ways and ultimately to destruction. He could not live the ordinary, skirt-chasing, hard-drinking, empty life of most of the Archdukes, and, as he was not allowed to lead any other, he had to perish.

But catastrophe was still a long way off and Rudolph did not concern himself exclusively with the frustrating affairs of the Empire. In spite of his preoccupation with politics, he was throughout almost his whole life a keen stalker and shot, as one would expect of Francis Joseph's son. Nowhere did the Emperor feel more carefree, more himself than when pursuing the fleeting chamois in the jagged rocks of the Alps or the stag in the lonely woods. His letters to his son, usually stilted and artificial, were human when he dealt with hunting and shooting. But while Francis Joseph was only interested in the shooting, Rudolph was for many years more preoccupied with the observation of wild life, particularly birds. 'In you the ornithologist's heart beats stronger than the hunter's', one of Rudolph's friends had once written. In later years, when his life was beset with troubles and his restlessness had increased, he began to shoot indiscriminately, but he never became quite a game butcher, like his cousin, the Archduke Francis Ferdinand, or Prince William of Prussia.

IV

The Crown Prince had always shown great interest in natural sciences and his nature observations were closely linked with this. Although he could satisfy much of his desire for varied observations in his native country, he went abroad as well on longer or shorter expeditions. Before, as after, his marriage his hunting was his best means of countering the effect of long hours at his writing-desk. The Hapsburg domains still stretched from Central

Europe far into the Near East, and the Crown Prince, driven by his interest in the animal world, went frequently to those regions which were not generally included in official visits. In this way he had a good opportunity of getting to know what was to be one day his heritage. These hunting expeditions, particularly as he grew to manhood, meant a minimum of comfort and often the entire absence of ceremony. Accompanied by only a gamekeeper he often spent many days living rough, sleeping in lonely hunting boxes, and the authorities concerned with his safety felt frequently embarrassed. He had a homely way of talking and knew how to put people at their ease, and what his gamekeepers or beaters told him on these lonely stalking parties or over the fire in the evening must have been refreshingly different from what his courtiers told him in Prague, Budapest or Vienna. The hereditary lands (*Erblande*), as Austria was called in the antiquated language of the Hapsburg family laws, in this way became a living reality to him. He no longer had to rely as much on official reports as his father did ; his judgements on far-away provinces and their problems could be based on his own observations, and his political opinions were often founded on experience. He knew the country, and his easy command of many of the languages spoken in the Empire made possible direct contact with people in all walks of life.

He spent a fortnight on the lower Danube, observing and shooting birds ; he went into the lonely mountains of the province of Siebenbürgen to hunt bears, and was there nearly killed by an animal which he had wounded. He had no shot left in his rifle and the bear, which had reared to attack him, was quite near when one of his companions saved his life by a well-aimed round. He was as much at home on the wide Hungarian plain as on the rocky or snowy mountain sides of the Alps or the Dalmatian islands of the Adriatic.

He was fond of travelling, as one would expect of Elisabeth's son, and, although he did not travel to the same extent as his mother, he visited Spain, Palestine and Egypt. Some of his official journeys gave an opportunity for an occasional shooting party, as in Berlin or during his mission to Turkey in 1884, when he went pig-sticking in Asia Minor.

As he had a literary bent and wrote well, he soon began to describe his hunting expeditions in the more out-of-the-way places. These descriptions are written in vivid language which makes them very good reading ; they would have roused interest, even had their author not been the Crown Prince of the Austro-Hungarian monarchy. It was important for his style that he was not restricted in his subjects to political topics ; the desire to make his readers experience the thrills and impressions of his travels made him write much more vividly than politics alone would have required. To depict nature, a much greater word-mastery and writing discipline are necessary to avoid trite-ness. When we read Rudolph's travel books we are impressed by his facile and at the same time precise way of writing — no other member of his family ever achieved this mastery. He could, had he not been born to his station, have earned a living by his pen — provided the censorship would have permitted it. The urge to write on nature topics also helped his political thinking. People writing on day-by-day politics are frequently tempted to use empty but high-sounding phrases, particularly in German — and still more in its Austrian variation. Such phrases are of no use in describing actual experiences.

Rudolph could avoid — both in his writing and in his thinking — smothering flaws in an argument by verbiage.

He published several volumes of his travel reports, some of them at first anonymous. They were all well received, especially *Fifteen Days on the Danube*, which showed a keen appreciation of the beauties of nature. *A Journey in the Orient*, which was first published in 1881, proved so popular that a new edition became necessary and was published in 1884 with over a hundred illustrations. A third edition was required a year later.

Thus Rudolph's life was fully occupied in those years ; it must be remembered that politics and hunting and writing had to be done in his leisure hours, that he held a military appointment which took up most of his time. His married life was not allowed to suffer. Where it was possible, and not too strenuous, Stephanie accompanied him on his various expeditions and he frequently discussed with her political problems, as is shown in his letter to Latour already quoted. He trusted her implicitly and confided to her his plans for a great and re-born Austria which was to stretch to the limits of Asia, if not beyond. When in Constantinople in 1884 on a state visit he promised, 'Here you will be Empress one day'.[4] The Crown Princess did not long maintain her interest in politics. This is certainly the impression she gives in her memoirs, and in his later letters to her Rudolph mentions politics rarely, so far as can be judged from those which she chose to publish. This statement cannot be made with certainty. Rudolph's friend Szeps, with whom he usually discussed political affairs, reported that whenever Stephanie was present during their talks she would take her full share in them, and that both husband and wife gave the impression of enjoying happy, undisturbed family life. At times

Rudolph would make statements which might have shocked his father and other members of the family, but he never toned them down because of Stephanie's presence. She was often content to sit through such discussions in an atmosphere blue with smoke. The fact that the Empress Elisabeth shrank more and more from public functions, or was away on her travels, meant more work for Stephanie, who had to deputise for her. She liked these occasions and already pictured herself as the future Empress. She took them perhaps too seriously, but she acquired deportment and dress sense, in both of which she had been sadly lacking during the earlier years of her married life. Not only Stephanie, but Rudolph too had an increasing number of public functions to attend ; he had to visit those outlying parts of the Monarchy which would have taken up too much of the Emperor's time. The better known it became that he fulfilled these duties well, with his easy grace and bearing and with his pleasing manner of public speaking, the more the young couple had to devote themselves to these often empty, but always tiring, duties. On the other hand, frequent travelling and representing together must have strengthened the bond between them. When in Berlin in 1883, one of the Prussian Ministers noted how they exchanged friendly, surreptitious glances.

V

Rudolph was very anxious to have a family, and on more than one occasion they had mistakenly assumed that Stephanie was pregnant. When early in 1883 medical opinion confirmed beyond doubt that they could expect a child they were overjoyed. Rudolph wished to tell his father the news personally and was pleased when his duties made a visit to Vienna necessary. The Emperor 'was extremely joyful'. The Empress was staying at the time at the German spa of Kissingen, so he wrote the news to her. The prospect of having a son brought home to Rudolph how strong his dynastic interests were. In his letters to Stephanie he referred to the unborn child as *Vaclav* (Wenceslas), the name of the sainted king of Bohemia. In the German-speaking regions of Austria the name Wenzel (the German version of Vaclav) was used as a nickname to indicate any Czech. He concluded a letter written during his wife's pregnancy with 'take great care both of yourself and the Vaclav, and think of me. Embracing you with all my heart, your faithful Rudolph.' [5]

When the time for Stephanie's confinement was near, the Emperor at last agreed to Rudolph's transfer to Vienna, and on September 2nd, 1883, the child was born at Laxenburg, where the couple had spent their brief honeymoon. When Stephanie learned that the child was a girl she wept, but Rudolph consoled her with, 'Never mind, a girl is much sweeter'.[6] She was named Elisabeth after her beautiful grandmother. Rudolph was very much the proud father. He wrote to his friend Szeps : 'Mother and child are very well. Stephanie looks blooming as usual, as if nothing had happened. The little one is a stunner of seven pounds weight, perfectly well and strongly developed, with many hairs on her head, very much alive ; she shouts terribly and drinks a great deal without the slightest difficulty.' This description does not bear out Stephanie's stricture : 'The Crown Prince was absolutely stricken, for he had set his heart upon an heir to the throne !' [7] When the child was four weeks old he again to wrote to Szeps while attending a Court shooting,

'The party goes on Sunday to Eisenerz, but I have had enough, I long greatly for wife and child'.

When Elisabeth was born Rudolph and Stephanie had been married a little under two and a half years. So far they had been reasonably happy together, but differences in temperament and taste boded ill for the future. Rudolph was fond of simple pleasure — listening to popular music and joining in a sentimental song about wine, women and beautiful Vienna. He enjoyed mixing and chatting with the people at the *Heurigen*, those places where the Vienna wine growers were permitted to sell their own produce in simple and unpretentious surroundings while they sang their sentimental songs. Stephanie accompanied him once or twice but found no pleasure in it — the air was too smoky, the crowd too noisy, the wine too sour. She remained always stiff and formal and could never relax and forget her position. Rudolph, like his mother, disliked the more formal Court occasions which delighted Stephanie, yet when he did attend such functions his natural grace was a delight, while she had difficulties in overcoming her awkwardness. After the birth of her daughter, Stephanie certainly gained in composure, and by this time had also a better command of the German language, which she spoke with an Austrian accent. Nothing now prevented her from joining in her husband's pleasures had she wished to do so. She was not yet twenty, young enough to adapt herself, yet old enough to feel instinctively what was needed to make her marriage a success. The Crown Prince had very few people to whom he felt near ; there would have been room for Stephanie. If she had ever loved him — and not only the position which he had provided for her — she would have tried to learn.

Although she had to undergo an operation whose

outcome made the prospect of bearing further children remote, marital relationship continued for many years, and there is evidence that it was continued not only for the purpose of providing Austria with a male heir. The Crown Princess in her memoirs denies any real interest on Rudolph's part in married life : 'The Crown Prince had neither tastes nor understanding of a kind that would have enabled him, if only for the sake of setting a good example . . . to lead the affectionate existence of a young married couple'.[8] This was not so. As late as August 1885 he ended a letter to his wife with : 'Pay great attention to all you are doing. I am very anxious. I am longing terribly for you and count the days which still separate us. Embracing you with all my heart' [underlined in the original].[9] Amongst Rudolph's papers there is only one letter, dated 1887, from Stephanie. It is written in French and shows an equal affection on her part. This suggests that for several years their marriage was a reasonably happy one.

By 1887 Stephanie had not again become pregnant and she was sent to Franzensbad, a spa in Bohemia much recommended at the time for overcoming sterility. Rudolph was greatly concerned that the cure should be successful. He wrote to Court Marshal Bombelles, who was with the Crown Princess, giving orders that all receptions and excursions were to be strictly avoided, lest they should hamper the treatment. 'I do not want to write to Stephanie on these points, or she becomes nervous, and a peaceful mind is the principal thing in such cures.'

Stephanie's cold and self-centred attitude so clearly revealed in her memoirs, seems to have been the same during the early years of their married life. In spite of her protestations, she showed no real desire to share the way of life which her husband had already mapped out, and she had nothing to offer in its place. Yet she resisted all his attempts to re-create a world which they could both share. Estrangement became unavoidable ; its main cause, as is so frequently the case, was the feeling on both sides of not being understood. At a time when it was accepted that men, whether married or not, were free to have their mistresses, Stephanie's attitude was more than unfortunate — it was fatal. Most women found Rudolph very attractive.

Stephanie's elder sister, Louise, described him as 'more than handsome, he was enchanting. Behind his fragile appearance lay reserves of strength and energy. He reminded one of a racehorse ; he had its temperament, breeding and caprice. His will power was only equalled by his sensibility. . . . Like his mother, the Empress Elisabeth, he had a way of talking that held everybody, and a faculty for setting all about him agog to solve the riddle of his personality.' [10] Stephanie, according to her memoirs, was more critical, even before their marriage. 'The Crown Prince could not be called handsome, but I found his appearance by no means unpleasing. His small light-brown eyes had an intelligent expression, but there was something unfrank and hard about his gaze ; he could not bear to be looked at directly in the face. About his wide mouth, which was half hidden by a small moustache, there was an expression which was difficult to read." [11] Although her memoirs were published when she was old and embittered, one would have expected more regard for the feelings of her own youth, if indeed she had had any at that time.

Rudolph had grown up in a man's world, lacking his mother's nearness in spite of all his longing for her. He needed the tenderness which only a woman can give. He was married, but remained alone, and he was ready to come under the spell of any woman who could offer him those qualities which he could not find in his wife.

REFERENCES

1. *Neue Freie Presse*, June 4th, 1933.
2. H.R.H. Princess Stephanie of Belgium, Fürstin of Lonyay, Ex-Crown Princess of Austria-Hungary, *I was to be an Empress* (Leipzig, 1937), p. 123.
3. Lonyay, *op. cit.* p. 123.
4. Henry Wickham Steed, *The Hapsburg Monarchy* (London, 1913), p. 212.
5. This letter is printed twice, once in Stephanie's memoirs, p. 144, and also in Juliana von Stockhausen, *Im Schatten der Hofburg* (Heidelberg, 1952), p. 95. In the memoirs the word 'faithful' is left out.
6. Corti, *Elisabeth*, p. 33.
7. Lonyay, *op. cit.* p. 146.
8. Lonyay, *op. cit.* p. 153.
9. Stockhausen, *op. cit.* pp. 99 f., and in a free translation in Lonyay, *loc. cit.* pp. 189 f.
10. The Princess Louise of Belgium, *My Own Affairs* (London, 1921), pp. 106.
11. Lonyay, *op. cit.* p. 94.

CHAPTER SIX

Strange Trends and Influences

I

RUDOLPH was doubly related to the Bavarian Royal house, the Wittelsbach, both his grandmothers being sisters who had been Wittelsbach princesses. Theirs was one of the oldest reigning families in Europe, they had been rulers since the early thirteenth century. Thus they could even beat the Hapsburgs by a few decades. In-breeding had been frequent. There had been several branches of the family, but by the early nineteenth century these were reduced to two, the ruling branch, the Dukes *of* Bavaria, and a minor branch, the Dukes *in* Bavaria. By the grace of Napoleon, the Duke *of* Bavaria became King of Bavaria in 1805. In 1780 the Duke *in* Bavaria married Maria Anna, sister of the Duke (later King Maximilian I) *of* Bavaria. Their grandson Max, Duke *in* Bavaria, in 1828 married his aunt Ludovica (called Louise), a daughter of this same King Maximilian. These were the parents of Elisabeth, Rudolph's mother. Sophie, another daughter of King Maximilian, married Archduke Franz Karl of Hapsburg. These were the parents of Francis Joseph, Rudolph's father. While Francis Joseph showed no weak hereditary strain, the Empress Elisabeth is generally described as being restless and strange. She showed definite signs of an eccentric disposition which may well have been the result of the frequent marriages within the family. Both their surviving daughters were entirely free from any signs of degeneracy — they were in fact rather ordinary women — but Rudolph's nervous energy and high intelligence may have been a consequence of this in-breeding.

The family tree (see pages 98-99) suggests that the in-breeding and hereditary strain in Rudolph was reinforced from the Hapsburg side. Here also there had been some in-breeding. The Emperor Leopold II, Maria Theresa's second son, was Rudolph's great-great-grandfather. His son, the Emperor Francis I, married his first cousin, Leopold's niece. The eldest son of this marriage, the Emperor Ferdinand, Rudolph's great-uncle, although not insane, had shown a definite imbecile trend. Francis Joseph's youngest brother, Ludwig Victor, showed a similar trend, again without being certifiable. The Viennese, with little regard for rank, called both mad when no policemen could overhear them. Instead of sixteen great-great-grandparents Rudolph had only twelve, and even among these there were some blood relations. Going still further back we find that at least one of his ancestors was 'restless, strange, pedantic and despotic, excessively violent, suffering from pathological fear of dangers and from imaginary illness'. To him is frequently ascribed the insanity in the royal branch of the Wittelsbachs.[1]

Certifiable madness became apparent in the Wittelsbach family during Rudolph's lifetime. King Maxmilian, grandfather to both Francis Joseph and Elisabeth, had been married twice. Francis Joseph's mother and Elisabeth's mother were both daughters by his second wife; the children by his first marriage inherited the Bavarian throne. In 1864 Maximilian's great-grandson, Ludwig II, became King when he was just over eighteen, and although

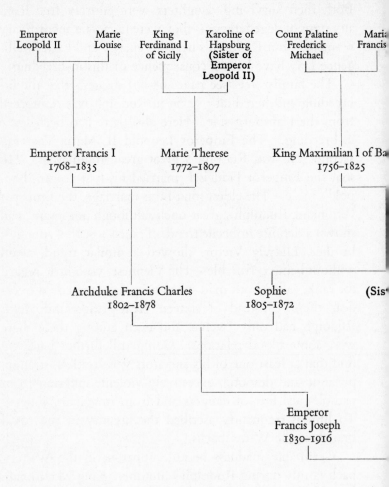

Emperor Leopold II	Marie Louise	King Ferdinand I of Sicily	Karoline of Hapsburg **(Sister of Emperor Leopold II)**	Count Palatine Frederick Michael	Mari Francis

Emperor Francis I
1768–1835

Marie Therese
1772–1807

King Maximilian I of Ba
1756–1825

Archduke Francis Charles
1802–1878

Sophie
1805–1872

(Sis

Emperor
Francis Joseph
1830–1916

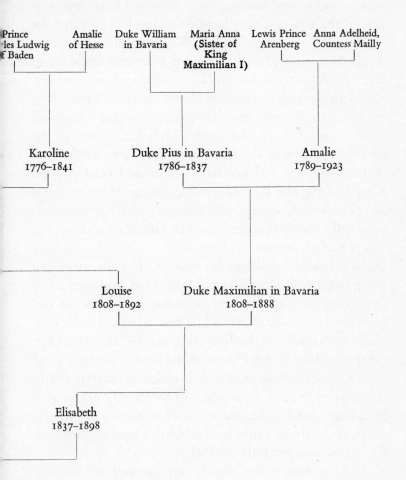

Prince
les Ludwig
f Baden

Amalie
of Hesse

Duke William
in Bavaria

Maria Anna
**(Sister of
King
Maximilian I)**

Lewis Prince
Arenberg

Anna Adelheid,
Countess Mailly

Karoline
1776–1841

Duke Pius in Bavaria
1786–1837

Amalie
1789–1923

Louise
1808–1892

Duke Maximilian in Bavaria
1808–1888

Elisabeth
1837–1898

thirteen years older than Rudolph they were of the same generation, second cousins. He showed a keen appreciation of the arts, was very handsome, and had captured the imagination of his subjects. When hardly more than seventeen years old he had shown a definite tendency to form passionate attachments to members of his own sex, a tendency which increased with the course of time. One of his friends was the composer, Richard Wagner ; another, much later, the actor Joseph Kainz, one of the greatest Hamlets of the German stage. Such attachments of themselves would not have constituted madness, but King Ludwig also had an ever-increasing desire to avoid all other human society, which made orderly government constantly more difficult. In 1872 his only brother Otto was certified insane. There were no other children. Ludwig himself, although his way of life grew more and more strange, was not certified until 1886, and died a few days later in mysterious circumstances which to this day have not been fully explained. Otto, who had to be kept under permanent medical supervision, died in 1916. The other members of this branch of the family, Ludwig's and Otto's uncles and aunts and their children, were perfectly healthy and lived to a ripe age. Consequently it may well have been possible that the strain of insanity was brought into this family by Ludwig's and Otto's mother, although she herself was perfectly normal.

Ludwig had never shown any interest in women, regardless of age, but his cousin the Empress Elisabeth certainly attracted him. He had no close relationship with his mother ; the only older woman to gain his confidence was his governess, Fräulein Meilhaus. Even with the Empress there was, whatever colourful novelettes and films may imply, no romance of any kind. Elisabeth was his senior by eight years and was already married before he showed any interest in her. His inclination was exclusively towards his own sex.

II

Through his mother Rudolph had learned at an early age of his cousin Ludwig. In 1865, when he was not yet seven, his mother had described one of his visits : 'Yesterday the King [Ludwig] paid me a long visit, and if Grandmama had not come in in the middle he would still be there. He kissed my hand so often that your Aunt Sophie, who was looking through the keyhole, asked me afterwards whether anything remained of it. He was dressed in Austrian uniform and scented all over with *chypre*.' [2]

In 1867 Ludwig, in order to satisfy public demand, became engaged to Elisabeth's younger sister Sophie. After a year's uneasy courtship the frightened King postponed the day of the wedding again and again and finally broke the engagement. For a time Elisabeth was hurt by his behaviour, but not for long ; perhaps she thought that he would not have been the right husband for her sister. Meanwhile Rudolph had grown older, and, when he met his cousin, he greatly impressed the older Ludwig by his easy grace. In 1875 Rudolph, then seventeen, paid a visit to the Bavarian Court, and for the first time the cousins had an opportunity for long talks together. Ludwig had made lavish preparations for this visit, and put the full splendour of the Court at Rudolph's disposal. He admired the young prince's erudition as much as his graceful bearing, and for some time after this visit they corresponded regularly. Their letters give an insight into both minds.

Francis Joseph, who had regular reports on Ludwig's strange behaviour from his Minister in Munich, had not cared for his son's friendship with him, but he had put up with it for the sake of the Empress, who seemed fond of her peculiar cousin. She was so easily offended and the Emperor studiously avoided anything that could cause her annoyance. But when Rudolph returned from Munich in 1875 he had had to give a detailed account of his visit. The Emperor had seemed satisfied with their relationship and had not forbidden any further contact between them, and so there had existed during Rudolph's most impressionable years an influence which cannot have been in any way healthy.

The young man had been naturally impressed by the attention shown to him by a ruling king. Although Ludwig had moderated his usual exuberance when writing to the Crown Prince, more than enough had remained to impress. A short time after the visit he had ended a letter with : 'You had the kindness to assure me in your last letter that you love me and esteem me. I too love and esteem you, dearest cousin, from the bottom of my heart and I beg of you, as you did of me, for the continuation of your friendship which I value so much. . . . In you lives the spirit of Maria Theresa and Joseph II ; this is the truth, and who would deny it I would hate as if he were my personal enemy. . . . For my whole life I shall in sincere rockfirm friendship remain happy in having met you. . . .'

In 1877 Rudolph had again visited Ludwig in Munich and a little later wrote to him from Gödöllö in Hungary a letter of thanks in which he answered Ludwig's protestations of eternal friendship. Although he expressed himself less effusively than his cousin, he showed sufficient enthusiasm to please him : 'You have in your kindness so often assured me of your friendship and commanded me to speak to you in the sincere language of the heart and not in the forced tongue which your high position requires. Would you therefore please forgive me when I assure you that you are my dearest and most valued friend, not on account of your dignity, but because of your spirit, your noble and really lofty nature, and that you will always be able to count on me and my loyalty. I appreciate fully and am proud that you, a gentleman, so much wrapped up in yourself and your knowledge, and who so rarely trusts anyone with your confidence and friendship, should select me as your friend.' [3]

Rudolph's mind must have dwelt long on the things told him by Ludwig and he was anxious to please his older cousin. He had never had any ear for serious music but he went to the opera to hear music by Wagner, who was Ludwig's demigod. Latour had already remarked on the Crown Prince's lack of sincerity and his desire to please. We are forcefully reminded of that observation when we read the letters which he painfully penned to his cousin in which he simulated an interest in Ludwig's excessive love for Wagner's music, as when he reported on Richard Wagner's visit to Vienna or on a *Lohengrin* performance.[4]

He was often lonely and in need of a companion who could understand him. When writing to Ludwig on subjects which really interested him he showed a confidence absent from his letters to other relatives. During his stay in Munich in 1877 or in a subsequent letter which was not kept, Ludwig must have discussed with him religious questions. These problems had occupied Rudolph's mind much at that time, so that even during his crowded stay in England he had taken time off to pen a long letter in which he had written frankly of his religious beliefs : 'You have graciously enquired after the books which influenced my religious views. I must confess that I do not like to come into the open with my creed, as I never know whether I hurt somebody else's feelings, but I can tell you everything that I feel and think, as I know your gracious friendship for me, and because I know you are also very enlightened in your views and not dominated by a religious mania which inhibits all spiritual development. I appreciate religion when it became in a really beneficial way the educator of the people and implanted in the common man the first beginnings of moral feelings, but I am afraid of it when it becomes the weapon and the means for the achievement of the purposes of a single class or party, when consequently it implants blind belief and superstition among the people instead of real culture. For an educated man who stands at that point of spiritual development which lifts him above everyday life, and who begins to investigate and to think systematically, for such a person I consider the Christian faith an entire impossibility within those narrow confines that our Church demands. He will have his religious, or rather his moral laws, which he sets for himself, and according to which he regulates his spiritual life ; but they will not be the confines which the Church wants to impose through the desire for Heaven or the fear of Hell, but only those chains by which the spiritual life of man dominates the physical life of the body.'[5]

Ludwig was very religious and throughout his life attended most of those services and ceremonies demanded by the Roman Catholic Church. But in order to please Rudolph he made concessions in his reply. Unfortunately part of the letter, the first sheet, is lost, but the remaining sheet gives Ludwig's opinion clearly enough. 'Let the people definitely stick to their good Catholic belief with its beneficial promises of life after death, its miracles and sacraments, but educated people can not, as you so rightly say, find these out-dated views satisfying. . . .' In the same letter he added an assurance of his unchanging friendship : 'I cling to nobody as firmly and as faithfully as to you and it is my sincere desire that you should receive Bavaria after my death. Goodbye my dear brother, keep your friendship for me which is dear and valuable to me above all else. . . .'

III

The last meeting between the two cousins had taken place in 1880 when Rudolph was on his way to Brussels to meet Stephanie. It had led to the repetition of all old promises of eternal faithful friendship, and they had remained together until morning dawned. This meeting had taken place in Ludwig's Wintergarten, whose splendours were a byword among the burghers of Munich. No record of their talk exists. We can only surmise that conversation in the normal sense must have been difficult. Ludwig's strangeness of behaviour had greatly increased during the previous two years and the ordinary government of Bavaria had almost ceased. It was a signal honour for Rudolph that Ludwig had come to Munich for his sake, but what the more systematically minded Rudolph had gained by their conversation is impossible to gauge. One thing is certain : the close contact between the highly impressionable Crown Prince and the confirmed homosexual King so near to insanity had been very unwise. After Rudolph's engagement and marriage the letters

became less frequent and soon seem to have ceased altogether. There were many reasons for this — Ludwig's
life became stranger and stranger as time went on, and any
man of his circle who married placed himself outside the
pale.

In 1886 Ludwig was certified insane and declared
unable to exercise his royal office. He was to be confined
to the castle of Berg on the lake of Starnberg, near Possenhofen, where the Empress Elisabeth's parents had their
country seat. On the second day of his restraint, neither
the King nor his accompanying alienist, Dr. Gudden,
returned from a walk. They were both found drowned
in the lake where the water was less than knee-deep.
Either Ludwig committed suicide and drowned Gudden
who tried to prevent him, or he attempted an escape in
which he was obstructed ; that in the ensuing struggle
Gudden was drowned and Ludwig, in a moment of realisation, then committed suicide. A third version, sometimes
told at the time, that Gudden murdered the King and
during the act was drowned by Ludwig in self defence, is
still less credible, although Rudolph believed it at first.
The Emperor sent Rudolph to represent him at the
funeral, which was probably a grave mistake, as the Crown
Prince had been seriously ill only a few months before,
and it is doubtful whether he was fully recovered.

The Empress Elisabeth was staying with her parents at
Possenhofen, accompanied by her youngest daughter
Valerie. She was much affected by her cousin's mysterious
death. She had been one of the few people who had never
lost her tenderness for the dead King and she behaved very
strangely when she learned of the tragedy. She cried
for hours and wildly accused the Bavarian Government
of having indirectly caused the King's death by having

him certified insane. For days she was in a state of wild agitation.

Rudolph visited his mother at Possenhofen before attending the funeral. He feared that the news of her cousin's death would have upset her, but he was unpreprepared for such violent outbursts of grief, and the thought struck him painfully that his beloved mother too might one day fall a victim to her cousin's horrible affliction. There were innumerable idiosyncrasies and traits, unimportant in themselves, which now might be interpreted as symptoms of the same tendency. He cross-examined his sister closely, but seemed satisfied with the result and was, during the stay, very amiable and full of tenderness, towards both his mother and his sister. The thought that his mother might be suffering from a still hidden hereditary taint was not far from the morbid idea that he himself might have the same streak in his blood. We know that Rudolph, although never a hypochondriac, was in many ways timid and easily afraid of hidden dangers. He would not show anyone his fears — there was nobody close enough for that — but they would be there, burrowing in his subconscious mind, undermining his will to live.

From his childhood he had shown a strange interest in death, and this had persisted into manhood. In April 1882 Szeps had made a note of an almost frightening talk with Rudolph, who had told him : 'From time to time I look for an opportunity to watch a dying person and to overhear his last breath. It is always for me a curious sight and of all the people whom I have seen dying, each has died in a different way. I observe with attention dying animals and try also to get my wife used to the sight. It is necessary to learn to take the last needs of life into account.' A few weeks after this talk, in which Stephanie too had joined, Rudolph was at Görgeny in Hungary, and in a fit of morbidness said to his companions : 'It is not I who will be Emperor of Austria but he' (pointing to the Archduke Francis Ferdinand, next in succession to the throne).

In 1886 — the year of Ludwig's death — Rudolph met Professor Zuckerkandl, an anatomist, who had a short time before married Maurice Szeps's daughter Bertha. He asked him if he did not find life among corpses uncanny. Zuckerkandl replied : 'No, even skulls have a certain beauty. One gets used to the idea that death is not a misfortune, but a necessary, even miraculous, fulfilment of life.' Rudolph immediately assented : 'One should face the idea of death straightforwardly'.[6]

Later, in 1887, Rudolph asked Zuckerkandl to let him have a skull, a request which was naturally granted and a specially prepared skull was handed to him which he kept on his desk in the Imperial Palace. According to one version [7] he is supposed to have brought the skull from Dalmatia, where he had found it in a cave, and Zuckerkandl had prepared and polished it for him. Whichever the case, the Crown Prince kept this skull on his desk.

There is no indication that he had a permanently diseased mind, but there can be little doubt about his morbidness, which increased as time went on. The attendance at Ludwig's funeral and his mother's strange behaviour, must have reinforced these tendencies. Ludwig's death, although their contacts had lessened with the course of years, must have been a painful reminder of the time when he was almost the only person who considered the views of the young Crown Prince seriously. Rudolph was not much older, but he felt frequently tired, and the days of 1878, or even those of 1880, seemed a long time ago. He must have felt the loss of his cousin keenly, for in 1887, when he bought a hunting lodge at Mayerling in the heart of the Vienna Woods, he hung a portrait of the dead king in his bedroom.

Rudolph was not the only young Viennese with this strange predilection for death, but he was the first to give expression to it. In the 'nineties suicide was a frequent subject on the stage and in fiction. The best-known writers of the *fin de siècle*, Schnitzler, Hofmannsthal, Stephan Zweig and later Rilke, all share the strange trend which the Crown Prince was the first to express. With an easily hurt mind, a tenderness of feeling which he often hid behind a screen of dare-devil bravado, Rudolph was very much a product of his time. He, at least in his early twenties, resembled much more the young *literati* of contemporary Vienna than an army officer. He was of the generation of which one of its members, Hofmannsthal, had written: 'So let us clear the stage, put on the plays we wrote, the comedies of our souls, tender, wise beyond our years, and sad'.

REFERENCES

1. Mitis, *op. cit.* p. 220.
2. Corti, *Elisabeth*, p. 129, and F. Mayr-Ofen, *Ludwig II of Bavaria* (London, 1937), p. 105.
3. Mitis, *op. cit.* p. 34.
4. Mitis, *op. cit.* pp. 406 f.
5. Mitis, *op. cit.* pp. 254 f.
6. Bertha Szeps, *op. cit.* p. 114.
7. Berthold Frischauer, 'Kronprinzlegenden', *Neue Freie Presse*, August 20th, 1921.

CHAPTER SEVEN

New Friends and New Foes

I

RUDOLPH had put a great deal of thought and work into his memorandum of 1881, but he realised that it had had no effect. Austria's home policy was then at a particularly critical stage. While the Taaffe government was reactionary and tried to suppress political Liberalism, its financial policy did not seriously impede economic progress. Moreover, the city of Vienna and most of the bigger towns were still administered by predominantly Liberal councils which were firmly wedded to the ideas of *laissez-faire* — eschewing all communal enterprise, frequently to the disadvantage of the inhabitants. This prejudice was unfortunate, as the unavoidable economic development from the more primitive to the more modern methods of production was a painful process which inevitably left a trail of many infuriated and pauperised victims. Not unnaturally, people who had to suffer from the changes resented them and acted instinctively, and not always rationally. They hated the new class of capitalists, who obtrusively displayed their wealth, frequently in the most tasteless and purse-proud way, but who were permitted to go on making money, even by the Taaffe government, to pay taxes, to provide the funds for the modernisation of the towns, for the arts and the theatres.

The first shock had occurred in 1873 when the crash at the Vienna stock exchange had caused heavy, frequently irreparable, losses to many people who had been carried away by a skilful, but not always honest, propaganda in their desire to taste the forbidden fruit of what they later called the Upas tree. Bankruptcies and suicides were the consequences of the breakdown of the unnatural inflation of speculation. It was conveniently discovered that many of the bankers and stock-jobbers had been Jews. Anti-Semitism had never entirely disappeared in Austria, but it had been less prevalent between 1867 and 1873. In 1867 the legal disabilities of the Jews had been removed, without establishing real equality. In 1873 the crash at the stock exchange had unleashed still latent forces of hatred which increased during the subsequent years, and in the early 1880s came into the open in a new guise, as a political party which blatantly proclaimed anti-Semitism as its party creed. Its foremost aim was to prevent Liberalism from gaining a hold in the country, if possible to achieve its total destruction. Although Liberalism was still young it had antagonised many people through its lack of awareness of social obligations. By equating it with Jewry it could be further discredited and ultimately destroyed.

Many Jews in their newly attained freedom may have acted indiscreetly, may have been pushing and snobbish and frequently reckless in their business dealings. Parts of the former Poland still belonged to Austria, and Jews from these provinces had been attracted by the relatively easier living in the western provinces, particularly in Vienna. They were sometimes uncouth and outlandish in manners and behaviour, but no more, and no less so than the Christians from those still backward areas. Their strangeness, particularly when they were orthodox in their belief and in their dress, drew attention to themselves, and there was sometimes friction and often cause for complaint. On the other hand, Jews formed an important part of the Vienna intelligentsia, and the enhanced cultural life of the city was largely due to their contributions. Both Court theatres owed their reputation to Jewish patronage, and the musical life of the city had undergone a remarkable change, so that no longer were composers like Brahms and Hugo Wolf forced to die in penury as Mozart, Beethoven and Schubert had done. The Jews 'were the real audience, they filled the theatres and the concerts, they bought the books and the pictures, they visited the exhibitions and with their more mobile understanding, little hampered by tradition, they were the exponents and champions of all that was new. . . . Because of their passionate love for the city . . . they . . . were happy to serve the glory of Vienna. They felt that their being Austrian was a mission to the world.'[1]

Whether the grounds for the anti-Jewish feelings were real or imagined, it was not at all difficult to convince dissatisfied people that Jews were the cause of all evil. In appealing to the basest instincts in the masses, to hatred and envy, the new political movement introduced into Austrian politics the atmosphere of a sewer. Taaffe and his Ministers possessed a certain *savoir-vivre*. While they did everything in their power to impede political progress they had recognised that economic development was necessary — if for no other reason, to keep Austria-Hungary sufficiently strong to remain a great power. The new political forces, on the other hand, were frequently led by uncouth backwoodsmen who were ready to use any arguments, no matter how unsavoury and dirty, provided their demagogy had its effect. In economic matters they

Moriz Szeps

Joseph Latour von
Thurnberg

showed no spark of understanding, they were prepared to make any demand regardless of the consequences. Some of the speeches of their leaders sound as though they had come from Hitler or Goebbels. Hitler himself confessed that he owed much to the anti-Jewish movement in Vienna, where he had received his first political education.

In the early 'eighties this movement was still in its infancy, but already it had begun to threaten the Liberal city government of Vienna and the whole spiritual life of the city. The barbarians were at the gates, and a wave of pessimism swept over the young writers, many of whom were Jews. In time Rudolph was bound to come up against these forces. As yet he had hardly noticed them — Taaffe seemed much more real and dangerous. Not content to be a mere onlooker, starved of real news by his father's government, he took a step which was to have important consequences. At his request one of his former tutors, the economist Menger, introduced Moriz Szeps to him in October 1881.

Szeps was editor-in-chief of one of the most important Liberal papers, the *Tagblatt*. To the Minister President and the reactionaries at Court he was a *bête noire*, as his was an influential paper which, even at a time not very favourable to the daily press, had achieved a circulation of forty thousand. He was Rudolph's senior by some twenty years, was highly cultured, well read and a good conversationalist, possessing a stupendous memory. Through him the Crown Prince was allowed a glimpse into the strange, yet fascinating world — that of the sophisticated, civilised higher middle-class, usually ignored by Court circles. It was considered poor taste for an Archduke to have anything to do with members of this class, other than of a possible fleeting amorous nature with their daughters.

In this case matters were much worse, as Szeps was not only a member of this middle class, but also a Jew, and as the anti-Semitic movement gathered momentum the association would cause embarrassment and possible danger for the Crown Prince.

To aggravate the situation still further, Szeps was not only a Jew, but a journalist as well. Journalists in Taaffe's Austria, and not only then, were looked upon with a feeling of dread and contempt. They were the modern counterpart of the medieval hangman, considered to be following a dishonourable calling. Public condemnation was not entirely without foundation ; most newspapers had very limited circulations and not sufficient advertisements to pay their staffs decent salaries, so that journalists were frequently venal and on the look-out for perquisites. But there were exceptions, people like Szeps, men of stature and discernment, beyond reproach. Taaffe and other Ministers considered it beneath their dignity even to talk to newspaper men, and the authorities from the Minister President downwards had a poor opinion of the press. The least important pen-pusher in a government office felt himself superior to any editor. Neither the government nor the public was aware that the press had a public duty to perform in a modern state.

Rudolph had acted boldly when he began his friendship with Szeps, but this did not worry him. His motto was 'I want to know', and the editor could supply knowledge better than anyone else in contemporary Austria, although his sources did not please the government of the day and made him still more suspect. Szeps had connections with France, he was related to Clemenceau and knew Gambetta well. Between 1871 and 1938 it was considered a crime in Vienna for a newspaper to have good relations with French politicians, whereas the acceptance of biased information and sometimes money from Germany was considered meritorious and patriotic. Particularly during the 'eighties, when Bismarck was still directing German foreign policy, his secret fund to influence newspapers had a wide circle of recipients, inside and outside Germany.

The Crown Prince was anxious to keep his association with Szeps from the government's knowledge. He was fully aware that the police, by orders of the Minister President, had devised a system of spying upon him under the guise of protecting his life. The system of police surveillance over all members of the Imperial House dated from the days of Metternich and his Imperial Master Francis I, but in Rudolph's case it had been perfected ; no aspect of his life was free from their prying. The Crown Prince had earlier stated to Latour that he had reasons to distrust the Imperial Austrian postal services. He had been fully justified. But supervision was increased as time went on, particularly when, in spite of all precautions, his connections with Szeps became known.

This was not due to lack of care on either Rudolph's or Szeps's part. An old trusted retainer, Nehammer, carried the letters to the editor ; on leaving the palace he had first to shake off the detectives shadowing him by using several trams and making detours. At Szeps's flat none of the servants was to know that he came from the Crown Prince. Although old and frail he had been introduced as a masseur who came by doctor's orders to massage the editor's daughter Bertha. When alone with her he could hand her the letters unobserved. On his part Szeps, when not writing his letters by hand, did not dictate them to his secretary but to his daughter, and the waiting Nehammer would take them back to his master. Szeps, when he visited Rudolph in the Imperial Palace, as he frequently did, came usually well after midnight, at a time when the vigilance of the police had abated. Nehammer would take him to the Crown Prince's room by way of servants' and tradesmen's doors and stairs.

Even when his visitor was safely in the palace there was still the danger of being overheard. On one occasion they had hardly settled down when 'the Crown Prince suddenly got up again and, pointing to the left-hand door, said : "I don't trust this door. Let's go into my wife's music room."' When away from Vienna Rudolph communicated with Szeps by post, but that was not safe either. On one of the first occasions he wrote, 'I have good reason to assume that my letters are opened'.

He himself was partly to blame for coming under suspicion, as he admitted : 'Unfortunately I was often careless in my remarks and since then I have been considered "wayward" in very high conservative circles. This is very awkward as, in regard to matters not otherwise connected with me at all, I am given distrustful glances.' Even had the Crown Prince been more careful in his utterances the police would have found out.

Rudolph may not have intended his relationship with Szeps to become very intimate, but partly because of the older man's interesting and attractive personality, partly because of the opposition which this strange friendship was bound to meet in Court circles, it grew into a firm bond. Yet Szeps never omitted to show the deference due to Rudolph's rank. Although much better informed than many people at the Court, he was always ready to hear the Crown Prince's views and took them very seriously — to him Rudolph was not 'just a talker'. The only drawback was that the relationship with Latour seemed to have become a little cooler by virtue of the new friendship. But while the former governor could be approached for advice on all matters that might have troubled Rudolph, Szeps was mainly enveloped in politics, and could never quite replace Latour's rôle of fatherly friend.

The hostility which the Crown Prince met in certain Court circles was not a consequence of this new friendship. Already in his first letter to the editor he speaks of 'malicious highwaymen, who permanently cause me annoyance and vexation'. This was to grow worse. After about a year's friendship, Rudolph summarised his experience in a letter to the editor : 'I must draw your attention today to a number of odd things. They are becoming very watchful and suspicious of me, and I see more clearly every day what a tight circle of espionage, denunciations and supervision surrounds me. Be very careful if ever you are asked about your relations with me. Even if you speak to Nehammer, or give him letters or messages, do not omit the slightest precaution. Watch him, too, to see if he commits any solecism. . . . I have already told you that I have good reason to believe that our relations are known in high quarters ; since then I have proof of it. . . . I know only too well the way in which my enemies work. . . . Open accusations and denunciations of me in highest quarters. All this I have been through already. I have been denounced as a Freemason, and complete proofs with dates have been supplied, whereas I do not even know the rules of the order. . . . There is a large circle and an active committee continually preparing complaints and intrigues of this sort. For a long time they tried to bribe me, but when this did not work they took to the technique of trying to terrorise me from time to time and creating many difficulties and much unpleasantness for me. . . .'

Mitis in his biography is not sure whether the Crown Prince's suspicions were based on fact or whether he imagined that he was being persecuted.[2] Since the publication of his work, however, evidence has been published which shows beyond the shadow of a doubt that the police supervised every moment of Rudolph's life. The book *Das Mayerling Original* (Wien, 1955), of which more will be said later, consists largely of reports from police spies and informers on every step he took.

Through Szeps Rudolph came into contact with other journalists. In comparison with other daily papers the *Tagblatt* had an excellent news service ; much more information was received than could be used, taking into account the censorship and a politically rather uneducated reading public. For many years Rudolph had complained of a lack of information, as he had stated in one of his letters to Szeps, 'Since I belong to the people least informed from official sources . . . what I say is decidedly my private view'. Szeps was able to supply better information than the official sources, and he put all his connections at the Crown Prince's disposal ; his reports on French conditions, based on direct contacts, were invaluable. Two members of the *Tagblatt* staff, Frischauer and Futtaky, frequently reported to him directly. Futtaky lived in Budapest and knew Hungarian political conditions well, and Frischauer, whenever necessary, was sent to investigate particular centres of trouble and could be relied upon to unearth the causes. The Berlin correspondent Heller was also a first-rate man and Szeps passed on many of his reports to Rudolph.

Count Kálnoky, the Austrian Minister for Foreign Affairs at the time, had a sovereign contempt for the press.

He relied entirely on the reports from the Austrian diplomatic representatives, which were not always good. Rudolph had a poor opinion of the diplomats of his time ; he said of them : 'It is a pity Europe wastes so much money on its diplomats. The damage they do is, God knows, much greater than the advantage they bring.' Even had he been given more information from the Foreign Ministry he would not have considered it reliable. His own source of information seemed to him more exhaustive and nearer the truth. This was important, as in those years he became increasingly interested in foreign policy. When it became obvious to Kálnoky that he could not prevent Rudolph from obtaining information he started to show him from time to time some official reports. In return the Crown Prince expressed his gratitude by sharing some of his unofficial reports with the Foreign Ministry. These items of information were almost invariably passed through Baron Szögyenyi-Marich a high official in the foreign service with whom the Crown Prince had become friendly and whom he held in high esteem.

II

Rudolph's letters to Szeps are available and are interesting in showing the gradual unfolding of his views on Austrian foreign policy. He held very outspoken opinions on home affairs, but his views in this field were already crystallised before he met Szeps. It was the older man's wider horizon which showed the Crown Prince that internal and external politics could not be separated. Although Austria had had an alliance with Germany since 1879 and although relations with Russia were at least outwardly friendly and cordial —

the common denominator was the conservatism of the three rulers — Rudolph's sympathies had been with the West, particularly with France ; there Liberalism was a political force. This preference was strengthened by Szeps, who was on friendly terms with many French politicians, but it would be wrong to assume that it was he who created the deep distrust which Rudolph throughout his life displayed towards Germany and Russia. He could not easily forget 1866, when the Hapsburgs had been driven out of Germany. Although he held the Prussian army in high regard as a fighting machine, he considered that its striking power had been reduced by the creation of the German Empire and he was deeply suspicious of Bismarck, whose Machiavellian foreign policy he detested. It was not, as is sometimes suggested in biographies, that Szeps fundamentally changed his political opinions. Liberalism, suspicion of Germany and Russia, predilection for the Western world, were present already in Rudolph's mind ; the friendship with Szeps served to reinforce them.

Already in one of his first letters, Rudolph wrote of the increasing strength of France which caused Germany to woo Austria. He also speaks disparagingly of 'Russia in her delirium tremens'. A little later he said, speaking again of France : 'I have great sympathies for that country, as long as she remains a republic. We have to thank France for a great deal as the fountain-head of all liberal ideas and institutions . . . she will always remain our model. What is Germany in comparison ? Nothing but a military state, as she was before, only enlarged. What was the benefit of the year '70 to Germany ? To the whole circus of little Kings and Princes they have added an Emperor.' The idea of the German Empire, Rudolph asserted, was maintained and drilled into the people by the military, police and civil service.

During the first two years a deep pessimism character-ised most of the letters. 'A dull and musty mood depresses Europe. It is not really a violent disease, but people feel so lousy, they fear internal as well as external eruptions.' In another letter : 'We are faced with very gloomy and ugly times ; one could almost believe that the old Europe has outlived itself and is now approaching its ruin. A great, a tremendous reaction must come, followed by social upheavals, from which after a long sickness an entirely new Europe will emerge.'

He feared for Austria's future, both externally and internally ; his letters were increasingly dominated by the two great dangers which he foresaw throughout his life — the unavoidable war with Russia and the reactionary policy of the government of Taaffe. 'Russia is the threatening spectre and, in the constant danger of war in which we live, civil life slackens and one pines away with one's own efforts to show strength. . . . Soon a solution of these abnormal conditions must come.' But even more danger-ous than the threatening war with Russia was Austrian government policy, or rather the lack of it. Now for the first time he referred to the new demagogic movement : 'Taaffe's Ministry does not contain any great men, but only clever gamblers, who live from one day to the next. They play with fire : delusion, fanaticism, stupidity, boundless cunning, lack of principles, unlimited lust for power, have combined to fight against modern culture, against the sound power of the educated middle-classes. Elements have been brought into motion and ghosts evoked which it is impossible to banish. How much has the proud, liberal and hopefully developing Austria changed within a few years. These are dismal times and yet it is only the first step on the path of reaction. I am curious to know how long it will take such a tough and old structure as this Austria to crack in all joints and to crash down.'

Rudolph disclosed his misgivings about the Austrian political situation not only to Szeps, but also in a letter to Chlumecky : 'I believe everyone who wants to be proud of his fatherland would agree with this judgement of the present political situation. . . . If those people, who call themselves Austrian patriots *par excellence* and at every opportunity parade their patriotism, were paid to destroy the Monarchy, they could not act differently.'[3]

III

It was natural that Rudolph with his gift for writing would try to influence public opinion as soon as his friendship with Szeps was sufficiently firmly established. The *Tagblatt* seemed to offer an excellent means of showing to a wide public how pernicious the system of Taaffe had become, but it would be difficult in view of the strict censorship. The Crown Prince was not dismayed. The precautions had to be doubled, lest the ever-vigilant police should find out who supplied the inside information. In order to allay suspicions he asked his friend to attack him occasionally in the paper.

When he sent a manuscript to the editor by the faithful Nehammer, Szeps immediately copied it in his own hand, and the original was returned to the author. In this way not even the staff of the paper knew of the connection. Those manuscripts which Rudolph did not himself destroy can be found among his papers in the Vienna Archives. Reading them, one is impressed by the easy flow of language, rarely is a word crossed out and replaced by another. Szeps, in his desire to escape the censorship which the Crown Prince in his writings so patently underestimated, toned down the manuscripts, and hardly two connected sentences in them can be found unchanged in the printed version. Rudolph never resented the use his friend made of his experience in circumventing the censor.

It can be taken as proof of unhealthy political conditions if the heir to the throne could not publish his views without their being censored, and Rudolph's concern as a patriot thus becomes understandable. Naturally he would not advocate bloody revolution or any other violent upheaval ; all he suggested was the peaceful and fully constitutional replacement of the Taaffe government by a more liberally minded one. He may from time to time have used strong terms, but a government which has to fear a strong expression in political controversy cannot have rested on safe foundations.

Frequently when other engagements prevented the Crown Prince from writing, he had to be content with suggesting articles for which he could supply information. But that too was dangerous — the police might tamper with his letters. Sometimes information given to Szeps by word of mouth was only to be used when Rudolph wrote 'the weather is good' ; 'the weather is poor' meant that the information should be withheld.

It was not, as has been suggested, the desire to see his words in print which prompted Rudolph to write for the *Tagblatt*, but his deep sorrow at the retrogression in Austria. This is shown in the letters to Szeps in a way which precludes any doubt, but there is further evidence of this deep concern. Minister Chlumecky told his son that the Crown Prince, whom he knew well, was convinced 'that his father's policy of hesitation and half measures could become pernicious to the Monarchy. He knew the truly living forces in the Empire and wanted to captivate and to use them for the rejuvenation of the country. He wanted to open wide the well-closed windows of the Imperial Palace and let fresh air and bright light enter.' Chlumecky was convinced that although possibly 'Rudolph's political aims were not yet fully thought out, it seemed a mistake on the part of the Emperor to have excluded the Crown Prince from all government business, although he was burning with the desire for great things'.[4]

Even had Rudolph's views lacked a certain maturity — he was still in his early twenties — he knew the basic defect from which Europe, and particularly Austria, suffered. On July 26th, 1882, he said in a letter to Szeps : 'The idea of nationality is based upon the most common brutal principle ; it is indeed the victory of the carnal instincts and sympathies over the spiritual and cultural advantages which cosmopolitanism, the idea of the equality of all nations, brings to humanity. I consider the enmity of nations and races a decisive step backwards, and it is characteristic that just those elements hostile to progress in Europe indulge in these principles and exploit them.'

IV

The Crown Prince was still stationed in Prague, but he came frequently to Vienna. On these brief visits he usually managed to see Szeps, sometimes only for a few minutes at dead of night. Much which was too secret for letters was discussed during these interviews which Szeps recorded afterwards. His records are available at the Vienna Archives where they were deposited after the Crown Prince's death. There was a particularly important interview in January 1883 at a critical time for Szeps. The government, after trying in vain to kill the *Tagblatt* by the constant interference of the censor, now forbade the sale of the paper in all shops licensed for the sale of tobacco — a state monopoly in Austria. At the time tobacco shops were almost the only places where newspapers were sold. Szeps, with great financial sacrifice, countered the blow by renting and staffing special shops for the sale of his paper.

Rudolph was very angry at this latest trick of Taaffe's. When he received his friend, as usual after midnight, his words show the great concern he felt : 'We have embarked on a catastrophic policy and it seems that nobody can alter it now. We are driven into the darkness by fate and it is partly the work of the Jesuits, who are closely connected with all the influential members of the Imperial family. I am not allowed to move, and I have grown so distrustful of everybody around me that life is becoming torture. And as far as people from the Court are concerned I dare not speak to anybody who is concerned with Count Taaffe.'

After a long conversation, Szeps felt it was time to leave and drew attention to the late hour, but the Crown Prince asked him to stay : 'Are you tired ? I never am. I don't sleep well, especially in Vienna. I always feel better and more at home in Prague than here.' It was then, in the Crown Prince's simply furnished room at the palace, during the small hours of the morning, that he unfolded a strange tale, speaking as if under a great stress, haltingly at times and at others very quickly : 'Two years ago I was in a dreadful situation. There was a kind of conspiracy to make people believe that I had become a member of the Freemasons or some other anti-religious and revolutionary society. These accusations became more and more open, and finally I had no choice but to declare : "As an officer I have given a solemn oath not to join any secret society whatsoever. I am now accused of belonging to such a society. I demand, as I have the right, that a military court be set up to investigate these accusations in detail." I insisted on this and the cowards retired, and they have never dared to say a word about it again.'

Strange as this story of persecution may sound, Rudolph had previously referred to it in a letter and, even assuming that he may have dramatised the situation, enough remains to show that his life cannot have been easy. The story which the Crown Prince told his visitor grew still more bizarre as he continued : 'For many months the Hungarians have been greatly worried about the way things are shaping. The Hungarians are now the only support of liberal and constitutional ideas. . . . Last summer Tisza [Count Tisza, the Minister President of the Hungarian half of the Empire], with two of his Ministerial colleagues and a third important politician, who at the time held no official appointment, met and discussed the idea of having me crowned King of Hungary. They adopted a formal resolution to this effect. Although there were only four people present at the meeting, Archduke Albrecht must have learned about it a few weeks later. He came to me and said : "Rudolph, I understand that they want to crown you King of Hungary. I must warn you against it, Rudolph. The title of Majesty which you would acquire would only flatter your vanity. Basically it would mean nothing. Moreover, if you were crowned, you would have to swear a solemn oath to observe the Hungarian constitution and then your hands would be bound for ever. Do not let yourself be crowned. Think about your own future and that of your family. Give no promises. One can never know what might happen and in certain contingencies such an oath would be an unsurmountable obstacle." There has been no further mention of the possibility of my being crowned King of Hungary.'

There is no direct corroboration of the facts stated by the Crown Prince, but conditions in the Austro-Hungarian Empire — especially relations between the two constituent halves — were such that the possibility of such a plan as outlined by Rudolph cannot be dismissed. There had been a previous occasion when an heir apparent had been crowned King of Hungary while his parent was still reigning Monarch of the Austrian Empire. Francis Joseph, although he had since made amends, was not very popular in Hungary after his cruel suppression of the Hungarian revolution in 1848–49. There is also proof that Hungary, where the Liberals were in power, viewed the way in which Taaffe tried to suppress Liberalism in Austria with alarm, and that Tisza had — unsuccessfully — tried to intervene. Rudolph was known to be a Liberal and the idea that he would therefore make a good King was likely to be discussed. He spoke the language well, he was the son of the Empress Elisabeth who, in 1867, had persuaded her husband to give Hungary the utmost degree of autonomy which was compatible with the existence of the combined Austro-Hungarian Monarchy. A possible

explanation is that there had been talk of Rudolph's eleva-
tion to the Hungarian throne, but that the matter had been
dropped when it was discovered that information about it
had been divulged. That there had been a mature plan
may be doubted, but the incident was not a figment of
Rudolph's imagination.

More important from a biographer's point of view are
the complaints about persecution. Rudolph repeated
them so frequently that they must be considered seriously.
Probable reasons for them are contained in his letter to
Count Bombelles of April 1883: 'I represent a tendency
which is an abomination to these gentlemen ; they fear
I could grow out of the common, comfortable pattern
and differ from most of my relatives . . .'. This was true.
Taaffe knew that the Crown Prince was his implacable
enemy and that he would let no opportunity pass to bring
down the government. The other Archdukes, who felt
quite comfortable whether the government of the day
pursued a reactionary policy or not, considered that
Rudolph's indifference to ceremony and protocol, and
his democratic tendencies, endangered their privileges ;
they may also have been jealous of his good looks and the
attraction he held for many people who thought of him
as their only hope.

This is not mere conjecture. Chlumecky stated :
'Rudolph frequently tried to disregard the boundaries of
Court etiquette and he consorted with people who knew
real life and learned a great deal from them. . . . What
attraction for people and whole nations could he have
exercised by his charm, which he possessed in such a high
degree.'[5]

Because Rudolph was considered a danger by some of
the members of his family and by the government of the

day, he was attacked. Because open hostility was not possible, more insidious methods had to be used. He was not fully aware of their extent ; his complaints to Szeps made this clear. Whether he was a Freemason or not may still be of importance to some devout Catholic, but it would not materially change the position which history concedes to him. Far more important is his moral standing. Even now, so many years after his death, many people, particularly in Austria, know him not as a Liberal, as the most progressive Hapsburg of the last century, but as a libertine, if no worse. All the rumours which are still repeated were current during his lifetime. Difficult as it may appear to establish after the passage of time whether they had any foundation, and if not, what their source was, the attempt must be made.

The rumours began early, when Rudolph was still living as a young man in Prague, and they continued throughout his life. For all that time there is ample evidence that he took his duties extremely seriously and that he also worked hard in other fields. There is also evidence that for most of the time his married life was fairly happy. There is little likelihood that he had time or felt the desire for a series of amorous adventures. In retrospect it seems much more likely that rumours about Rudolph's dissolute life were invented in order to discredit his political views.

In the Austria of the 'eighties, mud-slinging was a recognised weapon in the political struggle, even more so than later. It was, for example, considered perfectly legitimate to call an opponent by such epithets as a Jewish pig, a Czech dog, a dirty German, or whichever was the most apposite, whenever factual arguments were lacking. One could call Szeps or Frischauer or Futtaky Jews in order to discredit their political convictions, but Rudolph's ante-cedents were so well known that one could not call him a Jew. If he were generally considered a skirt-chaser that also would discredit him, although not as much as being a present or past adherent of the Mosaic faith. The appeal to feelings of sexual envy was frequently used in Austrian politics in place of an argument.

It is not without interest that another Hapsburg had had an undeservedly poor reputation. Count Polzer-Hoditz, in his biography of the Emperor Charles I,[6] described how, both as an Archduke and later when on the throne he was the victim of a number of entirely unfounded rumours. And in this category one may per-haps also include the numerous stories about the Emperor Joseph II, stories which survived him by many years, and even more than a century after his death sentimental novels and musical plays depicting unfounded highly romantic love episodes were enjoyed by gullible people. In both these cases there is also a factor which applies to Rudolph : Charles I was critical of Germany, whereas Joseph II was hostile to the excessive influence then wielded by the Catholic Church.

This can be no more than an attempt to explain why the Crown Prince had so persistently a poor reputation in the eyes of many people, whereas Archdukes whose depravity was beyond doubt were hardly ever mentioned.

V

The German Chancellor, Bismarck, considered the alliance with Austria one of the corner-stones of his foreign policy. In order to demonstrate to the whole world how closely

linked the two states were, he suggested frequent meetings between the members of the two Imperial houses. In
consequence of this policy Prince William often went
to Austria and the Crown Prince to Berlin. They
did not get on well together as they grew older, although
they had to keep up the appearance of friendship. William
wrote many years later in his memoirs: 'To my regret,
however, I was forced to notice that he did not take religion
at all seriously. . . . Nor could I help becoming aware of
other faults in his character so much so as to destroy
my original confidence and we drifted further apart.'[7]
Rudolph on his part was highly critical of his 'friend'.
In April 1883 when William was once more in Austria,
the Crown Prince wrote to Szeps that he could see him
in the evening only, not during the day 'since I have to
be a great deal with the Prussian Prince; in the evening,
however, he understands well how to find his own enter-
tainment and then I am free'. To Stephanie, he wrote :
'William is enjoying himself here. I had to lend him three
thousand florins — for an indefinite period. The Emperor
is greatly amused by these stories.'[8] It may be that
William's increasing hostility was caused by his realisation
that his show of self-righteousness had not deceived
Rudolph.

The relationship between the two Princes had no bearing on the fact that the Austrian Crown Prince fully
realised that the alliance with Germany was necessary for
his country. He was convinced that war between Austria
and Russia was ultimately unavoidable if the Monarchy
were to extend its influence in the Balkans. The necessity
of such an expansion was a basic article of his political
faith. Austria alone, he feared, would hardly be able to
defeat the Eastern colossus. Consequently, although he

was highly critical of Germany, he tried at least to maintain an outward show of good relationship.

He disliked his frequent visits to Berlin, but when there he did his best to make the Germans see the Austrian point of view. He was well aware that Bismarck, the all-powerful master of German politics, had a weakness for Russia. Whenever Rudolph saw him he discussed the situation fully, trying to emphasise the Austrian point of view. The highly strung Crown Prince made not the best impression on the 'Great Man', though Bismarck was naturally very complimentary in his diplomatic utterances on these occasions. He told the Austrian Ambassador in Berlin after Rudolph's visit in March 1883 : 'Your Crown Prince was very amiable, as is his wont. But as far as the development of his mind and the maturity of his opinions and views are concerned, they have by far surpassed my expectations. His political understanding is not an ordinary one and has surprised me. It proves that, in spite of his youth, he has reflected seriously and independently about many things. We were not always of the same opinion, but he defended his point very well and what struck me was the caution which he showed.' [9] In private, the Chancellor was less flattering. He told some of the Prussian Ministers after the same visit : 'The Archduke Rudolph has given me the impression of a timid weakling, like a man who looks round to see whether a stone is about to fall on his head. The Lord does not favour those Monarchs, to whom he grants only such "*chétive*" [weakly, puny] offspring as now in Austria and in Russia.' [10]

Rudolph had no illusions about Germany — 'Prussia is only affectionate when she needs someone', but Bismarck had impressed him at least during the first few meetings, and only later did he become aware that the Chancellor used Austria as a pawn in his diplomatic game.

VI

To the many problems Rudolph had to contend with, a new one was added in 1883 — Hungary. Until then politics in the Hungarian half of the Monarchy had seemed relatively peaceful and progressive. On January 1st of that year he had written to Latour, 'My hopes are solely based on Hungary, which is so happily and ably led'. He may have been influenced in his judgement by his good relations with Hungarian politicians, by Tisza's suggestion to have him crowned King of Hungary. Later in 1883 conditions in the Eastern half of the Empire deteriorated suddenly. The Magyars, who were numerically less than half of its population, had dominated Hungary since the settlement with Austria in 1867. The Slav inhabitants were the largest minority but only a few had the right to vote and they were consequently severely restricted in their minority rights. When the Magyarisation of the Slav province, Croatia, was speeded up, riots broke out in its capital, Zagreb. Rudolph became alarmed and Szeps immediately sent his diplomatic correspondent Frischauer to get first-hand information which was duly passed on to the Crown Prince. He now realised that his hopes were doomed, that he could no longer expect Hungary to force in time a more liberal course on the Austrian half of the Empire. While outwardly Liberal, the Hungarian government could be very illiberal towards its minorities.

In a letter to Szeps he discussed the Hungarian situation and came to the conclusion that in the last analysis the riots were due to the lack of a healthy middle class. 'Hungary is badly administered . . . the true basis of a modern state, a strong middle class, is lacking.' The prospect that Hungary would be prone to internal disorder and would no longer be a bulwark against the forces of reaction, alarmed him. He asked : 'Should I write something about these problems ? For instance : The power of the bourgeoisie as the basis of the modern state ?' This article and others were duly written, but the censorship or Szeps's precautions left little standing of Rudolph's original pungency. The storm in Croatia subsided after a few weeks, but it had clearly shown that Hungary, so far considered a country with few problems, had enough of them too. The political scene became increasingly difficult and disturbing. Rudolph had to look on while his heritage was crumbling — he was helpless and could not set things right.

In his anxiety it must have been a welcome break to open the Electricity Exhibition in Vienna while the crisis in Hungary was still at its height. As usual he had himself drawn up his speech, and his old love for Vienna, sometimes obscured by political considerations, came to the fore again. The Crown Prince had always been a good public speaker, but the words he found for the Electricity Exhibition were probably his most apt, 'May a sea of light radiate from this town and new progress flow from it'. In the *Tagblatt* he wrote of the technical progress. 'What man creates in the realm of facts does not belong to him alone, but becomes the common property of all human beings. . . . The fairy tale is an aristocratic dream ; its realisation by research and the consequent invention is democratic reality.' The middle classes were enthusiastic and Rudolph's remarks were the talk of the town. A

Hapsburg who favoured progress was something quite unique! Never was the Crown Prince's prestige higher in Vienna than during the first few days of the Exhibition.

But Vienna and its liberal middle-class was not Austria. Within the new forces of reaction, not yet very vocal and articulate, but nevertheless present, the speech had hardly found an echo. Opposition from this side was not very important as yet ; more eloquent was the fact that the Minister President had not been at the opening ceremony, and nearly the whole aristocracy had stayed away. They had boycotted the Exhibition ; either they had not sufficient intelligence to realise the importance of technical progress, or their boycott was a demonstration against the Crown Prince. His would be a hard struggle, when he ascended the throne. But he was still young, full of energy, and in spite of all difficulties, full of optimism.

REFERENCES

1. Stefan Zweig, *The World of Yesterday* (London, 1943), pp. 28 f.
2. Mitis, *op. cit.* pp. 83 f.
3. *Neue Freie Presse*, June 4th, 1933, 'Zwei Briefe des Kronprinzen Rudolf an Handelsminister Baron von Chlumecky'.
4. Leopold von Chlumecky, *Erzherzog Franz Ferdinands Wirken und Wollen* (Berlin, 1929), p. 38.
5. Chlumecky, *op. cit.* pp. 30 f.
6. Graf Polzer-Hoditz, *Kaiser Karl* (Zürich-Leipzig-Wien, 1929), pp. 72 and 277.
7. William II, Ex-Emperor of Germany, *My Early Life* (London, 1926) p. 229.
8. Lonyay, *op. cit.* p. 143.
9. Mitis, *op. cit.* p. 191.
10. Lucius von Ballhausen, *Bismarck-Erinnerungen* (Stuttgart, 1921), p. 377.

CHAPTER EIGHT

'A Looker-on Here in Vienna'

I

THE Crown Prince and Princess had moved to Laxenburg near Vienna in May 1883, but Rudolph's official transfer from Prague was dated December 22nd of that year. He was appointed Officer Commanding the 25th Infantry Division. Soon after their child's birth they moved to the Hofburg, but Rudolph kept also his modest bachelor quarters there which he had used during his brief visits from Prague. The Crown Princess did not find the Hofburg to her liking. There were no bathrooms, other sanitary arrangements were equally deficient, and although gas had been in use in Vienna for some time and electricity had been recently introduced, in the young couple's quarters oil lamps were the only source of light. There was, as Stephanie stated in her memoirs, not even running water in any of their rooms ; she had to use a rubber tub for her ablutions and the water was carried in wooden buckets.

Equally distasteful to her was the way in which the rooms were furnished. Vienna, too, had its time of anti-macassars and aspidistras — it was called the Makart period after the painter Hans Makart. Neither Francis Joseph nor Rudolph had any artistic pretensions and the Empress hardly cared for Vienna or its furnishings, so that Stephanie

The Imperial Palace (Hofburg) in Vienna in the 1880s

had to fight for improvements. As she was never popular at the Vienna Court, it cannot have been easy for her.

Family life at the Court in Brussels may not have been exemplary, but the cuisine certainly was, and here also Stephanie was disappointed. The kitchen quarters were near the living-rooms which were permeated with the smells of the various foods, particularly that of the ever-present onions and garlic. The food itself was stodgy and heavy. Francis Joseph was known to be a lover of simple home-cooking and had no taste for French elaboration ; even the Kaiser speaks of the Emperor's preference for beef stew — the ubiquitous *goulash* whose smell is unsurpassed in penetrating power. To her father-in-law's horror the Crown Princess insisted on a French chef.

Rudolph did not bother about the domestic arrangements. Not only did he find his duties in Vienna much heavier than those in Prague, but his search for a solution of Austria's problems also took up much more time. He was nearer the heart of things, and the more he considered the problems which confronted him, the less it seemed possible to solve them. Hungary had been showing distinct signs of strain. Foreign policy now required more attention ; conditions in the Balkan peninsula, which the Berlin Congress of 1878 had attempted to settle, showed signs of becoming fluid again. Austria might soon have to assert her claims, but was Kálnoky the right man to press them with the necessary energy ? All these questions were more important to the Crown Prince than any domestic problems.

Whatever the future held in store for him, he was not frightened. He was at the height of his creative power, he would master all difficulties in good time and create a great and happy Austria. On New Year's Day 1884 he wrote to Szeps : 'Out of the darkness which surrounds us . . . from the night of reaction, may we at last awake to the dawn of a better time in which our ideals will be victorious. First let us free ourselves from the grip of pessimism which is tantamount to submission to fate and to the loss of self-confidence. Let us always be aware that better times must come, when we shall have to answer for those principles to which we have devoted our lives.' He was pleased to be in Vienna now ; it gave him an opportunity of increasing his and Stephanie's public duties. He wrote to Szeps early in January : 'In a time like the present, members of dynasties must show themselves frequently and work hard, to prove their right to exist. This is the reason why my wife and I intend this winter to visit many establishments. . . . It would be good if the people were to learn from your paper what we are doing so that we are not taken for useless parasites.'

This was a wise move. Rudolph's popularity was threatened by the increasing fury of anti-Liberal propaganda, which came now from two sources — the government itself, and the new anti-Semitic demagogic group. Early in 1884 Austria experienced a period of social unrest which had a definite anti-Monarchical flavour although it was not only incited by the new movement but also by government supporters who wanted to use the workers as pawns in their fight against Liberalism.[1]

This unrest, caused by the dissatisfaction of the workers, spread to such an extent that the government, in spite of the part it had played in furthering it, now thought it necessary to declare a state of emergency. Rudolph realised how much certain reactionary circles had welcomed the dissatisfaction to make use of it for their own ends. He told Szeps : 'The fight against the sound Liberal bourgeoisie, against the truly progressive but orderly principle in the state, this is the slogan of the so-called Conservatives. . . . Now they incite the workers to fight. They want to play off these elements, but thereby order, livelihood, trade and commerce, the possibilities of regular development are endangered. It can reach a point in Vienna where the army . . . will take the matter in hand. And then not only anarchism, but the root of all evil will be cured in a most energetic, though I admit not very gentle, manner.'

The idea that the army might take a hand in the political struggle was wishful thinking. Rudolph knew that his uncle, the Archduke Albrecht, the Supreme Army Commander, was as good a Conservative as Taaffe himself. He was at the time deeply immersed in military matters, and this may have been the reason why he overrated the army's importance as an instrument of politics. He frequently dined with officers — he always enjoyed the atmosphere of the mess — so that their opinions were familiar and doubtlessly many of them, especially those of middle-class origin, held fairly progressive views. Moreover, whatever the political convictions of the officers, Rudolph was rightly convinced that 'the army was the only connecting element which represents the idea of the Empire in this chaos', but it was childish to assume that a *coup d'état* by the army would ever have been a progressive step.

A few weeks later, when this period of unrest had passed, Rudolph set his mind to the new task of bringing out a comprehensive work on the Austro-Hungarian Empire. He had established himself as an author and was aware of a keen interest in his descriptions of Austrian landscape. Now he drew up a scheme for *The Austro-Hungarian Monarchy in Word and Picture* in twenty volumes, to be written by the finest experts in their subjects. He would not act as editor, but would reserve for himself the ultimate decisions as to the contents. There were to be German and Hungarian editions, each with its own editor. He wrote the introduction and contributed a number of articles. The scope of the work can be gauged from the petition which he wrote to ask his father to give his blessing to the project : 'Where is there a state with such contrasts in topography, combining within its boundaries such a splendid variety of landscape, climate and natural history, and which could, owing to its ethnological composition of various nations, furnish a great work with the most interesting pictures. . . . This work shall show at home and abroad what a rich treasure of intellectual strength this Monarchy possesses in all its peoples and lands, and how they combine in a glorious achievement, which must serve the consciousness and the power of the great common Fatherland.'

The German edition had a sale of fifteen thousand copies and brought a substantial profit, but the Hungarian edition was less successful. Rudolph saw the first few volumes through the press but did not live long enough to see the completion of the work. In it he created, unaware, a memorial not only to himself, but to the Austro-Hungarian Monarchy. Reading it now, many years after the Empire has disintegrated, one still feels that in spite of all its shortcomings it must have been a state which could attract a great deal of patriotism.

During the time when he was engaged in the preparations for this work the University of Vienna awarded Rudolph the honorary degree of Ph.D. While honorary degrees for members of ruling families were quite frequent, in this case it was a painful reminder for Rudolph that he had not been permitted to work for his degree as he had so much desired. There is a note of resignation and regret in his acknowledgement of the honour. Very properly, he expressed his thanks to one of his old tutors, Dr. Krist : 'This distinction which has been awarded to me by Vienna University I consider a great honour which has given me much pleasure. But what grieves me is the humiliating feeling . . . not to have earned the doctor's degree . . . by my own efforts. In any case it will be for me a new spur to serve enlightenment and progress incessantly and to work for them as much as is possible. . . .'[2]

II

As early as 1883 an extensive tour of some of the Balkan states had been planned for Rudolph and Stephanie, but it did not materialise until the following year. Officially this journey, which was to include Romania, Turkey and Serbia, was not to be considered as a series of state visits, but simply as a journey to invite the governments of these countries to take part in an exhibition to be held in Budapest. An official state visit by the Austrian heir to the throne could have been interpreted as an attempt to increase Austrian influence and consequently a contravention of the Berlin Congress of 1878, which had defined the spheres of influence in the Balkans. It is indicative of the Crown Prince's position that the Austrian Foreign Minister had so little trust in him that his toasts were drafted for him by the Ministry.

Despite these restrictions, Rudolph was glad to have an

opportunity to show what he could do. He had always been attracted by the Near East, and for years had held that it was Austria's historic mission to carry Western culture into these small states which had been established on former Turkish territory, and into Turkey itself. Although the mood of the Balkan nations was no longer Austrophil, although Hungary by her suppression of both Yugoslav and Romanian minorities had destroyed much of the pro-Austrian sympathies which had once existed, Rudolph succeeded in creating new friendships for Austria. The tour was a signal success. The official Russian gazette, *Nowoje Wremja*, reported that it was a political event and concluded, 'A surprising change has taken place in the mind and character of the Austrian heir to the Throne, and this splendid development must be taken into account in our policy'.[3]

While Rudolph succeeded in captivating sympathies for Austria in the Balkans, he himself was still more captivated by what he saw there, both in reality and in imagination. From 1884 onwards his belief in Austria's mission in the Balkans became as firmly a part of his political creed as was Liberalism. In consequence of this belief, he used all his powers of persuasion to get the distrustful, half-demented Sultan Abdul Hamid interested in a railway line from Vienna to Constantinople, to be built with capital supplied by a Baron Hirsch. In doing this he was carrying out instructions from the Foreign Ministry, which in this instance coincided with his own ideas. It was no easy task; the Sultan was evasive and prevaricating, he had to be carefully induced into making up his mind to give the orders necessary to get construction under way. In Vienna it was whispered that the Crown Prince was using his position to obtain the railway concession for a rich financier interested in the Turkish railways. It was alleged that he was heavily in debt and that in return for the concession Hirsch would settle his accounts. In this case the absurdity of the allegation can be proved, as the instructions from Kálnoky have been preserved. Rudolph had been in Constantinople in April 1884 and a month later the Austrian Ambassador could report to Vienna that the Sultan 'had in fact, on account of the suggestion made by H.I.H. the Crown Prince, given orders to expedite the matter'.[4]

Rudolph submitted a detailed report after his return, summarising his experiences. He described the journey, and gave his opinion on the suitability of the Austrian diplomatic representatives in the capitals he had visited. Generally, he had not been impressed by them. He described briefly the political conditions in the countries as he found them, and he gave an evaluation of their military worth. But, important as all this may have been at the time, his conclusions are the most characteristic part of the report. They are written in plain, matter-of-fact language and represent one of the basic chapters of his political creed; Austria's future was to him inextricably bound up with the Balkans.

It was the age of growing Imperialism. Austria, unlike the other great powers, had no colonies, insufficient maritime resources to emulate their conquests, and no treaties of protection in overseas continents. But she too would extend her dominion, although nearer home, in the Balkans. Here was the future Greater Austria. 'Undeniably we have great interests in the Orient and the state of the Balkans is for us a vital question. . . . I found the ground better prepared than I had expected. The moment is favourable. Austria, closely allied with Germany, creates an imposing impression upon these nations, and as the nearest civilised state connected by a river which is foremost an Austrian line of traffic, everybody is impressed by the idea that our geographical position alone allots to our Empire a great civilising rôle to play in the Balkan peninsula. Russia is far away, separated by the sea, and is herself still an undeveloped state, not much more cultivated than the Balkan countries.

'From Austria and through Austria west European and central European culture thrusts into those districts still fallow. . . . Financially, economically and educationally we must place those countries under our own dominating influence and win them for ourselves. In Constantinople as well as in Romania, Bulgaria and Serbia, people feel and realise that Austria, thanks to her geographical situation, is called upon to play an important part in the Orient; I believe they think there more of it than we in our modesty would have dared to believe. I have always taken Austria's mission in the European Orient as a law of nature and now after this journey my belief in our great future in these regions has only grown firmer.

'A partition of the sphere of influence with another great power, *e.g.* Russia, is an idea frequently voiced in Austria. I consider this a clear impossibility since all the Balkan countries form a connected whole, and instead of making peace one would only lay the foundations for incessant quarrels and complications. One shrinks from the war with Russia, and looks for means . . . to buy peace by . . . concessions. But nothing can spare us this struggle save a voluntary surrender by Russia of her present policy in the Orient, which . . . is hardly possible.

'The European Orient is better prepared for us than

we believed ; if we succeed by the establishment of railways and shipping connections, by supporting the already
strong Austrian communities, and by all means at our disposal . . . to drive incessantly towards the one aim regardless of what Russia says — with her, whatever happens,
war is unavoidable — then will it be inevitable that we
shall be the masters of the European Orient.'

From the time of this journey onwards, the 'unavoidable war with Russia' became almost an obsession. To
Rudolph the whole foreign policy hinged on it. And
since Austria by herself did not seem strong enough
to be sure of the outcome, the alliance with Germany
became more and more important, and he devoted still
more thought to the readiness and preparedness of the
army.

Whatever the preoccupation with foreign policy and
other problems, he did not overlook his friend Szeps's
fiftieth birthday on November 3rd, 1884. His letter of
congratulations was a whole-hearted declaration of his
belief in progress and liberalism : 'I wish for your sake
and for all our sakes that you continue for many years as
a courageous fighter in the front rank, to profess and to
champion the principles of true enlightenment, genuine
education, humanity and liberal progress. Related by the
same ideas and convictions, we strive after the same aims.
Although times may temporarily deteriorate, although
it may seem that reaction, fanaticism, brutality as well as
a return to old conditions are unavoidable, let us have
confidence in a true and great future, in the final success
of those principles which we serve, because progress is a
law of nature.' It was a profession of faith in a future
which seemed to fade more and more as Rudolph pene-
trated into the jungle of Austrian politics.

III

At the urgent invitation of Bismarck, the German Chancellor, Austria had concluded an alliance with Germany in 1879, swallowing her pride so deeply hurt in 1866, in the hope that Germany would help her in a possible war with Russia. Although Rudolph's belief in the inevitability of such a war was not shared by many Austrians in influential positions, its possibility could not be ruled out, and taking into account the discrepancy in population, an ally in such a struggle was very necessary. Bismarck, however, had little, if any, intention of permitting Austria to come into conflict with Russia. At this time his foreign policy was aimed at preserving peace, and making use of strong conservative forces in Austria, to which Francis Joseph too belonged, the Chancellor succeeded in bringing about an understanding between Austria and her north-eastern neighbour. This of course presupposed a policy of no expansion in the Balkans, which was in direct contradiction to all that Rudolph considered Austria's vital interest.

Such a *rapprochement* was not easy to achieve as the Tsar was suspicious in spite of all the assurance given by Bismarck. In order to overcome Russian doubts, a meeting of the three Emperors concerned was arranged at Skiernewice in Russian Poland. Rudolph was incensed by the idea ; he considered that his father, by visiting the Tsar, who was so much younger, was lowering his dignity. He was still more angry when the meeting ended with the agreement that Austria and Russia would in future discuss any problem arising in the Balkans before taking action. The spheres of influence as laid down by the Berlin Congress of 1878 would be fully adhered to. On account of this he had already, during his journey in the Near East, felt humiliated. The arrangements for his brief stay in Bulgaria had taken too much into account the fact that this country was considered a Russian protectorate. Although he knew well the Prince of Bulgaria, Alexander of Battenberg, his stay there had been much shorter than those in the other countries he had visited. In spite of this he had seen how much Bulgaria had become a Russian satellite, and that the Russians were much more active than were the Austrians in their spheres.

His uneasiness was aggravated when in 1885 he went once more to the Balkans to visit those countries which had not been included in the previous tour. This second journey had not the immediate freshness of the earlier one, but there were sufficient impressions to reinforce his conviction that an offensive foreign policy in the Balkans was necessary. Yet the official policy took no account of his views, and as though to drive home the humiliation the Tsar came to Austria, to Kremsier in Moravia, in the summer of that year, to repay Francis Joseph's visit. The Crown Prince had to be present and all his opposition to his father's policy, which he considered so extremely misguided, came to the fore in a venomous letter in which he reported to Stephanie on the *entrevue*.

It was not only venom ; there is in this letter a certain note of cynicism. The sneering tone which now creeps into some of his letters seems a direct consequence of the increasing feeling of frustration. So far he had been in opposition to Austrian home policy ; this was important, but not vital. Governments come and go even if their position seems to be secure, and it is relatively easy to embark on a new policy in home affairs. Mistakes in foreign policy are not so easily corrected — unique opportunities may be lost for ever. Rudolph felt increasingly exasperated because he was convinced that Austria was throwing away her future by a docile foreign policy.

Bismarck had driven the Hapsburgs out of Germany ; they had irrevocably lost most of their Italian provinces, and Rudolph saw the only way to expansion in the Balkans. The old Hapsburg idea of a supra-national empire was gravely endangered by the growing strength of nationalism ; both West and South the time was past for a supra-national state, but the derelict, neglected former Turkish provinces of the south-eastern corner of Europe was a region where the Hapsburg Monarchy could still show its function as a civilising force. This last hope was being sacrificed by his father's government, thrown away at Bismarck's bidding and with his father's connivance. What was the good of his training, his analytical faculty, of his power of observation ? The future was to be sacrificed to the principle of conservatism and expediency.

He told Stephanie in this letter from Kremsier : 'The Tsar has become colossally fat ; the Grand Duke Vladimir and his wife, as well as the Tsarina, look old and decrepit. The suites, and particularly the servants, are terrible. In their new uniforms they have become quite Asiatic again. At the time of the last Tsar the Russians were at least elegant and some gentlemen of the entourage looked very distinguished. Now they are an awfully common lot.'[5]

The Crown Prince also gave his impressions in an article which he had hoped Szeps would print in the *Tagblatt*. But the editor had to disappoint him ; the censorship would never have passed the article, although it was, as Rudolph assured his friend, 'in accordance with the true facts'. He had written it in the vein of righteous indignation which he felt : 'With Russia, no honest friendship is possible, not even a more or less permanent *modus vivendi*, as long as we aspire to parts of the Balkan peninsula . . . and desire a sphere of influence in the Orient for our future . . . Skiernewice has caused us great harm. . . . [It] is the gravest mistake committed by our Foreign Minister who has been so much influenced by the Russians. . . . While the Emperors protest their friendship and embrace one another, the Russians use the gullibility and short-sightedness of our diplomats . . . to send agents into the Balkans and to establish arms depots in order to prepare for a revolt in our occupation territory. . . . At Kremsier splendid festivities are being held. . . . The statesmen will be negotiating — about what they do not know themselves — but in all this hollow splendour the established fact remains : we Austrians must either resign all influence and authority in the East or prepare for a difficult but inevitable struggle.'

IV

Taaffe and foreign policy were not the only worries which lay so heavily on him. In Vienna he now had a better opportunity than previously at Prague to see that all was not well with the Austrian armed forces. He had earlier considered that those people responsible, particularly his uncle the Archduke Albrecht, were neglecting the army, but now, when a show-down seemed more or less imminent, the Crown Prince became convinced that Albrecht's influence was pernicious. In many of his letters he expresses helpless opposition to the aged Archduke who enjoyed the Emperor's full confidence. Much of the opposition may have been due to the difference between youth and age, yet the Crown Prince was undoubtedly right in his contention that the Archduke was too old to adopt modern methods in his office.

He disclosed his fear to Latour : 'The Archduke is getting old physically and still more so mentally. Beck [the Chief of Staff] is tired and exhausted, moreover he is not equal to his job. His entourage is not happily chosen. These symptoms are noticed by all officers and diminishing confidence is the serious consequence.'

Uncle Albrecht was not the only black sheep which became blacker as Rudolph's preoccupation with foreign policy increased. The Foreign Minister, Kálnoky, came in for his share of blame, and with him almost the whole Ministry and most of Austria's foreign representatives. Both Latour and Szeps were the recipients of letters in which Kálnoky was accused of stupidity : 'In the Balkans things are again on the boil. . . . At the Ballhausplatz [the Foreign Ministry] they know little about it and treat matters with sovereign stupidity. Russia uses the short-sightedness of Kálnoky and the so-called *rapprochement* with Austria unashamedly to set up committees and to send money, arms, etc., into Bulgaria, Rumelia, Macedonia, Serbia and even Bosnia. I have good sources.' In another letter he stated : 'Matters in the Orient can take a serious turn very soon. In my opinion much could now be done, but all strength to arrive at firm decisions is lacking. They are more vacillating than ever before.'

Events were soon to prove Rudolph right. There was unrest in Bulgaria, and Austria had to take sides ; a diplomatic mission was sent. Russia, who considered Bulgaria within her sphere of influence, took this amiss and the *rapprochement* with Austria came to an end. In December 1885 the Crown Prince sent a brief memorandum to Kálnoky in which he summarised his views on the Balkan situation : 'Our most important problems consist of the maintenance of our present influence and the acquisition of a position of strength in the European Orient and in the creation of the most favourable situation for the moment of opening the attack. . . . Much, certainly our position generally, and particularly in the Orient — perhaps even to be or not to be — depends on the next days, on swift decisions ; many mistakes of the last years can be corrected or new ones, and this time decisive ones, made. Not only is our present at stake, but still more the whole future, for which we are responsible to the coming generation.'

The last phrase gives the clue — the next generation, he and those who, like him, believed in a liberal Austria with a mission. It was this that was at stake, and it was so exasperating that those in power did not feel the same urgency. The mistakes which could now be so easily made would endanger his heritage, his Austria which he loved so desperately. Kálnoky in his answer poured cold water on Rudolph's suggestions. 'Certainly our aim must be to secure Austria's influence and position of strength in the Orient . . . but we must not take any risks. We must avoid war with Russia by all means at our disposal. . . . I know that I take the chance of being reproached for a policy which is not resolute and energetic enough, but this is the lesser evil ; a greater evil would be to involve the Monarchy in a war of unforeseeable consequences, if it can be honourably avoided ; to involve it in a war under conditions which admit doubts as to Germany's obligations to help.'

Kálnoky's argument concerning Germany's treaty obligations struck home, because Rudolph's former suspicions that Bismarck did not really want to help Austria in a war with Russia were deepening as time went on.

He was basically as convinced as Kálnoky that Germany was no reliable ally ; but as he held very strongly that to avoid war with Russia meant giving up hope of saving Austria from becoming a second-rate power, or even worse, from disintegration, the Foreign Minister's reminder was a painful one. During the following months, when there was so much unrest in the Balkans that the danger of war seemed imminent, he followed keenly every move of Bismarck.

Certainly he was no pacifist, but it would be wrong to consider his belief in the inevitable war with Russia — he even wished that such a war would break out soon — a sign of war-mongering. Fighting Russia was equated with fighting black reaction, and both in Austria and in Germany people who normally condemned war were ready to fight against Tsardom, as was shown by the enthusiasm far into the left-wing circles in 1914.

V

In the winter of 1885–86 the Crown Prince thought it necessary to sum up once more his views on the problems facing the Austro-Hungarian Monarchy. The memorandum which he wrote during those weeks is a much more mature work than the earlier one of 1881, but it lacks much of his earlier idealism. He had not jettisoned his ideals, but as he could see no straightforward approach, he came to the conclusion that the ends justified the means. In his introduction he described himself as 'a quiet observer, who is near all political activities, but does not interfere', and goes on to talk of the disappointment which had gripped so many people, who had been full of optimism only a decade earlier ; that parliamentarianism had been reduced to a childish plaything, and that internally as well as externally there was insecurity and fear of the future.

How much the situation in the Balkans had captivated his imagination can be gauged from the fact that he started the memorandum with a consideration of it. In this section there was little new, except the idea that during the Russo-Turkish War of 1878 Austria had been confronted with a choice of either helping or attacking Russia when her armies were unable to overcome the Turkish resistance. Neither was done, and an opportunity wasted unlikely to occur again. Next Austro-German relations were examined. 'Germany needs the alliance more than we do . . . but Bismarck . . . taught us . . . to believe that Austria could not exist without this close alliance.' Germany was weaker than was generally believed, she was not really united. Only a republic would achieve full unification 'and then not a centralised republic like France, but a federal republic like the United States'.

He then developed his ideas on the Balkan problems. Appeasement of Russia would have to cease, she should be pressed back behind an enlarged Romania, and Poland would have to be resuscitated. He even had a King for this new Poland, his uncle, Charles Ludwig. Preventive war with Italy was also unavoidable, to secure Austria's rear. He had generally few sympathies for the Italians, consequently his demand that they, both in Trieste and in the Southern Tyrol, should be Germanised by force.

There is much ill-considered *Realpolitik* in the memorandum, as, for instance, when Rudolph demands that in internal politics the wishes of the Germans should be satisfied ; Czechs and Slovaks could only create minor difficulties, a Czech state would not be viable and the Czechs would be glad to form part of Austria. The Polish provinces should be united with the new Poland.

In the Hungarian half of the Monarchy things were easier, as the Hungarians had no related nation (as had the Germans) and were therefore dependent on Austria. Although they had a number of solid achievements, their weak point was their arrogance towards their minorities which formed the majority of the Hungarian half, and nothing could be achieved by ill-treatment, contempt and vehement suppression. It is interesting to note that the Crown Prince, who was so righteously concerned with the minorities in Hungary, suggested for them the same treatment in the Austrian half as he condemned in Hungary.

Finally, he questioned why, considering all these difficulties, the Austrian Empire did not perish, and suggested in reply, 'Because the great mission of this state is still unfulfilled. It has yet to play a great part in the European Orient which it will then reform basically. . . . I go so far as to maintain that a great war which forces us to fight out the whole issue of the Near East would be of great advantage to our internal conditions and for our whole right to exist. . . . One must not despair. Only he who gives himself up is lost.'

The memorandum is given at some length as it illustrates the change in Rudolph's outlook. Expediency was permitted to overrule his ideals. It is a far cry from the professions of the letter on Szeps's fiftieth birthday. How far these new suggestions were seriously meant and how far they sprang from a momentary despair cannot be decided, for they are contradicted by later statements. Whatever the Crown Prince's real conviction, whether or not some of the proposals in the memorandum point to a lowering of ethical standards, it discloses in parts a surprising immaturity. It seems that his increasing frustration, his nervous impatience, seriously reduced not only his analytical faculties but also impeded his capacity for self-criticism. It may even have been that he now suggested startling solutions as he was aware that reasoned and sensible arguments had been persistently ignored.

We do not know whether this memorandum was submitted to the Emperor and his Ministers or only to personal friends. It was privately printed and a number of copies must have been distributed. Szeps received a copy, and he acknowledged it in a letter which, though in terms of praise, is not free from criticism. 'The pamphlet is a positive programme and from it Your Imperial Highness will one day draw *what is mature* for realisation.' *

VI

More than four years had passed since Rudolph had drafted his earlier memorandum, and his position had hardly changed, except perhaps for an increase in military duties. His influence was now as negligible as it had been then, but the international situation was much more fluid and he, after his tours of the Balkans, painfully aware of its inherent dangers. What had been bearable at twenty-three was much more difficult to put up with now at twenty-seven. Then he looked forward to a field of responsible activity, now he was sometimes near despair at having to be an onlooker while a timid foreign policy, matching an unimaginative reactionary home policy, might irretrievably damage his country's future.

Little, if anything, of this mood was generally known,

* (My italics. R. B.)

but those few who did know of it and who also knew of his hostility to them and their policy made good use of this ignorance : the rumours of amorous adventures, for which he had neither time nor inclination, were persistently encouraged and believed.

Rudolph's letter to Szeps on New Year's Day 1886 clearly shows that his mood must have been far too serious for light-hearted adventures : 'In the life of our Fatherland which we all hold so dear, we may have to expect exciting times ; perhaps they will be gloomy, but they may be great. We do not enter into a quiet year. Whatever may happen, we shall do our duty. . . . The future may be overcast and bloody. But even the most serious time and the most dismal mood cannot force me into doubting our mission. It is not yet all over with us. A state which cannot be wrecked by the biggest mistakes, by clumsiness and misfortune, does not perish at the moment when it is confronted with the consummation of its cultural mission and its justification. . . . Do not overrate me — because to make a few not too poor speeches, to write rather good books and essays and to have enjoyed a modern education are things which are far removed from great success in the course of world history. Who knows what the new year may bring, perhaps it will soon show what one is worth.'

An incident which probably took place during this time shows the extent of his preoccupation. At a shooting party he had his place next to his father. A herd of deer was driven past his stand towards the Emperor's. He shot, and, when the stags were already a fair distance away, left his stand against all rules and shot once more. The second bullet hit his father's gun-bearer in the arm, missing his father's head by a few inches. The Emperor was understandably extremely angry and forbade him to go shooting next day, but the incident was kept a secret at the time.*

Early in the new year Rudolph fell seriously ill. Although at the time it was stated that he was suffering from peritonitis and cystitis, some biographies express doubt of this diagnosis and apparently agree with the rumours that his illness was venereal disease. There is no evidence to support this view. He was so seriously ill that he was sent to the Island of Lacroma (Lokrum) in the Adriatic, and his mother changed her travel programme to visit him there.

The rumours of venereal infection seem to be without foundation. According to the letters available his married life was still reasonably happy. When Szeps sent him a letter of congratulation on his fifth wedding anniversary, the Crown Prince replied : 'It is always a beautiful celebration for me. May God grant that it remains so.'

Two events in 1886 were of great consequence in his life. One was the death of his cousin Ludwig II of Bavaria, and the other the *coup d'état* in Bulgaria. Here the ruling Prince, Alexander of Battenberg, had fallen foul of the Russians, who considered themselves Bulgaria's protectors. In August 1886 he had been kidnapped by a group of Russian officers, forced to abdicate and leave the Balkans. Rudolph was greatly perturbed ; he knew him well — they had been brother-officers in the Austrian army before Battenberg had gone to Sofia. When some of his actions had seemed to threaten Russian authority it became evident how far Russia would go to assert herself. Why should not Austria, with the same determination, assert her rights

---

* There is no contemporary evidence. Mitis learned of the incident from a gamekeeper and recorded the evidence of the two surviving witnesses some forty years after the event.

in the Balkans ? Rudolph was annoyed when Kálnoky refused to interfere. The matter became still more intriguing when the Austrian Archduke John Salvator was for a time seriously considered as a candidate for the Bulgarian throne in Alexander's place.

Archduke John Salvator, a little older than Rudolph, was, like him, a rebel who would not be satisfied with the accepted life of an Austrian Archduke. He was ambitious and was a man of ideas. In 1875 he had published anonymously a pamphlet on problems of the Austrian artillery which had not suited the authorities. For this he had been severely reprimanded by the Emperor and had been more or less in disgrace since. He was now offered the vacant throne of Bulgaria. The Crown Prince was opposed to his candidature ; in a letter to Kálnoky he condemned John Salvator's rôle in the affair : 'I have experienced much incorrect behaviour by this gentleman, but dealings with a foreign deputation in foreign affairs in this critical time without permission and behind the backs of the Emperor and the Minister of Foreign Affairs, this is behaviour in an Archduke which must be most severely punished. Where shall we get if such things are possible within the Imperial family and the army, if the Emperor can no longer rely on these elements, which must not know any other principle but that of unconditional obedience and complete faith.' Rudolph had had to suffer many rebuffs, but at this stage he was still convinced that absolute obedience was the first duty of an Imperial Prince.

Even without Austrian interference Austro-Russian relations were disturbed as the Tsar, suspicious by nature, saw Austrian manœuvres behind any difficulties arising in the Balkans. The danger of war now became very real.

Would the German alliance stand the test? For a time Rudolph had faith in it. In September 1886 he wrote to Szeps, who had warned him that Germany was no longer a reliable ally. 'With regard to Germany you are too pessimistic. They are senile there [the German Emperor was 89], they definitely want to avoid war, but friendship with Russia is out of the question.'

War was to him a way out of all difficulties — the Dual Monarchy seemed to be disintegrating more and more. An Austrian officer had laid a wreath on the grave of a fellow officer killed in 1848 when fighting the Hungarian revolutionaries — or patriots, according to one's point of view — and he had been so violently attacked by the Minister President in the Hungarian Diet that even Rudolph's sympathy for Hungary was forgotten. He wrote to his usually despised Uncle Albrecht to obtain 'brilliant satisfaction' for the insult to the army. The Archduke refused to act — conditions were so delicately balanced that he thought intervention would merely aggravate matters.

VII

Bismarck too was aware that war might be imminent and he was more than usually interested in Austria. The German Ambassador, Reuss, had to supply reports about all important people. In a long report on Rudolph he wrote : 'As for the Crown Prince, he is easily impressed. What he feels intensely and gives voice to, passes as quickly as it comes. Therefore his attitude of opposition, although frequently shown, is not feared by the Ministers.' 6 The Chancellor was disquieted when he received Reuss's report and told him 'it must cause us concern that the Crown Prince has close connection, not only with *literati* and journalists, but according to your own statements is impressed by editors who have formerly obtained French money and have still close relations with Paris. If the Crown Prince continues in this way it must fill us with apprehension for the future and make us doubly careful in our political relations [with Austria].' [7] Reuss had little idea how consistent Rudolph was in his basic concepts. He may have changed some of the passing ideas from time to time — he was still young, but he remained distrustful of Bismarck's policy throughout his life and his sympathies for Western democracy were never shaken. The German Embassy was aware that the Crown Prince had, through Szeps, good connections with France — that was probably one of the reasons why Bismarck was so interested in him—but in spite of all surveillance by German agents it remained unknown that in December 1886 he had had a talk with Clemenceau, whom Szeps brought to the palace. In this talk he stated in unmistakable terms his belief in Austria's mission. Much as the 'might have been' must remain taboo to the biographer, it is sometimes difficult to resist temptation. Would this creed if carried into effect have preserved Austria, and would the survival of a great power in the Danube basin have been better than some of the agonies caused by its forcible destruction? In reply to Clemenceau's remark that for France's good she required a free and independent Austria, Rudolph replied : 'Our Hapsburg state has actually long since put into practice, in a miniature form, Victor Hugo's dream of a "United States of Europe". Austria is a *bloc* of different nations and different races under a united rule. At least that is the basic idea of Austria, and it is an idea of enormous importance to the civilisation of the world. Because the present execution of the idea is, to put it diplomatically, not altogether harmonious, it does not mean that the idea itself is wrong. It simply means that such an idea requires a liberal rule for its harmonious and balanced execution. . . . This is one of the main reasons why, in my opinion, Austria should co-operate with the Western democracies. It is among them that can be found the real liberalism that we require, personal freedom and the absence of racial hatred and dissension.'

When Clemenceau remarked that Germany was trying to entangle Austria in Balkan politics, Rudolph became heated : 'Our Balkan policy! This is a mission which, alas, is often misunderstood in France and England. It is our noblest mission to bring enlightenment and civilisation to the East. You in France do not realise what work has been done in Bosnia . . . since its occupation. . . . It is one of my greatest dreams to fulfil what I call the "*pénétration pacifique*" of the Balkans. Only Russia bars the way, drunken, threatening Russia, who means to keep the Balkan people imprisoned in barbarism and darkness. . . .' The visitor interrupted Rudolph to say how important it was for Austria to come to terms with England to find understanding for the Balkan plans. The Crown Prince eagerly took up the idea : 'The Prince of Wales is friendly towards me. We see each other whenever he comes to Austria, and I am quite positive that when we both come to the Throne, England and Austria will come to a complete agreement. . . .' [8]

Rudolph had great plans. 'When we both come to the throne. . . .' But though Queen Victoria prevented the Prince of Wales from having any real influence, just as Francis Joseph prevented his son, the Prince of Wales could afford to wait, while Rudolph could not. Britain was in an unassailable position, but Austria was showing clear signs of disintegration, and the Emperor's policy, as it appeared to the Crown Prince and others, increased the strain to breaking point.

On December 31st Szeps sent his usual New Year's congratulations. He must have been aware of the need for encouragement and was more than usually fulsome in his praise : 'Your Imperial Highness can count on hundreds of thousands and millions of devoted and faithful followers, enthusiastic admirers . . . but I feel that not many have had, as I have, the good fortune of gaining such a deep and splendid insight into the grand qualities and the supreme gifts of him with whom the future of a great Monarchy is inseparably connected. . . . Accustomed to hard, energetic, independent and self critical work, borne by great ideas and accompanied by the love of millions of sincere hearts, you will achieve and fulfil that which we wish and hope for you and the Monarchy. . . .'

Rudolph might have been irritable of late, shown signs of strain and been hasty in some of his judgements, yet he was still the hope of those who believed in Austria's future as a modern state that would take its rightful place in the concert of the Great Powers.

REFERENCES

1. Ludwig Brügel, *Geschichte der österreichischen Sozialdemokratie* (Vienna, 1922), Vol. III, pp. 293, 303.
2. *Neue Freie Presse* (Wien, February 11th, 1889). Josef Krist, 'Kronprinz Rudolf und seine Lehrer'.
3. Mitis, *op. cit.* p. 165.
4. Mitis, *op. cit.* p. 423.
5. Lonyay, *op. cit.* p. 189, and Stockhausen, *loc. cit.* p. 99.

6. E. V. Wertheimer, 'Kronprinz Rudolf und Fürst Bismarck', in *Archiv für Politik und Geschichte* (April 1925), pp. 349-363.

7. Wertheimer, *ibid.*

8. The quotations are taken from Berta Szeps-Zuckerkandl, *op. cit.* pp. 110 f. This is the only record of the talk and there is unfortunately no corroboration. The book, while certainly serious, is not without mistakes in small items, such as dates, but the account of the interview gives the impression of being genuine. Moreover, Mitis (p. 430) assumes such an interview as probable.

CHAPTER NINE

Anxiety and Frustration

I

RUDOLPH acknowledged Szeps's New Year letter for 1887 on January 2nd. 'We have begun a serious and dark year. It may bring us great decisions, hard struggles, world-shaking upheavals. Should this be so it will either end with nothingness, with our physical and spiritual annihilation, or with the inauguration of a great time, as I foresee it, which will usher in splendid days. Let us hope for the latter possibility ; all our work, the earnest striving and the fact that behind us culture stands ready to penetrate further eastwards — all this cannot easily be defeated by the Caesarean mood of a Mongol state.'

War with Russia seemed now imminent not only to him. The Emperor Francis Joseph, not easily alarmed, told his Ministerial Council on January 7th, 1887, that 'regardless of all care to maintain peace the required measures are to be taken, so that events due to a deterioration of the political situation in the near future would not come as a surprise'.[1]   The Tsar's agents were busy throughout the Balkan countries, particularly in Bulgaria. Austria, with her large Slav population, had to prevent any increase in Russian prestige lest the Tsar should appear as the natural protector of all Slavs. An armed show-down seemed almost unavoidable.

Austria's principal ally, Germany, had seemed doubtful in her attitude since the crisis began in August 1886. Kálnoky at that time told the German Ambassador, Prince Reuss, that Germany, 'at the first opportunity when the political interests of Austro-Hungary were at stake, turned towards Russia'.[2] Bismarck's speeches in the Reichstag occasioned by the Bulgarian crisis were like a blow to Austria's expectations. Now almost everyone was convinced that Austrian interests did not matter to the German Chancellor. He had stated : 'What's Hecuba to us, what Bulgaria ? It is all the same to us who rules in Bulgaria and what becomes of Bulgaria ; the whole question of the Orient is for us no question of peace or war. . . . Our friendship with Russia is more important. . . .'[3] The Archduke Albrecht wrote a memorandum for Berlin in which he declared : 'The Austro-German alliance must be bilateral, but it is so no longer. . . . We are sacrificed to Russia in spite of the agreement or perhaps because of its incorrect interpretation. . . .'[4]

Rudolph for once agreed with his uncle and wrote to Kálnoky: 'You know that I do not agree with the Archduke the Field Marshal in all things and that I have more frequently spoken against than for him ; but on this occasion I think it my duty to draw your attention to his plans'.

He was firmly convinced that Austria's alliance with Germany was useful only if she could rely on help in a war against Russia. 'As the situation is now, we are forced to stick to the German-Austrian alliance and to try to draw as much profit from it as possible for our policy in the Near East. . . . For us Austrians it is essential to count on the definite help of the German army', thus he had stated in his memorandum of 1886. Now, not even a year later, it looked as if German help would not be available, although the decisive struggle seemed close at hand. He had to go to Berlin in March 1887 on the occasion of the Emperor William's ninetieth birthday. Here was an opportunity to discuss the questions of the alliance with Bismarck. He went well prepared ; he had Archduke Albrecht's memorandum, another from Foreign Minister Kálnoky, as well as private information. Only a few days before his departure he had asked Szeps, always well informed about France, for news from Paris. He could now face the wily Chancellor well armed.

Bismarck felt uneasy. He may have realised that he had gone too far in his attempts to maintain 'the wire to St. Petersburg', and he was charming, as he knew well how to be, when talking to the Crown Prince. He tried to explain away his words about Bulgaria and, according to the record which Rudolph submitted to the Foreign Ministry after his return, he succeeded in dispelling some of the Crown Prince's doubts about German reliability. He even spoke 'with great warmth and admiration of our army which, as he said, he had seen fighting in 1866'. That this admiration was artificial and *in usum delphini* was unknown to Rudolph — he could not know that Deines, the German Military Attaché in Vienna, had stated at the time in a letter to his chief, Waldersee : 'The more one gives the Austrians their due, the more easily they will be led by us. However they will accept our advice in all circumstances.'[5]

Although the Crown Prince was unaware that his country was intended to be used as a pawn in the German game, he cannot have been deceived long by Bismarck if indeed he was as much deceived as his report suggests. He had several talks with Frederick William, the German

Crown Prince and his wife, Princess Victoria, Queen Victoria's eldest daughter. Frederick William and Princess Victoria were both extremely suspicious of Bismarck and may well have warned Rudolph not to trust him. The Chancellor had his spies everywhere in Berlin, even in the German Crown Prince's household. He was well aware of these talks and it was easy for him to guess the subject under discussion. Rudolph greatly impressed the Prussian couple. The Austrian Ambassador in Berlin reported to him later : 'The recollections of you here are particularly cordial and truly appreciative. The Crown Princess is unmistakably enthusiastic and does not hide the delight which she has found in the contact with your I.H.' [6] The Ambassador knew of the oppositional attitude and of the isolation of Frederick William and his wife, and continued : 'The vivid intercourse which you, most gracious Prince, cultivated with the Crown Princely couple . . . had been very much noticed here and also amply commented on. On this account it is asked whether it does not mean a cooling off between you and Prince William.' [7]

Bismarck's aim was to keep France isolated, and he had long been suspicious of Rudolph's relations with Szeps, who was on good terms with a number of anti-German French politicians. His suspicions were sharpened by Rudolph's friendship with Crown Prince Frederick William and his wife — also Liberals whom he both feared and disliked. In his usual manner he sought for all possible information, personal, private and public. He obtained from an anonymous 'authority' — either a member of Rudolph's suite or, more likely, the Duke Ludwig *in* Bavaria, the Empress Elisabeth's brother — a report which was as far removed from the truth as could be, but which was nevertheless circulated to the more important German missions abroad : 'Because of Rudolph's intimate relations with journalists of extreme views who flattered his vanity and which both Majesties so deeply deplore, indiscretions had been feared, so that the idea of his becoming a member of the Ministerial Council had been abandoned. According to the same source the personal relationship between the Monarch and his son lacked that character of affection which is usually the rule in the highest families. It is significant that both Majesties agree [in this]'.[8] The report ended with the piquant remark that Duke Ludwig declared his readiness to go to Vienna if required, to influence the Empress and through her the Emperor, in favour of Germany. It is a fair inference that the report on Rudolph was the Duke's fabrication.

Prince William was entirely under the Chancellor's influence at the time, and consequently at loggerheads with his parents. He disliked the idea of Rudolph being on a good footing with them and in his usual impetuous way tried to create the impression that he too was a man whose opinions mattered.

While his mother wrote to Queen Victoria, 'Rudolph . . . spoke with marvellous clearness, intelligence and common sense, and is quite *au fait* of everything . . .',[9] William made a speech at Potsdam in April 1887 in which in his tactless way he deliberately gravely offended Rudolph.

It can no longer be ascertained what expressions were used, but Rudolph was sufficiently annoyed to ask the Austrian Military Attaché, Lt.-Col. Steininger, to find out more about it. Steininger's reply, despite its length, is not sufficiently explicit as to what was actually said, but makes it clear that the remarks were not only offensive to

Rudolph himself, but to the whole house of Hapsburg and to Austria generally.

Steininger admitted 'that one has here in Germany generally little or no understanding for our polyglot state' and that it was not the first time that he had had occasion to discover this. He also stated that William, who was 'coarse and reckless by nature', must have been 'in an almost irresponsible state of mind', as he had not only abused Rudolph 'in the filthiest manner, but also his own parents and his wife'. This was cold comfort, and Steininger's subsequent talks with Waldersee, who tried to excuse William, did not improve the situation. Rudolph did not know that William's anti-Liberal attitude, which may have been responsible for these attacks on him and the Liberal German Crown Prince and Princess, was aggravated by Court Preacher Stöcker. Stöcker, a violent reactionary and anti-Semite, was in close contact with Vienna circles of like persuasion — such men as Vogelsang and Vergani. We are left to guess how much gossip and falsehood in this way reached the ear of the malleable and gullible Hohenzollern Prince.

Steininger had also spoken of rumours that Prince William favoured German aggrandisement at Austria's expense, but said he hoped that when the Prince would have had time to become reasonable his views would change. Rudolph did not find this very convincing, particularly when he learned a little later that William's father, Crown Prince Frederick William, was seriously ill, although it was not yet realised that he was fatally ill. The old Emperor was ninety, his son ailing, and the grandson, a self-declared enemy of Austria or at the very least an immature talker, might be called to rule fairly soon. Although the immediate crisis had by now passed and war with Russia seemed less imminent even to Rudolph, the prospect of the unreliable William as German Emperor was frightening.

II

When preparations were being made for Queen Victoria's Golden Jubilee in 1887 relations between Britain and Austria were very cordial. As early as February the Queen had the Austrian Foreign Minister informed that she would be very pleased to receive the Crown Prince. The invitation was eagerly accepted and considered a great honour, although it seemed a little inconvenient to be away at the time. Rudolph wrote to Kálnoky : 'I fully realise that we must not offend the old Queen at this moment and I am consequently as usual prepared to go wherever the Emperor orders me. All private considerations and pleasures are of no importance whatever and I am pleased to be useful and able to serve in any respect.'

The Prince of Wales was particularly pleased when the Crown Prince arrived. On the first night of the visit they were at the Marlborough Club until the small hours of the morning, and throughout the stay they spent much of their time together. The Prince of Wales introduced many of his friends to Rudolph, Mrs. Langtry, Lord Rothschild, etc., and one morning took him to see Buffalo Bill, then the vogue in London. Both Princes were so interested that they did not return until 1.30 although the Queen had been expecting them to lunch half an hour earlier. Even this did not lessen her good opinion of Rudolph, whom she invested with the Order of the Garter, 'fixing it herself and tickling me as she did so, so that I could hardly refrain from laughing'.[10] The Prince of Wales told Rudolph's adjutant Count Kinsky of the Austrian Embassy that 'he was very glad because it was a particular, quite exceptional distinction, as the order was usually only granted to members of the family or to reigning princes'.[11]

In the festive London of the Golden Jubilee Rudolph represented his country worthily. He showed the graceful Austrian bearing (*österreichischen Anstand*), greatly impressing the many illustrious guests, and was 'loaded with honour and kindness' by the Queen. On one occasion he led her in to dinner, preceding all kings. He amazed not only the foreign guests, but Kinsky too, who said in his report to Kálnoky : 'It was very interesting to meet the Crown Prince, whom I did not know, or rather I did not know the Crown Prince as he is today. I cannot assure your Excellency sufficiently how pleasantly surprised I was to see how much he has changed to his advantage, or how wrong perhaps my opinions and my ideas about him had been.' Kinsky's 'ideas and opinions' about the Crown Prince were of course those of the Austrian aristocracy. When the diplomat met Rudolph outside Vienna society the necessarily close contact gave him an opportunity to revise his ideas. Naïvely Kinsky tried to explain why he was so different. 'I fancy that I have found the reason why he has improved in his relations to journalism. It appears to me that formerly nobody told him anything and that all information was withheld from him. As he is intelligent and eager to learn he consequently tried to get information from journalists, from whom he received it with the journalistic manner and bias. When he approached your Excellency you were not aloof in your contact with him, but enlightened him more and more so that now he draws his knowledge from the right source, is satisfied with it and has confidence.' [11] Although Rudolph's connections with Szeps and his other journalistic friends remained as strong as ever, the fact is eloquent that Kinsky sought an explanation for his surprise at finding the Crown Prince so different from the picture he had had of him.

Rudolph saw the German Crown Prince and Princess frequently while in London and they charged their Court Marshal Radolinsky to tell Kinsky how charmed they were with him. The good relationship between them may have contributed to Queen Victoria's liking for him, as the old Queen valued her eldest daughter's judgement. The diplomatic agreement between Great Britain, Austria and Italy, concluded later in 1887, may well have been made easier by the confidence in Austria's future created by Rudolph's consummate tact.

III

Back in Austria again, Rudolph returned to his old way of life and its many empty duties. In England his charm and good nature had met with respect. Now, in Austria, he was once more unimportant and little notice was taken of his views and opinions. It seems almost incredible that the Rudolph who represented his country so graciously at the Golden Jubilee and the Rudolph of the summer of 1887 in Austria could have been the same person. Soon after his return the frustration which he must now have doubly felt increased his cynicism alarmingly, as his letter of July 27th to Stephanie clearly showed. 'Yesterday morning I drove from Laxenburg into town, went to see Tilgner the sculptor and then to the Hofburg. Afterwards I had a frightfully hot journey to Baden and lunched at 3 o'clock with Uncle William. . . . There were Aunt

Elizabeth, a terrible sight . . . a few old women . . . then Pateneg, half woman, half man, half German Knight, half priest. . . . You can imagine what frightful jabber went on. The food was excellent, but the drinks had not been properly cooled which annoyed me greatly. . . . Then to Vöslau where there are only Jews.'

Here the Crown Prince inserts a quotation from a Hungarian political song, *minden szido gazember* (all Jews are criminals), a thing which would have been unthinkable earlier. 'They all came to see me off at the station. In the evening I returned to Vienna. Here the air was thick, so hot and heavy, so that I had to take very many drinks. Indeed it was too hot to sleep, so I stayed up for a long time and at length fell asleep at the open window when the cool of the morning came. Slept until 10 o'clock. Then came Weilen [the writer, who, together with Rudolph, was editing his book on the Monarchy] whose hands sweat more disgustingly than ever. He was gasping with the heat and foaming at the mouth as he talked so that he looked just like an old pointer. He . . . is writing a play — poor mankind! He only comes to Vienna once a week, to . . . greet me with a damp handshake. As soon as I have finished this letter, I shall get into a bath, where I shall smoke, sleep and sing. Then I shall have a good meal. Sacher [the most famous Vienna restaurant of the time] has greatly improved this year and in the evening I am going to Bruck [a garrison town]. There it will be frightfully hot with much dust, perspiration and smell.' [12]

This kind of bravado may of course have been assumed to show off to his wife, who by now was no longer interested in really serious problems. On the other hand, he had of late put on this act so often that it may have become second nature, although he avoided showing it in his letters to Szeps. Archduke John Salvator stated at the time : 'So far his political views are entirely irrelevant, since our Emperor, in accordance with the constitution, decidedly refuses any uncalled for influence. The Crown Prince is intelligent enough to avoid any temptation to do this. But that is also known to the gentlemen who hold the reins of government. They are, as long as they enjoy the Emperor's confidence, safe in finding his assent in all important questions — thus they need not take any notice of Crown Prince Rudolph." [13]

Had Francis Joseph been able to forget his office and talk to his son as man to man, explain to him the reasons for his policy or, alternatively, given him an appointment in which he could have shown his mettle, much of his later difficulties might have been avoided. Nor could Rudolph look for help from his mother. While he never felt a nearness to his father, he loved his mother deeply, but her love for him was not strong enough to overcome her almost pathological urge to travel. She was away most of the year, and, during the brief interval she spent with her husband she seldom saw her son. She was abnormally shy and reserved — she rarely even spoke of everyday happenings to the Emperor. An understanding word from her would have eased Rudolph's often troubled mind, but it was never spoken. It could have changed his whole life.

Thus he was lonely at a time when this solitude was fatal to his state of mind. If Stephanie had not been so petty-minded and lacking in womanly instinct she could have helped. Highly strung and frequently restless, he was not an easy husband, but Stephanie, in her laboured pretentiousness, lacking tact and warmth of heart, was not an easy wife either. Yet their conjugal life had not entirely ended, or Rudolph would not have sent her to a spa to increase her chances of having another child. It may have been more dynastic considerations than regard for his family life which made the Crown Prince so concerned, but the tone of his frequent letters to Stephanie suggests that he still felt affection for her ; yet she had no comfort to offer him, to help him in his loneliness.

In these circumstances the Crown Prince tried to drown his worries in a vortex of activity. He concentrated on military duties and he increased the time he spent hunting. Hardly a day passed when he did not go shooting at least for a couple of hours. Both Vienna and Budapest were sufficiently near game reserves to permit this, even when he was busy on other pursuits. The unfortunate fact was that he had now become so cynical. What had at first been protection for hurt pride was now habit. Frequently not taken seriously himself, he now refused to take others seriously. He began pouring scorn over everyone and everything. He had always been impatient and ready to find fault in people, he had not been easy to satisfy, but now this tendency increased alarmingly.

At this time, possibly a little earlier, Rudolph seems to have begun a relationship with a dancer, Marie Kasper, a good-looking, vivacious girl who had many friends among the artists of Vienna. She was superficial and easy-going, and her gaiety and lack of pretension were a relaxation. He turned to her frequently, and she seems to have accompanied him later on some of his unofficial journeys. Marie, generally called Mizzi, was on friendly terms with a lawyer, Florian Meissner, who acted as an informer — paid or unpaid — and many of Rudolph's movements were reported to the police.[14] Meissner acted in a professional capacity for the German Embassy in Vienna, which he had represented in a few out-of-court settlements of a delicate nature. It is therefore reasonable to assume that reports of Rudolph's movements were also passed on to the German Embassy.

In a discussion with his younger sister Valerie about the possibility of war in 1887 he said : 'In a war there is the possibility of leaving one's mark', but Valerie retorted, 'It costs so many human lives and you are endangering your own'. He made a disdainful gesture and said dreamily, 'When one has enjoyed everything, one has no interest left'.[22]

IV

Towards the end of 1887 the news of the Prussian Crown Prince's illness became more and more alarming. There could no longer be any doubt that he was suffering from cancer of the throat and it seemed unlikely that he would live to see the new year in. He would probably die before his father.

Anyone who knew Frederick William as Rudolph did realised how frustrated he had felt at having to watch idly his father's foremost adviser, Bismarck, wasting by his personal rule the good-will which had gone into the newly created German Empire. The parallel must have been in the mind of the Austrian Crown Prince that he too had to watch a Minister, Taaffe, threatening the very existence of the Austrian Empire. So far Rudolph could console himself, as Frederick William had done, with the thought that his time would, must, come and then all wrongs could be righted. But would it come, could one rely on it ? Frederick William had been deceived by a cruel fate, he had waited in vain. Would he, Rudolph, too be overtaken by inexorable fate? If one could not be sure that there was any sense in waiting, what sense was there in living at all, in putting up with the many humiliations an impatient heir to the throne has to endure. Moreover Rudolph's father was relatively young, not yet sixty, his family known for the longevity of its members. How long would he have to wait? Would death be kind and not overtake him? Would there still be time to set his house in order or would it then be too late to save Austria? He had always been preoccupied with death, now he feared it.

At times he seemed greatly changed; not in all respects, but sufficiently to become untrue to some of the ideals of his earlier days. He was now often too restless to concentrate on memoranda or many long articles; it was as though part of his vitality were ebbing away. Talk and gossip about him, which had never stopped since he had been declared of age, intensified — this time apparently not without reason, although some of the puerile pranks and drunken excesses which were ascribed to him were not of his doing. In February 1888 Engelbert Pernerstorfer, a member of the Austrian parliament, told the House: 'A tale has reached me according to which a young gentleman in an extremely high position, after a drunken spree with his fellows, wished to bring them back with him into his wife's room. . . . Then there is another tale, about another exalted personage, who, with his friends, all of princely blood, galloped over the fields. From a distance they caught sight of a funeral procession. They halted, and all these noble princes amused themselves by jumping over the coffin. The patriotic indignation of the Minister for Education will be all the greater, since the position of the young gentlemen is so exalted.'[16]

A few days later, two men gained admission into Pernerstorfer's flat and horsewhipped him. When the police investigated, the two men could not be found, but it was discovered that they were soldiers. The Archduke to whom the deputy referred was in both cases Otto, the younger brother of Francis Ferdinand, Austrian heir apparent after Rudolph's death. Some people, however, took Rudolph to be the Archduke who had jumped with his horse across a coffin. Although he can be acquitted of this charge, he was nevertheless an accessory after the fact by obstructing the course of justice and possibly by having a hand in the outrage on Pernerstorfer. On March 5th, 1888, he wrote to Stephanie : 'The police have given me some anxious hours ; they have been on the trail and have discovered the regiment from which the riding-whips came. They could not get hold of the "guilty parties", for we spirited them away in good time, one to Southern Hungary, and the other to the Hercegovina. Still it needed all my cheek and ingeniousness to save myself . . . from trouble.'[17]

What a decline! 'O what a noble mind is here o'erthrown.' The man who had once, only nine years previously, stated 'thank God I do not feel in myself the calling to pursue the so-called accustomed courses, the foolish triviality of my relatives with their blinkers', now took part in or condoned their criminal behaviour.

V

The life which Rudolph had so far led had been a hard and onerous one in spite of all the splendour attached to it. He had taken his duties seriously, however empty and senseless they had seemed. He had worked hard, but the problems with which he had had to contend remained insoluble. The Minister President continued to enjoy the Emperor's unlimited confidence ; war with Russia remained a spectre on the horizon, and yet Austria's ally, Germany, went on flirting with Russia. In 1886 his cousin King Ludwig II of Bavaria had died mentally deranged, and his successor and younger brother Otto had been insane for many years. Rudolph was related to the Wittelsbach line. With his thorough training in biology what would be more likely, in his moods of frustration, than to ponder over the dreadful possibility that he too might one day succumb to the insanity which had claimed as its victim a cousin with whom he had spent many happy hours. Insanity could attack him as cancer had attacked Frederick William of Prussia. Is it not possible that the fear which at times tormented his soul may also at times have disturbed the balance of his mind ? Such thoughts must frequently have overwhelmed all other considerations and sapped his usual will to work. On these occasions he became an Imperial playboy. Yet for most of the time he still followed his old pursuits. He went on writing and taking an interest in politics, and he could still fit the word to the occasion. In his opening speech to the Hygiene Congress in Vienna during that year he said, 'Man is the most precious capital of state and society'. But now all this required more effort and seemed no longer so important.

His health, never robust, was impaired by frustration : he often felt tired, drank a great deal 'to buck himself up', and drank more than was good for him. This increased the feeling of fatigue, of which he complained so much in his letters. In 1887 he had been given morphia to combat a chronic cough, but he probably took too much. He wrote to Stephanie : 'I cannot get rid of my cough. Sometimes . . . I have frightful attacks which are especially inconvenient at . . . ceremonial occasions. I am keeping the cough under with morphine, although it is an injurious drug.'[18] Combined with alcohol, morphia may have lowered his standards. His personality changed slowly and imperceptibly only, but someone who had not seen him for any length of time would notice the change.

His friendship with Szeps continued and they seemed to have met quite frequently, though there were fewer letters than before ; perhaps because the problems seemed more difficult than ever, perhaps because he had at times given up hope of finding a solution. They seemed less urgent. The Prussian Crown Prince too had wrestled with the problems of his country, and what good had come of it, now that illness had befallen him and death could not be far off ?

Frustration and the combined shock of King Ludwig's death and Frederick William's illness had some sort of paralysing effect on Rudolph. It is frequently suggested in biographies that he was of unsound mind in his later years, due to his inherited tendency. It is, of course, almost impossible to suggest a diagnosis on the basis of the scanty and not always fully reliable evidence, but there are strong grounds for assuming that the Crown Prince was not suffering from genuine schizophrenia. True, he showed at times some of the symptoms of split personality, but there is not enough evidence to draw the conclusion that dementia praecox was the reason. He was too rational, even when he was an Imperial playboy. It may have been an anxiety neurosis which developed when frustration became overwhelming and the thought of his demented cousins was juxtaposed with it and with the fate of the German Crown Prince. Liberalism, the creed of his future government, was endangered by the new forces of pan-Germanism and anti-Semitism which gained more and more hold over the people in Austria. He must have been maddened by the contradictions inherent in his position. He could do nothing to save his country, though he was the heir to the throne. He said to the Austrian politician, von Chlumecky : 'The least Imperial Councillor [a courtesy title usually granted to civil servants after twenty-five years of service] has a bigger field of action that I have. I am condemned to be an idler.' [19] Yet there was so much that needed doing. 'Conditions in the East become gloomier and gloomier and the lack of decision here becomes greater and greater', he wrote to Szeps in December 1887.

From all the evidence one has the feeling that during this year, or even later, Rudolph's personal distress was not beyond a fairly easy remedy, and this would certainly not have been so had he shown evidence of inherited insanity. It is only necessary to read his letters, his pronouncements, to feel — and since no better evidence is available, reliance on such feelings may be admissible — that an improvement of his position, a clearly defined field of real responsibility might have, probably would have, averted disaster.

Rudolph had still some time to live, and there might have been time to prevent the catastrophe for which he was heading, had someone, his mother for instance, found strength to break through the barriers of custom, etiquette and reticence and talked to him in a human and understanding way. Even so the outcome could not have been certain. The Crown Prince was suffering from two ills :

frustration was one, the other was beyond an easy remedy — his country's malady. Had personal calamity not aggravated matters, the optimism inherent in the healthy mind of a person of Rudolph's age could have overcome the difficulties. But his soul was weighed down by the inescapable juxtaposition of private distress and anxiety for the future of his country.

REFERENCES

1. Corti, *Franz Josef*, Vol. III, p. 79.
2. Mitis, *op. cit.* p. 143.
3. Arnold Oskar Mayer, *Bismarck, der Mensch und Staatsmann* (Stuttgart, 1949), p. 594.
4. Glaise-Horstenau, *op. cit.* pp. 303 f.
5. *Aus dem Briefwechsel des General-Feldmarschalls Alfred, Grafen von Waldersee*, herausgegeben von Heinrich Otto Meisner (Stuttgart, 1928), Vol. I, p. 164.
6. Mitis, *op. cit.* p. 135.
7. Mitis, *op. cit.* pp. 135 f.
8. Public Records Office, German Microfilm No. 3021, Document 100.
9. *Letters of the Empress Frederick*, edited by Sir Frederick Ponsonby (London, 1928), p. 212.
10. Lonyay, *op. cit.* p. 210.
11. Mitis, *op. cit.* p. 372
12. Lonyay, *op. cit.* pp. 211 f.
13. Heinrich P(ollak), *Erzherzog Johann* (Wien, 1901), pp. 76 f.
14. *Das Mayerling Original,* pp. 110 f.
15. Corti, *Elisabeth*, p. 383.
16. *Stenogr. Prot. des Abgeordnetenhauses*, X Sess., Vol. VI, p. 6991.
17. Lonyay, *op. cit.* p. 221.
18. Lonyay, *op. cit.* p. 206.
19. Chlumecky, *op. cit.* p. 31.

CHAPTER TEN

Lengthening Shadows

I

ON March 9th, 1888, the Emperor William I of Germany died. The first reports to reach Vienna of the Emperor's death were premature and had embarrassing consequences. The Crown Prince, in a cynical letter to his wife, gave her the story. 'There has been a frightful rush since yesterday. At 7 o'clock news of William's death came from Berlin. Special editions of the newspapers had been issued and all Berlin believed in the death. Apparently the old man was wrongly supposed for a time to be dead. Here the Correspondence Bureau and the newspapers disseminated the news, so that at nine o'clock special editions with a mourning border were issued, and there was great excitement throughout the town. . . . I . . . was at the point of sending off my telegrams of condolence, when at the last moment Szeps came up with a telegram — it was all a mistake and the Emperor was still alive. To avoid confusion, I sent instantly for Kálnoky, who was about to announce the false news. At midnight there was still a great deal of bustle. . . . To-day genuine news of the death has come, at the Stock Exchange, Lord knows why. The public mood was priceless as usual. Yesterday evening a great fuss. People were not sympathetically moved, but simply excited. When the news came that William was not dead after all, the general opinion was "how boring, he even cheats us when dying". Then, when telegrams arrived saying that during the night he had taken food and drunk champagne, people were amused. The genuine tidings of the death were received with indifference, or with the feeling, "thanks be, at last there will be an end of these stories, one way or the other". . . . Another thing which distracted attention from William's death was a great fire which broke out in the Bauermarkt [a street in the centre of Vienna]. . . . Ladies in their nightgowns had to jump into stretched canvasses, while terriers, pugs and other trash were brought down to safety through the tube fire escapes. . . . Truly Vienna, as the song says, has a charm of its own . . .'.[1]

But it was not all cynicism; Rudolph in his old manner as a keen observer also wrote a character sketch of the deceased Emperor for Szeps which was published in the *Tagblatt* on March 11th, in which he criticised him sharply, though not unfairly. 'He was deeply religious, God-fearing and full of trust in the Lord, and he had the talent to be always convinced that all his actions, no matter how unjust they were, were God's will. He was only the tool which the Lord used. . . . He was never proud of his great deeds, but was convinced they made for the natural development of the Hohenzollern power, desired by God's will. . . . He considered himself the protector of all good conservative ideas, but notwithstanding stole his neighbours' countries. He was greedy after land, he dethroned kings and princes, but disliked it, acting solely under the force of Providence which wanted a powerful Prussia for the protection of all that was good and old in Europe. This confusion of ideas was not with him a comedy, it is genuine old Hohenzollern tradition. . . . In the selection of his advisers he was always lucky. . . . He was a Prussian, body and soul . . . neither his son nor his grandson resemble him. . . .' The article caused quite a stir, but nobody could guess its author. Even Frischauer was in the dark, and when he asked Szeps who had written it he was told 'an old diplomat'.

The German Emperor's funeral had been delayed to permit the new Emperor to reach Berlin from San Remo. Frederick William, now Frederick III, was himself a dying man, and when Rudolph represented his father at the funeral he must have realised that after many years of waiting the new Emperor was at best a shadow whose days were numbered. He must also have seen William, the next in succession, full of his own importance, already seeing himself as Emperor. No written evidence of Rudolph's impressions is available, but they cannot have been happy and must have added to his already troubled mind.

At Easter 1888 the Crown Prince, Stephanie, Archduke Otto and some friends went from Abbazia for a cruise on an Austrian man-of-war, the *Greif*. This part of the Adriatic is treacherous, studded with small islands. On the first evening the men had consumed more alcohol than was good for them and were all very merry. After midnight the ship struck a reef and the captain decided to send his guests to the nearest island. There was no danger of sinking, as the sea was quite calm, but the ship leaked considerably. Rudolph and most of his company, however, had not yet slept off their potions and were unable to get into the boats. They had to be lowered into them, almost trussed like birds. The matter had to be reported to the Emperor, and some of the details soon became common knowledge and did great harm to Rudolph's already impaired reputation.

It would be wrong to exaggerate the importance of this episode of which so much has been made at the time and since, but it is an indication that the Crown Prince had changed. This is also shown by his greatly reduced interests in all serious pursuits. Hunting had once given him a welcome opportunity to observe and describe nature. Now asked by Szeps to write about his hunting experiences for a French journal, he had declined. He went on hunting, killed more animals than before, but was no longer interested in describing his experiences. Instead of scientists and politicians — men like Brehm and Menger, Szeps and Chlumecky — he now preferred the company of Archdukes and his aristocratic hunting fellows, some of whom might have been well-meaning, but were hardly his intellectual peers.

II

When transferred to Vienna in 1883, Rudolph had been appointed commander of the 25th Infantry Division. In 1888 he was due for promotion when the command of an Army Corps fell vacant. The Bavarian Minister in Vienna reported to his government on March 18th, 'As I understand, His Imperial Highness, Crown Prince Rudolph, will take over the vacant appointment of General Officer Commanding the Second Army Corps and thus become General Officer Commanding the Vienna garrison'. Five days later he added, 'The Crown Prince has been called to take over the office of General Inspector of Infantry and consequently will not take over the command of the Second Army Corps which is due to him as senior officer commanding a division'.[2]

The appointment to which Rudolph was thus promoted was doubtlessly higher ranking than the one which had been due to him. On the other hand, it was an office especially created and was more or less a sinecure. Szeps sent a warm letter of congratulations : 'The sphere of action is widened, natural gifts and serious endeavour find room for higher development, genius and energy achieve supreme success. All those who have had the good fortune of coming into close contact with Your Highness hope and look for this.' Rudolph in reply said he was very satisfied with the new appointment, and after a few weeks experience in this new office he told Latour: 'My position is as though it had been created for me, and I am very happy about it'. But was he really happy ? The letter to Latour seems in one point not sincere : he knew full well that the position had been created for him, and he may have written both letters not only to reassure the recipients, but also himself. Bibl in his biography assumes this. Whether or not the Crown Prince was really satisfied — he may have felt slighted — the promotion contributed materially to his misery. As a General Officer commanding an Army Corps he would have had a well defined field of duties, as General Inspector he had none. Regular work would have alleviated his frustration. Rudolph seemed to have felt soon after his appointment that it was not too easy. A few days before telling Latour that he was happy he wrote to Stephanie : 'I am rushing all over the place. Was a long time in the War Office and with the Emperor ; from the service point of view everything agreeable and flattering, but privately considered, lots of vexation.'[3] But a few weeks later he seemed more satisfied when he wrote again to Stephanie: 'I like my new position, it brings movement into my life, and suits me very well'.⁴ Such movement may have been welcome to him in his restlessness, but the staid duties of an ordinary command would have helped him to overcome it.

He eagerly grasped the opportunity which the inspectorate seemed to afford to improve the army's readiness for battle. Events in Serbia suggested possible developments in the Balkans, and there was much to be done as the Archduke Albrecht had, he felt, let things slide. For a time at least his former vigour seemed restored. When Szeps congratulated him on his wedding anniversary he replied, 'Were your expectations only partly fulfilled and I be allowed to realise at least half of my plans, I could then, when the time comes, be content to vanish from the scene'. But the physical exertion of his new office proved too arduous. He was not strong enough to stand the strain of 'a laborious life', riding 'sorry screws' and eating poor food, and he was not prepared to forgo hunting and the frequent quest for pleasure which had now become an important part of his life. He went on taking morphine, and in many of his letters there are references to hard drinking. This burning the candle at both ends showed in his face; he looked poorly and much older than his years.

The *Tagblatt* had for some time been the target of sharp attacks from the anti-Semites, whose leader, Schönerer, seemed aware of Rudolph's association with Szeps. In a mass meeting in February he had indicated his intention of intensifying these attacks and had declared 'the close season of the Jewish newspaper scribblers and their associates is now past for all times'. Rudolph considered that the allusion was meant for him and remarked to Szeps that 'to be attacked by Schönerer is an honour'. That Rudolph was right in his assumption was confirmed

when, after the *Tagblatt* had produced an extra edition
with the premature news of the Emperor William's death,
Schönerer, carrying a heavy stick and accompanied by
a few of his followers, entered the editorial offices and
threatened the staff.

Schönerer's attack on the editorial offices of the *Tagblatt*
had at last roused the government. The Emperor had
become interested as Schönerer had repeatedly announced
that as a German he owed his allegiance to Germany and
not to Austria. Rudolph hoped that 'this time the black-
guard would perish'. Schönerer's immunity as a member
of parliament was withdrawn by the House and he was
tried for unlawful entering and sentenced to five months
solitary confinement and loss of his political rights for
five years. The rather severe sentence transformed a knave
into a martyr, and after his appeal had been rejected a
demonstration of his followers took place on the evening
before he was to enter gaol. Empress Maria Theresa's
monument was to be unveiled on the day following, and
thousands of Schönerer's followers marched past the still
draped statue shouting wildly, 'Down with the Hapsburgs!
Down with Austria! Long live Germany!' until the police
intervened. A number of the more affluent followers
drove in carriages, among them Schönerer's wife accompanied by Dr. Lueger, now one of his champions, although
they later parted company.

The demonstration, particularly the participation of
Lueger who had a large following among the Catholic
petty *bourgeoisie*, was an ugly reminder that there were
many people to whom Austria meant nothing, and it cast
a sombre shadow on the following day's unveiling ceremony. This united all members of the Imperial family,
even the Empress was present. She had not seen Rudolph

for some time, and the change in his appearance must have been more evident to her than to those who saw him fairly regularly. His younger sister, Valerie, was about to become engaged to the Archduke Francis Salvator, whom he heartily disliked, and whom he considered to be too near a relative for marriage. Elisabeth was in favour of the match but feared her son might object to it. She decided to overcome her shyness and to discuss the match with him when the whole family was together at the unveiling. 'Never be unkind to Valerie,' she said, 'it would bring you bad luck. I am Sunday's child and I am in communication with the other world. I can bring good or bad luck. So think of May 13th.' Rudolph was a little bewildered. 'I shall certainly never wrong Valerie, Mama', he answered. Elisabeth was satisfied with this promise, but was uneasy to see him so pale. His eyes were unsteady, and there were deep shadows under them. 'Are you ill?' she asked. 'No, only tired and run down', he replied.[5] Elisabeth enquired no further. She valued her own privacy so much that her son's was also sacred, even when inquisitiveness would have been her duty.

III

In June 1888 the Crown Prince had the welcome duty of visiting Bosnia and Hercegovina, the two recently acquired Austrian provinces. As this was not only a military occasion but also an inspection of the provincial administration, Stephanie accompanied him. Had Rudolph known that during his absence the army council, of which he was now a member, would come to important decisions about the speed of army mobilisation, he would have been less pleased with his assignment ; but unaware of what was to take place he was glad of the mission. To both, the journey through an entirely new country, still characterised by strong oriental influences, was a stimulating experience. The Crown Prince particularly was impressed by what he saw. This had been Turkish land and neglected for centuries. After ten years of Austrian administration it was already showing signs of new life. Over part of the way they travelled on a railway built by Austria during that time. Enthusiasm was reawakened in him, and in Sarajevo, the provincial capital, it broke all the bounds of formality when at his great reception he had to propose his father's health. He embarrassed the Austrian Foreign Ministry by rousing Russian suspicions in proclaiming publicly that it was Austria's mission to carry Western civilisation into the Near East. 'We begin our real task of carrying Western culture into the Orient and the result will be great progress for the whole of Europe', he had said in his 1886 memorandum, and now this view had been strengthened.

Austrian official sources asserted that nationalist circles in Serbia were contemplating Rudolph's assassination during that journey, but no such attempt was made. The Crown Prince in spite of the danger was very enthusiastic about his experience and wrote to Latour : 'The journey in many respects meant taking risks, but it succeeded splendidly and was a great achievement. I was quite enchanted with what I saw down there. We have undertaken a great cultural mission and in ten years achieved incredible success. I would not have credited the old Austria with so much strength.'

During his stay in Bosnia, the German Emperor Frederick III had died and William, six months Rudolph's

junior, was now William II, King of Prussia and German
Emperor — the Kaiser. When he opened parliament on
June 25th he promised to tread the same path as his grandfather. Rudolph rightly interpreted that as a continuation
of the foreign policy which had favoured Russia at
Austria's expense. This could not reduce his confidence
in the Kaiser, as he had none. On the other hand, when
William instructed General Waldersee, who as his envoy
was to announce his accession in Vienna, he charged him
to give his regards to the Emperor and such Archdukes as
Waldersee would meet, but there was no special message
for Rudolph, the Crown Prince.[6] Soon afterwards
Rudolph gave in a letter to Szeps the following character
sketch : 'William II will do well ; he will probably soon
stir up great trouble in old Europe ; this I too believe.
He is just the man to do it. Of a heaven-inspired limita-
tion, but stubborn and energetic as a bull, he considers
himself the greatest genius. What more can one want.
Quite likely, he will in the course of a few years reduce
Hohenzollern Germany to the level which it deserves.'
Waldersee, who stated in his memoirs that he had found
everywhere in Vienna great confidence in his young
Emperor, was mistaken, at least so far as the Austrian
Crown Prince was concerned.

After his return from Bosnia Rudolph had again to
take up his military duties which were now even more
arduous. Parliament had voted additional means for
army reinforcements and a new deployment of the armed
forces was carried out, particularly a strengthening of the
garrisons near the Russian borders. In various letters to
Stephanie Rudolph stated that he was 'on the go from
morning till night'.[7]

This increased work should have pleased him. It was

the consequence of his old and now generally accepted contention that war with Russia was unavoidable. Even the Emperor, usually reluctant in committing himself, had said to Waldersee : 'How we can get out of it is not clear to me'.[8] Now, if ever, Rudolph should have felt happy, but he seemed weary and listless, 'tired and longing for a rest'. How he could in such a condition have borne the stress and strain of a war is difficult to see, yet he still considered it the only solution for his own and his country's troubles. When Szeps wrote an encouraging letter for his birthday on August 21st, he replied : 'The age of thirty marks a dividing point in life, and one that is not very pleasant either. Much time has passed, spent more or less usefully, but empty in real actions and success. We live in a slow, rotten time. Who knows how long this will continue. And each passing year makes me older, less keen and less fit. The necessary daily routine is in the long run very tiring. And this eternal preparing of oneself, this permanent waiting for great times of reform, weaken one's best powers. If the hopes and expectations which you are placing in me are ever to be realised, war must come soon, a great time, when we shall be happy, because after its glorious end we could build the foundations of a great and peaceful Austria. . . . *One must believe in the future.* I hope and count on the next years.' *

'One must believe in the future!' He had to force himself now to be optimistic ; no longer was belief in the future natural to him. Many factors were responsible for such a profound change, among them the events in Berlin. Rudolph could eat his heart out while William, the friend of Russia, did as he pleased. A few months before, Reuss had informed Kálnoky that 'nobody could guess when

* My italics.—R. B.

Russia would start the war, but it could be very sudden and unexpected'. Much as Rudolph wanted this war, German help was more doubtful than ever — probably Austria would have to fight alone.

Foreign policy was not his only headache. Taaffe with his miserable reactionary policy would have to give up sooner or later, but it now seemed certain that his régime would not be followed by a revival of Liberalism. The musty smell of Austrian politics had been intensified by the anti-Semite movement. Jailing Schönerer had not reduced it ; on the contrary, it seemed to be still growing under the leadership of Lueger, who, just as much of a demagogue as Schönerer, was more intelligent and consequently more dangerous.

The masses, attracted by the new creed, were as yet almost entirely excluded from the franchise, which could not, however, be withheld from them much longer, and, once Liberalism was beaten at the polls, Rudolph as Emperor would be without the political force to support and carry out his programme. No progressive government could be envisaged any longer since the demagogues would soon command the majority of the German vote in Austria. Yet it would hardly be possible to suppress such a popular, if reactionary, political force. The present was stale and unprofitable and the future fast losing its attraction.

IV

In September 1888 the Prince of Wales came to Austria to attend the army manœuvres and to enjoy some shooting. This visit was very welcome to Rudolph as both had so much in common : both were easy-going and disliked ceremony, and, most important, both were free from prejudices and were subject to a great deal of vilification and calumny.

The Prince of Wales attended the Austrian army manoeuvres in Croatia, went hunting and riding with both the Emperor and Rudolph. He and Rudolph shocked public opinion by lunching openly in a famous Viennese restaurant with a Jewish financier and philanthropist, Baron Hirsch, whom both had known for some time. Hirsch was fabulously rich and interested in railway concessions in Turkey — an interest which ran parallel with that of the Crown Prince and of the Austro-Hungarian Empire. Probably on Rudolph's suggestion the banker had helped Szeps when a few years previously the *Tagblatt* had been in financial difficulties owing to the censorship and the machinations of frightened shareholders. Again on Rudolph's instance he had invested capital in Austrian shipping lines in the Eastern Mediterranean which otherwise, through the lack of capital, would have had to close down. He also seems to have lent money to Rudolph personally ; this, when discovered, was considered a sufficient reason to hint — even by otherwise serious biographers — that the Crown Prince was in his pay.

Rudolph welcomed the opportunity of repaying the Prince of Wales for the hospitality which he had enjoyed in Britain. He told Stephanie : 'Wales . . . is in fine fettle and wants to see everything, take part in everything ; indefatigable, he remains his old self. Nothing seems to tire the old boy.' He ends on a note which clearly shows his sympathies, 'I gladly invite Wales, but I would invite William only to get rid of him by an elegant hunting misadventure'.[9]

William, who wanted to show himself in Vienna in

the full splendour of his new dignity, had announced his
arrival during the time of the Prince of Wales's stay.
This caused some trouble as the Kaiser refused to meet his
uncle. The Prince of Wales did not want to embarrass
his Austrian friends, gave way and went to Romania
during his nephew's stay in Austria. Rudolph would
naturally have preferred the Prince to remain with him
and the Kaiser to remain at home, but was unable to do
anything about it. He had, moreover, an important function to fulfil during the visit. Francis Joseph, although a
staunch supporter of the German alliance, had become
suspicious when William had made his first visit as Emperor to Russia. Remembering recent disturbances by
Schönerer's followers and their demonstrative preference
for the Hohenzollerns, he had no wish to see the Kaiser
dominating the scene, and he instructed Taaffe to forbid
a torchlight procession which the Vienna German nationalists had planned in honour of William's visit, and recommended the Minister-President generally 'to keep his eyes
open'. Rudolph had been given special commissions from
his father — he had to see that the Kaiser would never be
alone while in Vienna. Archduke Francis Ferdinand was
away hunting but by Francis Joseph's orders had to return
to the capital to assist the Crown Prince in his supervision
of the guest. Rudolph wrote to him : 'I feel very sorry
for you ; strong stags are far better than the German
Emperor'.[10] He told Kálnocky in a letter, 'The Emperor
wishes me to tell you that he is fully in agreement that
I should take part in the *déjeuner* given by Reuss, but he
was of the opinion that the matter must be done with
extreme care, so that the real intention, not to let the
German Emperor walk about alone in Vienna, cannot be
discerned'.[11]

There were the usual instances of tactlessness on the Kaiser's part during his stay. It was obvious from his distribution of honours during and after the visit — the Hungarian Minister-President was invested with a high order, the Austrian Minister-President not — that he had no idea of the intricacies of Austrian politics. The German Military Attaché, Deines, reported to his chief, Waldersee, who in turn recorded in his journal, that there was a sharp difference of opinion between the German Emperor and Rudolph, but no indication of its character was given.[12] *

While William was in Vienna at least some of the population must have shown a certain lack of enthusiasm. Those Viennese who had not been poisoned by Schönerer's venom demonstrated their feelings unmistakably. Szeps, in a letter to Rudolph, wrote that 'it was a beautiful Austrian day' when many Viennese showed the Kaiser that they were not enamoured with him. Rudolph had to bear the brunt of the Kaiser's consequent ill-humour, which was further increased by constant poor weather during his hunting trips, and must have felt relieved when, after William's departure, the Prince of Wales returned from Romania for a further few days.

V

In the autumn of 1888 attacks on the Austrian Crown Prince became widespread. Until then rumours had been spread insidiously, but now matters received much more publicity. Neither in Austria nor in Hungary were open

---

* It is strange that Mitis in his careful biography does not mention such an incident. But he, as nearly all Austrian biographers of the Crown Prince, is reserved when dealing with Germany.

accusations possible, so his enemies used their foreign connections for their calumnies.

In October a book was published in Paris, *La Fin d'un monde* by a certain Édouard Adolphe Drumont, in which the Crown Prince was openly attacked. The book dealt with French political conditions in a rabid anti-Semitic manner. The attack on Rudolph formed no part of the book proper, but was contained in a preface, which had no bearing on the subject. It was a restatement of Perner-storfer's speech in the Austrian parliament, and the Crown Prince was named as the culprit. Szeps, conversant with French political conditions, informed his friend that this attack had its origin in Austria, and in this he was right. Drumont was editor-in-chief of a Catholic paper *L'Univers*, and was on good terms with members of both wings of Austrian political Catholicism — the older Conservative wing and the newer anti-Semitic persuasion. The Conservatives had, in their daily paper *Vaterland*, repeatedly helped Drumont by attacking French Liberals ; in 1883, at the time of the death of Léon Gambetta, they had published a particularly vicious obituary. The anti-Semitic group also collaborated with Drumont. In 1889 a new anti-Jewish and anti-Liberal daily, *Das deutsche Volksblatt*, was published in Vienna in which Drumont was frequently mentioned in the most fulsome terms. The editor of the paper, a particularly crude Jew-baiter named Vergani, a few years later declared in a public meeting that Drumont — at the time serving a prison sentence for defamation of character — was the only sane politician in France.

But this attack on Rudolph in a foreign paper was not the only one. An Italian paper, *L'Epoca*, stated on November 15th, soon after Drumont's attack, that 'it was well known that Prince Rudolph led a most dissolute life'.

The Italian government in its paper *Riforma* published an official statement that this was not true and that 'it was well known that this Prince was leading a life of study and work, far removed from the scandal which had been the subject of complaint in parliament'.

In October French Liberals came to the defence with an article in the Paris daily, *Figaro*, in which Rudolph was highly praised. The Austrian people, so it said, expected something quite extraordinary from their Crown Prince, who would one day be a factor to be reckoned with in European politics, and he did not want Austria to be a vassal of her allies. In a similar vein, a new Vienna weekly, *Schwarzgelb* (the Imperial Austrian colours), wrote a few days later about Austria's relations with Germany, without mentioning the Crown Prince. In this article hostility towards Germany was sharply expressed: 'Just as Bismarck said that Bulgaria was Hecuba to him, so we say that Alsace-Lorraine is Hecuba to us, and that we would not risk the bones of one of our soldiers to defend Prussian domination there'.[13] Another paper, the *Pester Lloyd*, published in Hungary in the German language, discussed the possibility of a change of orientation in Austria's foreign policy; it would be easy to find other allies in place of Germany.

There is no evidence to suggest that Rudolph had anything to do with these articles, although they reflected to a large extent his ideas. The matter could have rested there had it not been taken up by a certain Paul Dehn, a follower of the notorious Schönerer. The mouthpiece of Schönerer's movement was a weekly paper, *Unverfälschte deutsche Worte* (Unadulterated German Words), which was the basest of all the Austrian periodicals at the time. In it were frequent references in praise of Herr Dehn and his anti-Liberal, anti-Semitic pamphlets, parts of which were reprinted. In November 1888 Dehn took up the gauntlet. He was owner and editor of an obscure news service whose handwritten, stencilled articles were offered to a few subscribers, mainly German periodicals. He seems to have maintained his service mainly through their help ; he probably obtained financial support from the Berlin Foreign Ministry, which at the time subsidised several German nationalist papers in Austria. We do not know whether the attack on Rudolph which this service handed out to its subscribers was in fact done at Schönerer's request, but it is possible. Schönerer had declared a few months previously 'the close season for the Jewish newspaper scribblers and their associates is past'. His direct attack on Szeps had miscarried and landed him in gaol ; an attack on Rudolph — one of the associates — had to be carried out more discreetly. The censorship kept a wary eye on the *Unverfälschte deutsche Worte*, but Dehn's news service, with the majority of its subscribers in Germany, out of reach of the Austrian censor, was both safe and effective.

Paul Dehn did not mention the Crown Prince by name, but stated that a 'very high personality — not, however, Emperor Francis Joseph', had an almost pathological dislike, sustained by hatred and envy, of the German Emperor. Consequently a certain type of journalist hoped to do good business by discounting a bill of exchange, whose day of payment would be determined by history. After enumerating the anti-German attacks in the Austrian press Dehn concluded by saying that Germany should insist on her need for a strong ally, and not one dominated by high finance — the Golden International — which tried hard to sow dissension between Austria and herself.

This attack on the Crown Prince, whose connections with Szeps and Hirsch were probably the reason for the obtuse reference to the Golden International, would have been without consequences had not two German daily papers, both of some standing, promptly printed the article. Thus wider circles became involved. Two Austrian papers, the *Fremdenblatt* and the *Pester Lloyd*, published articles in defence of Rudolph, but as they were both known to be mouthpieces of the Austrian Foreign Ministry their defence had little effect. Their half-hearted arguments were that Austria was at liberty to determine her own foreign policy and that the Crown Prince could not be held responsible for it. Bismarck now entered the lists. He had for some time been interested in all possible information about Rudolph, and a new rumour seems to have disturbed him. On November 22nd he asked Reuss whether it was true that the Crown Prince's domestic staff consisted entirely of Czechs and whether he was generally in favour of employing Czechs instead of Germans. The Embassy's first secretary, Count Monts, denied this and added, 'One does an injustice if one makes the Archduke responsible for things which he cannot change, even with the best intentions in the world'.[14] Bismarck was still not satisfied. In the *Norddeutsche Allgemeine Zeitung* — which voiced German Foreign Ministry opinions — and the *Neue Preussische Kreuzzeitung* — the official paper of the main government party, the Prussian Conservatives — articles were published accusing Rudolph of anti-German sentiments. This was not true, although he was suspicious of Germany. Rudolph's first concern was for Austria, and he would have been the most faithful adherent of the German alliance had he been convinced of Bismarck's sincerity. But his opinions on Germany did not matter ; what was important was the fact that he was a Liberal, and Bismarck was determined with all his might to smash Liberalism. Using all means, fair or foul, he had fought the Liberal Emperor Frederick III and his Consort, and Rudolph too was to be destroyed before he could become dangerous. The *Norddeutsche Allgemeine Zeitung* could not have printed any article of political consequence without Bismarck's knowledge, and the attack must have been his responsibility.

Waldersee in his journal blamed Herbert Bismarck (a coarser and clumsier replica of his father) who 'carried the main responsibility if Austria resumes her old distrust of us'. Deines, the German Military Attaché in Vienna, reported that 'the fact was particularly resented in Vienna that the attacks on the Crown Prince, which were as tactless as they were unfounded, were repeated in our most important conservative papers'.[15] Szeps tried to discover who had written the article in the *Kreuzzeitung* and found that it had been inspired, if not actually contributed, by Austrian reactionary circles. The fact that Bismarck's attitude was basically anti-Catholic and that reaction in Austria was based on political Catholicism did not disturb German reactionaries. This became obvious a few years later when political Catholicism had gained control of the Vienna City Council, and Austrian banks, distrustful of its intentions and frightened of its demagogy, withheld their credits. Berlin banks immediately opened their coffers — a sure indication that Berlin Protestants and Austrian Catholics got on very well together when fighting Liberalism was concerned.

The Crown Prince was not very excited by these attacks. He told Szeps at the beginning of November : 'I believe that he [Frischauer] was almost scandalised by my philosophical calm. I am no longer capable of getting annoyed about anything, least of all about things which concern myself.' Even when the attacks grew worse he asked Szeps only, 'What kind of rubbishy pamphlets did they write?' Had he decided to hit back, the *Tagblatt* was at his disposal, yet he did not feel that the matter deserved so much attention. Only a half-hearted article, probably written by Szeps, was published.

Rudolph's phlegmatic attitude was not the expression of genuine equanimity. Stephanie noticed at the time that he was much more restless than before, and this co-incided with other observations. Normally he would not have avoided a pitched battle. Looking at the Crown Prince's photograph at the time, we can also believe Stephanie when she stated that 'he was frightfully changed; his skin was flaccid, his eyes were restless, his expression had completely changed'.[16]

The Crown Princess took an entirely unorthodox step; she went to see her father-in-law to acquaint him of the change in her husband's behaviour and to ask for his help. He should send Rudolph on a voyage round the world. It was no good. The Emperor just told her that there was 'nothing the matter with Rudolph. . . . He is rather pale, gets about too much, expects too much of himself. He ought to stay at home with you more than he does.'[17] Francis Joseph had never understood his son, he understood him now less than ever, and Rudolph was past caring.

REFERENCES

1. Lonyay, *op. cit.* pp. 223 ff.
2. Quoted in Viktor Bibl, *Kronprinz Rudolf: die Tragödie eines sinkenden Reiches* (Leipzig and Budapest, 1938), p. 281.

3. Lonyay, *op. cit.* p. 229.

4. Lonyay, *op. cit.* p. 230.

5. Corti, *Elisabeth*, p. 401.

6. *Denkwürdigkeiten des General-Feldmarschalls Alfred, Grafen von Waldersee,* herausgegeben von H. O. Meisner (Stuttgart, 1923), Vol. I, p. 407.

7. Lonyay, *op. cit.* p. 237.

8. Glaise-Horstenau, *op. cit.* p. 324.

9. The first quotation in Lonyay, *op. cit.* p. 238, and Stockhausen, *op. cit.* p. 117. The second quotation in Stockhausen only.

10. Staatsarchiv Vienna, Exhibit Nachlass Erzherzog Franz Ferdinand, by kind permission of His Highness the Duke of Hohenberg.

11. Mitis, *op. cit.* p. 144.

12. Waldersee, *Briefwechsel, op. cit.* Vol. I, p. 209.

13. Mitis, *op. cit.* p. 382.

14. Wertheimer, *op. cit.*

15. Waldersee, *Briefwechsel*, p. 209.

16. Lonyay, *op. cit.* p. 240.

17. Lonyay, *op. cit.* p. 241.

CHAPTER ELEVEN

The Road to Mayerling

I

WHEN the Prince of Wales was in Vienna in early October he and Rudolph lunched together one Sunday in the Grand Hotel. In the afternoon a race meeting was to take place in the Freudenau, the race-course in the Prater, just outside Vienna, near the Danube. Rudolph wanted his friend to come, but the Prince of Wales declined the invitation; to attend a race meeting on a Sunday would have outraged public opinion in Britain. When, however, they went on talking about the events to take place in the afternoon his power of resistance weakened; he was too much of a racing enthusiast not to be interested. Finally it was arranged that he would go, but that Rudolph would use his influence with the Press to prevent any mention of the Prince of Wales's presence.[1]

It was a beautiful day and the two friends enjoyed the races. At the course, Frischauer stated, the Prince of Wales met a young lady whom he had previously met at Cairo, the Baroness Vetsera, and he introduced her to the Crown Prince. Frischauer was mistaken. The Prince of Wales had met her before, but he had not been in Egypt at the time when Mary Vetsera was there. In a letter to his mother he wrote: 'I met the poor young lady frequently at Homburg and Vienna. . . . I pointed her out to him [Rudolph] in a box at the opening of the new

"Burg Theater" [October 14th, 1888] and said how handsome she was — he spoke I thought disparagingly of her. . . .'[2]

Countess Larisch, Rudolph's cousin, states in her memoirs that Mary Vetsera, without being introduced, had written an admiring letter to Rudolph, who in his reply had suggested a meeting.[3] A third version, told more often and confirmed both by Count Hoyos[4] and by Mary's mother, that Countess Larisch introduced Mary Vetsera to the Crown Prince, seems more likely.[5] It is of little consequence how the introduction came about; Mary Vetsera had adored the Crown Prince for some time. She was very young, and he was handsome with a romantic, often melancholy air, and m any stories about his amours were told. When during the race meetings in the spring of 1888 Mary had seen Ru dolph, she had told her maid : 'I have seen the Crown Pri nce today. He was so handsome.'

The family Vetsera had n ot been long established in Vienna. Mary's mother, Helene, was Greek by birth, and had married one of the officials at the Austrian Embassy in Constantinople. Helene's father, Themistocles Baltazzi, a very rich banker, had provided large dowries for his three pretty daughters and all of them had married members of the Austrian nobility. There were also brothers, two of whom, Aristide and Hector, had lived for a time in Britain and were well-known sportsmen and racing enthusiasts who had once owned a Derby winner. The Prince of Wales mentioned in his letter that he had known Mary's mother as well as her aunts and uncles. In Austria, where the cleavage between higher and lower nobility was more marked than in most other countries, the family had not been introduced at the Court, and the members of the older aristocracy looked down on them, although there were many of the younger set who did not decline invitations to the splendid dinner parties at the Vetsera home, more like a palace, in the most exclusive quarter of Vienna.

Mary Vetsera, then seventeen years old, had been brought up in an atmosphere of luxury. In the autumn of 1887 she had accompanied her parents and her brothers and sister to Egypt, because of her father's precarious health. After her return to Vienna, if indeed not earlier, Rudolph became her ideal and she fancied herself in love with him, in spite of the fact that she had an understanding with Duke Miguel of Braganza, a member of the Royal house of Portugal. This, however, did not amount to a formal engagement. He lived in Vienna and was frequently out shooting with the Crown Prince, and from him she was able to learn small details about her idol without rousing suspicion. She was an attractive girl who looked more than her age. The Prince of Wales said of her : 'She seemed a charming young lady and certainly one of the prettiest and most admired in Vienna. I have known her Mother as well as her Aunts & Uncles for the last 16 years when I was at Vienna.'[6] She was not only prettier than Stephanie, but different in every respect, much more petite, much more feminine, than the angular Crown Princess.

She had fallen in love with Rudolph ; in the spring of 1888, when her mother discovered this infatuation, she had taken Mary to England for the summer ; yet the girl's desire to meet Rudolph had not diminished while she had been away. Soon after her return to Vienna she wrote to her former governess: 'Do not believe that I have forgotten him. I only love him much more dearly.' Now her main problem was how to get into touch with him. According to the custom of the time she was constantly chaperoned and could never go out unless accompanied at least by her maid. As the family was not introduced at Court she had little hope of meeting the Crown Prince in society, but she managed, in spite of difficulties, to meet him secretly.

The autumn of 1888 was very beautiful. Summer seemed to linger, the sun was still warm as though it could never be veiled by mists, and in the vineyards on the hills outside Vienna the grapes hung heavy and sweet. It was in this atmosphere of summer's long drawn out farewell that the two lovers met. Life had been cruel to Rudolph, and he now felt more powerless than ever before. How long would his father keep the Monarchy together? While he had to look on and see his heritage threatened by a fatally mistaken policy, William in Berlin, dull and reactionary, was the master of Germany. He had lost the urge to write; life seemed not worth the trouble. He needed somebody to believe in him, in his mission, somebody to tell him that his strength was not failing, that there was yet time to right the wrongs in disintegrating Austria. He needed someone who was yielding and feminine and not argumentative and domineering. He was not in love with Mary at first, but ready to fall in love with someone who could soothe his jaded nerves. He was carried away by her intense femininity, by her credulous youth, by her veneration.

She was not a cold-headed and cold-hearted schemer: she was warm-hearted, a little empty-headed perhaps, but she gave him the warmth of a little animal. Like a prisoner, who can lose his heart to a mouse sharing his cell, so Rudolph lost his heart to Mary, who understood nothing

Mary Vetsera

of politics and did not care for them, but who knew with the safe instinct of her womanhood that his aching nerves needed peace.

II

Countess Marie Larisch was Rudolph's first cousin. Her father, Duke Ludwig *in* Bavaria, and not *of* Bavaria as she misstates in her memoirs, was the Empress Elisabeth's brother. When young he had fallen in love with a beautiful actress of Jewish origin, Henrietta Mendel, and after renouncing all ducal rights had married her morganatically. His wife had been given the rank of a Countess Wallersee, and Marie was their only child.

The Empress Elisabeth met her niece for the first time when Marie was a little girl and was quite captivated by her natural manner. Some years later she invited her to stay with her, doubtless motivated by the desire to show that she had no prejudice on account of her sister-in-law's origin. The Imperial family was in Hungary when Marie arrived. Rudolph was sixteen at the time and his cousin two years older. He did not care for her very much, nor did she feel any fondness for him. Later in her memoirs she retailed some stories to discredit the Crown Prince, and in order to make them more credible makes him two years older. Whether she entertained any designs on him is an open question, but during this visit she was married off hurriedly to Count Larisch, who was as little in love with her as she with him.

It was not only against Rudolph that she directed her wrath in her memoirs, but also against the Empress. There are so many palpable untruths recorded that we are fully entitled to question her explanations as to how

Rudolph and Mary Vetsera met. We can more readily accept the young girl's own evidence contained in her letters to her former governess, Hermine. In the first, in which she speaks of her love for Rudolph, she wrote : 'I cannot live without having seen him or spoken to him. Dear Hermine, don't worry about me, I know that everything you say is true, but I cannot change the facts. I have two friends, you and Marie Larisch. *You* work for my soul's happiness and *Marie* works for my moral misfortune.' [7]

According to Mary's letters, Marie Larisch arranged the first meeting between her and Rudolph in the Prater just outside Vienna, and a little later, on November 5th, 1888, took the girl to the Crown Prince's bachelor rooms in the Imperial Palace, telling the girl's mother that she was taking her on shopping expeditions. Mary confided fully in her former governess — the experience so over-whelmed her that she had to open her heart to someone on whom she knew she could rely. 'Today you will get a happy letter because I have been with him. Marie Larisch took me shopping with her and then to be photo-graphed — for him of course. Then we went . . . to the Burg. An old servant was waiting for us ; he led us up several stairs and through several rooms until we reached one in which he left us. At our entrance a black bird — some kind of raven — flew at my head. A voice called from the next room "Please come in". Marie introduced me, then he said to me "Excuse me, but I would like to talk to the Countess privately for a few minutes". Then he went with Marie to another room. I looked around me. On his desk was a revolver and a skull. I picked up the skull, took it between my hands and looked at it from all sides. Suddenly Rudolph came in and took it from me with deep apprehension. When I said that I wasn't afraid, he smiled. You must swear never to tell anyone about this letter, neither Hanna [her sister] nor Mama, because if either of them heard about it I would have to kill myself.'

Meetings soon became difficult, as Marie Larisch left Vienna for her home in Bohemia. Mary Vetsera wrote to Hermine : 'Marie Larisch has departed and I cannot see him. I wither with longing and cannot await the day of her return. . . . I count the hours, because since I have met him and talked to him my love has so much deepened. I ponder night and day how I could contrive to see him.'

They found means of exchanging letters by way of Rudolph's valet and Mary's personal maid, whom she had taken into her confidence. Things became a little easier when the Vienna Opera began a Wagner cycle on December 11th. Mary's mother and sister attended the opera frequently but Mary invented a thousand excuses for staying home — at one time needing to dry her hair, at another pretending to have a headache. As soon as mother and sister were safely away Mary would go to meet Rudolph, and using the length of the Wagner operas to her own advantage found time even to visit him a few times. How much she loved him ! 'He is my god, my everything !' He now seemed as much in love with her as she with him. In a letter to her he assured her that he could not live without her and that he would go mad if he could no longer see her.

III

The Kaiser's play-acting had become second nature to him, and he believed himself to be the superman. He was deeply hurt that Rudolph refused to take him seriously and was determined to show him how powerful he was. Frischauer stated that someone in the Austrian Ministry of War had made a serious mistake.[8] The Army Council had ordered a new rifle for the infantry which proved unsuitable. It was a quick-firing weapon and several hundred thousand had been ordered. Only when deliveries of large numbers began to arrive was it discovered that the calibre was far too big (8 millimetres) and consequently the amount of ammunition required by a quick-firing weapon would be too heavy to be carried by an infantryman. As Rudolph was Inspector-General of Infantry and a member of the Army Council, the Kaiser, Frischauer asserts, held him responsible for the mistake. The order for the rifle must have been given before Rudolph had been made Inspector-General in March 1888, and as he was not a member of the Army Council before that date he could not be answerable for the mistake.

According to a Russian source, the journal of Foreign Minister Lamsdorff, the Kaiser complained officially about Rudolph's unsuitability for his appointment. Lamsdorff referred to a private letter from the Russian Ambassador in Brussels which contained a description of events during the Kaiser's visit to Vienna : 'The German Emperor made his inspection not as a guest Monarch but as an inspector assigned the task of carrying out a most careful review. The results of the inspection proved unfavourable and His Majesty did not conceal his displeasure : *he particularly criticised the infantry* [italics in the original] the chief inspector of which at the time was the Archduke Rudolph. Wilhelm II did not spare the heir to the throne and expressed his opinion to the Emperor and Empress with extreme openness. The latter was offended and declared that she did not wish to remain in the presence of the German Emperor, who was obliged to apologise. On his return to Berlin His Majesty wrote a letter to the Emperor Francis Joseph in which he explained that he had the right and was obliged to draw the attention of his ally to the state of affairs in his army, because they must defend their common interests, shoulder to shoulder, and asked that a more experienced person than the Archduke Rudolph should be appointed to the post of chief inspector of infantry. A result of this letter was a violent scene between Francis Joseph and his son, who refused to retire voluntarily.' [9]

There are thus two statements concerning complaints about Rudolph's capacity as Inspector-General of Infantry. The first, mentioned by Frischauer, need not be taken too seriously, because a number of German military writers at the time openly dealt with the lack in the Austrian army of a rifle equal to the German quick-firing Mauser rifle. Not one mentions Rudolph.

The second report of a complaint is more convincing. Contrary to the usual custom on such occasions, the Kaiser took all military inspections extremely seriously. Still more important, the phrase 'shoulder to shoulder' (*Schulter an Schulter*) is unmistakably German and quite in keeping with the Kaiser's usual style. Had the report been invented by a Russian he would have used 'side by side' (*bok bo boku*). The reference to a violent scene between the Emperor and Rudolph seems to be based on conjecture ; Francis Joseph disliked such scenes. Waldersee's cryptic references to differences between Rudolph and the Kaiser during the Vienna visit may have had their source in a remark the Kaiser had made about the turn-out of the Austrian troops. There remains in both statements a sufficiently strong residue of truth to permit the conclusion that Rudolph, at a most critical time, was being made to bear unnecessary humiliations.

He was himself fully aware that the Austrian army was not as well trained as it should have been, and had suggested the introduction of a new official manual on infantry training, as his inspections had shown him that this was necessary. Although the Supreme Commander, Archduke Albrecht, stated in a letter 'it is important to strengthen the zeal which the Crown Prince shows' [10] he nevertheless a few weeks later reserved for himself the right to see to the necessary revision of the training manual.

Frustrated from all sides, Rudolph's life became more and more unbearable. He talked to Mary about his troubles and found in her the sympathy he needed. Their love had become deeper. Here was not the possessiveness of frigid Stephanie, but the understanding he longed for. Although so young, her intuition gave her the maturity of an older woman, who knew instinctively what Rudolph needed. He gave her an iron wedding ring, which she wore on a thin chain round her neck. In it he had had engraved : 'ILVBIDT' which at their next meeting he explained as meaning '*In Liebe vereint bis in den Tod*' (United in love till death). Mary wrote to her governess : 'If we could only live together in a hut, we would be so happy! We constantly talk of this, and love doing so ; but alas, it cannot be! If I could give my life to see him happy, I would gladly do it, because I do not value my own life.' In another letter she seemed afraid that the affair might become known. For this contingency, Mary told Hermine, they had a suicide pact. They would kill themselves after a few happy hours. 'But', she continued, 'he must not die, he must live for his nation. All that surrounds him must be splendour and glory.'

At the time the Empress Elisabeth was captivated by the works of the German-Jewish poet Heine. Rudolph succeeded in acquiring some of the poet's letters. For the latter part of his life Heine had lived in Paris and Szeps's French connections had been of great help in securing the letters. At Christmas 1888 Rudolph presented them to his mother as a Christmas and a birthday gift — both days coinciding — while the Emperor, to whom poetry was a closed book, looked on, smiling ironically.[11] Rudolph had as little feeling for poetry as his father, but he had imagination, and pleasing his mother gave him much joy.

This time Elisabeth did not notice that Rudolph looked ill and tired, although being together in the family gathering at Christmas she had ample opportunity. He was very much on edge. A few days later he wrote what proved to be his last letter to Szeps. 'In foreign policy there is a lull at present ; the dangers have been put off for the moment, but this most unnatural quietness gives me the feeling of the stillness before the storm. It cannot continue so, this is my consolation.' The editor must have felt what Elisabeth had failed to realise, that the Crown Prince was again at a critical stage, but this time Szeps felt that it was more serious than usual and his reply, which was at the same time his letter of good wishes for the New Year, was long and contained such direct encouragement as he had never before thought necessary : '"this stillness is uncanny", so your Imperial Highness writes in your last letter, "like the stillness before a storm". The past year will be counted in history as an undertaker's year [referring to the death of the two German Emperors William I and Frederick III] ; it was no more. But this may in certain circumstances be enough, because if all that is withered, rotten and old is removed to make room for what is fresh and young it is an act of rebirth and rejuvenation which is necessary for the world. The undertakers of 1888 have, however, not rejuvenated and removed much — and the stillness which broods over Europe is truly uncanny.

'What will become of all this? When will the thunderbolts of Fate give those decisions which will be the beginning of a new era? The oppressiveness cannot last for ever, the year of change will certainly come. Not to slacken in the time of oppressiveness, to keep body and spirit strong for the period of action, that is the task which your Imperial Highness has set yourself, and this task is being fulfilled daily with tireless tenacity and activity. You do not slacken as do so many who, being tired, have submitted to the apparently inevitable. And because the Crown Prince does not slacken we maintain our hope for a great, glorious, free and prosperous Austria. You, Imperial Highness, have had to experience much malice and perfidy, but you have shaken it off with remarkable equanimity. It is well known that you desire great things, that you are capable of accomplishing them, and he who does not know feels it. This is why you are now being attacked by various means and your way into the future barred and you have already today many adversaries and enemies. But you rely on yourself, on your disposition, on your genius, on your strength and your endurance, and you may justly depend on it. To all this just a little luck — not even as much luck as your sincere admirers and friends wish you — just a little of this luck and you will accomplish great things for this Monarchy, for our Fatherland, for your own glory and for the people who are attached to you.'

On January 2nd the Crown Prince wrote much in his usual way to Frischauer: 'May the year 1889 not be too

bad for all of us. May it bring us stirring, interesting months.
I hope we shall meet this year again a few times on political
expeditions.' These expectations of stirring political conditions looked like being fulfilled. Schönerer had been
released from prison, and although he personally was out
of politics there were many who carried on in his place
spreading the poison throughout the body politic of
Austria. Lueger, at a meeting in the previous November,
had attacked the Papal Nuncio Galimberti and the Archbishop of Vienna, Ganglbauer, because these two Church
dignitaries were opposed to the lower clergy becoming
leaders in the anti-Semitic movement, and had declared,
'Schönerer is a great man who has gained imperishable
merits'.[12] Early in January Szeps gave an account of the
quickly deteriorating political situation in a letter to
Rudolph and summarised his opinion: 'The struggle
intensifies. . . . In order to uproot the Liberal Party they
[the government] have looked on maliciously while the
evil grew like a cancer, not considering that a cancer does
not stop. . . .'

Neither Szeps's letter, nor the knowledge that it was
based on undeniable fact, could rouse Rudolph from his
apathy, which like an incubus took possession of him in
ever-shortening intervals. Stephanie had gone south to a
warmer climate. He wished her happiness in the New
Year in a letter as conventional and cynical as were all
the letters he had written to her for a year or longer, but
there is a genuinely affectionate reference to their little
daughter Elisabeth: 'The little one has a cold, but
thanks be, no sore throat. She is very cheerful and romps
about.'[13]

His relations with Mary Vetsera continued. On
January 13th she went to see him in the Hofburg and

afterwards told her maid : 'If only I had not gone to see him today it would have been much better'. Now she could do only what he wanted of her ; she belonged no longer to herself but to him alone. Next day she wrote to her former governess : 'I was with him last night from seven till nine. We have both lost our heads. Now we belong to one another life and soul.'

In spite of his relationship with Mary, Rudolph maintained his old connections with Mizzi Kaspar. In December he had made her the strange proposal of a suicide pact. He had several times since the summer spoken to her of shooting himself, but never before had he been so definite. He now suggested that they should go to the Vienna Woods and there shoot themselves. Mizzi merely laughed — she did not take the proposal seriously.[14] During the winter of 1888–89 he had frequently asked his friends and shooting companions, 'Are you afraid of death ?' Count Hoyos enumerated five men to whom he had put this question. Major Fritsche, one of Rudolph's adjutants, later reported that at this time whenever the Crown Prince had news of anyone's death he would say, 'He is fortunate'.[15]

IV

In Austria, as is usual in Catholic countries, Carnival, the time between Epiphany and Ash Wednesday, is a period of festivity and jollification. Stephanie had returned to Vienna, but neither she nor Rudolph could attend any of the many balls of the Vienna society for some time, as the Empress Elisabeth's father had died a few weeks previously; but there were a number of receptions which they had to attend.

As the Kaiser had paid a visit to Vienna in October, a return visit to Berlin was expected. The Emperor discussed this with Rudolph and suggested that he accompany him to the German capital. Rudolph saw no reason for this visit ; his deep distrust of Germany appears now to have made him revise his ideas on Austria's alliances and it is reported that he suddenly advanced the view that a visit to the Tsar would serve Austria's interests better. 'Initially this project met with strong opposition, then it was decided in principle that after Berlin the Crown Prince could go to Russia. This prospect delighted him infinitely. From it he derived consolation in the numerous griefs which his position had occasioned him.'[16] The Russian Foreign Minister's account is based on the report of a talk between Szögyenyi and the Russian chargé d'affaires Prince Kantakuzene. No other evidence has yet come to light, consequently we cannot give the reasons for this revolutionary change of mind. We can only surmise that Berlin's policy of playing off Austria against Russia had made the Crown Prince reconsider Austria's position. He may now have favoured her participation in a new alliance with a distinct anti-German flavour. France and Russia were on the point of coming to terms — Bismarck's nightmare. Did he now consider an agreement with Russia to divide the spheres of influence in the Near East and to turn some of Austria's expansionist desires towards the West, with the possibility of reversing the outcome of 1866 so that the Hapsburgs could stage a come-back into German affairs ? There is no certainty, but it is a fair assumption.

Rudolph had not been as outraged as one would have expected by the recent attacks in the German press, but they may well have been responsible for a reconsideration of his attitude towards Germany. He felt her to be weaker since the Kaiser's accession, and by no means as strong as many Austrian circles believed and the Germans considered themselves to be. He might even have thought — he had expressed as much in his letter to Szeps — that William's impulsiveness and ill-conceived policy would reduce still further her value as an ally. On the other hand, an Austrian state visit to Russia would show Germany that Austria could beat her at her own game of double dealing. A pro-Russian, anti-German Austrian policy would be a blow to Bismarck — and Rudolph knew well that the insults in the Berlin paper had been tolerated, if not inspired, by him.

Little is known about the Crown Prince's activities during the first four weeks of January 1889. They are largely obliterated by the wholesale removal of documents which took place after his death, while the reports by witnesses, although not lacking in numbers, are so unreliable that they can hardly be used. There were, however, a few incidents which are beyond doubt.

It is asserted repeatedly that at this time Rudolph sought to divorce Stephanie. He is believed to have made application directly to the Pope to have his marriage declared invalid. The Pope, so the reports say, unable to grant the request, informed Francis Joseph. The Emperor demanded an explanation from his son and the ensuing discussion led to an angry scene. There were no witnesses, but it is reported that the end of the argument was overheard. The Russian Ambassador Prince Labanov told the Foreign Minister Count Lamsdorff that Rudolph had stated, 'After this I know what I have left to do', to which his father had replied, 'Do what you like, but I shall never agree to your divorce'.[17] The evidence on this point is by no means conclusive ; there is no application to be found in the secret Papal Archives.[18]

On January 20th Rudolph, with a few of his usual companions, went shooting in some woods on the Danube near Vienna. In the company were Stephanie's brother-in-law Prince Philipp of Coburg and Count Hoyos. The Crown Prince invited both to take part in another shoot during the following week at Mayerling, south of Vienna, where he had his hunting lodge. He could not give an exact date as he was too busy to fix the day in advance.

At the time the Hungarian Parliament had begun to discuss a new defence law which was being opposed by many of Rudolph's friends. On January 25th his closest friend in Hungary, Count Pista Károlyi, spoke vehemently against it and his speech was eagerly commented on by the press. Some papers reported that Károlyi had received a letter from the Crown Prince before he rose to speak, and the conclusion drawn was that Rudolph too opposed the bill because of his enmity towards Germany. The bill had been introduced 'to develop the defence potential of Austria-Hungary in the same way as had been done in Germany and to lift it to the level which would ensure the Monarchy being an equal ally'. Thus Károlyi was fighting Rudolph's battle — such was the assumption.

The British Ambassador in Vienna, Sir Augustus Paget, planned to give a ball at the end of January. Rudolph and Stephanie were not expected but Sir Augustus and Lady Paget dined with them a few days before, on Thursday, January 24th. Lady Paget found the Crown Prince greatly changed. 'He seemed, somehow, different, less sarcastic, less down upon people, and for the first time he looked me in the eyes while speaking. He said how sorry he was he could not come to us on account of his mourning, and then he alluded with great warmth to our mutual friend M. de Szoegenyi. . . . The only person he mentioned with bitterness was the Emperor of Germany, once his devoted friend (*sic*), and he said : "How horrible is this constant fight with the ghost of his father"'.[19]

In this narrative the reference to the Kaiser's devoted friendship is certainly strange. One would have expected the wife of the British Ambassador at the time, when Queen Victoria's eldest daughter was German Empress, to be better informed about the Kaiser's friendships.

V

On the Sunday, January 27th, a reception was held at the German Embassy on the occasion of the Kaiser's thirtieth birthday, to which both Francis Joseph and Rudolph went. At this party the Crown Prince talked to Lady Paget 'in the same strain as he had done on Thursday'.[20]

Others too noted the depressed mood of the Crown Prince.[21] He had a long talk with the sculptor Tilgner, whom he knew well. Not far away stood Mary Vetsera, who was on that evening even more attractive than usual. Rudolph was in German uniform and told Tilgner, pointing to the heavy epaulettes, 'Unbearably heavy, anyway this whole uniform is distasteful to me'.[22] General Beck noticed during the reception that Mary's glance was fixed on Rudolph during the whole evening and that he looked at her several times.[23]

Lady Paget noted that the Crown Prince greeted his father reverently when Francis Joseph came in ; he 'bent low over his father's hand, touching it almost with his lips'.[24] Szeps's daughter, Frau Zuckerkandl, said that a scene took place between father and son. 'The whole Court and aristocracy were standing in a circle awaiting the arrival of the Emperor. When he entered the ball-room he walked round the circle, stopping with each person for a moment and speaking a few words of greeting. But when he came to the Crown Prince, who bowed deeply, the Emperor abruptly turned his back on him. A shudder of horror ran through the guests. The Crown Prince halted for a moment as if he had been struck, then left the room.[25] Lady Paget was not the only person who saw nothing of this scene, Beck did not see it either. Each would have mentioned it unhesitatingly had even an affront amounting to part of the scandal described by Frau Zuckerkandl taken place. Francis Joseph was far too conscious of the dignity of his position to cause any public scene.

Neither of these witnesses noticed any fracas between Stephanie and Mary Vetsera; Lady Paget did not even notice the latter's presence, although she knew her. Coun-tess Larisch, however, who was not present, speaks in her memoirs of a scene between the Crown Princess and her rival : 'The eyes of the two women met, and I am told they looked for all the world like tigers ready to spring. . . . Just as everybody wondered what would happen next, Mary stamped her foot once — twice — and then flung her head back with a movement of supreme contempt. The Baroness Vetsera, who had watched the scene in terror, now came up, crimson with anger and shame. . . . She seized Mary by the arm and made a hurried exit from the ball-room.'[26] Stephanie never omits any record of an offence against her dignity, but she makes no mention of this scene. It probably belongs to the realm of fairy tales, like so much of Countess Larisch's memoirs.

Beck noticed that Mary Vetsera left early and that the Crown Prince too did not remain long afterwards. He had arranged that the shoot planned at Mayerling was to take place on 29th and 30th. He had seen Count Hoyos at the reception at the German Embassy and had told him to contact Prince Coburg so that both would come to the hunting lodge on Tuesday the 29th. He himself would go there on the Monday.

There are two reports that the Crown Prince spent the rest of the night with Mizzi Kaspar, but in other respects they disagree. While the Comptroller of the Imperial household, Burghauptmann Kirschner, later declared that Loschek, Rudolph's factotum, had brought the lady to the Palace,[27] the police file contains a report from Meissner that the Crown Prince went to her flat.[28] According to this source he remained there until 3 A.M., drank a lot of champagne, and on leaving made, quite unusual for him, the sign of the Cross on Mizzi's forehead.

Both are reliable sources, but as the Crown Prince could not have been in both places at once, one report at least must be invention. This contradiction and those in the reports of the German reception are fair samples of many similar accounts, although the invention is not always so easily discerned. It may well be that many of the reports on which biographies of the Crown Prince are based are as unreliable as these two, or Countess Larisch's narrative.

Szeps's daughter asserts that Rudolph asked her father to call on him after the reception. As many interviews with the editor took place at dead of night that talk with Szeps seems plausible enough. Less likely seems the report which he gave his daughter of the words used by Rudolph. According to this Rudolph was 'in a dreadful state of nervous excitation. Again and again he repeated "The Emperor has openly affronted and degraded me. From now on all ties between us are broken. From now on I am free." [29] If this report is true the words must have referred to another incident and not to that supposed to have taken place at the German Embassy. It is not known what Rudolph discussed with Szeps that night. Frau Zuckerkandl interpreted her father's account as referring to the incident at the German Embassy which she had described. Such an incident cannot have taken place. She must have connected Rudolph's statement with the wrong motive, or the matter discussed was of such a confidential nature that the editor put her off with an invented story.

It had been asserted that the Crown Prince may have been involved in some conspiracy concerning Hungary and her desire for greater independence from Austria. Events in Budapest began to move faster when early in January the Defence Bill had been introduced in the Diet. It was being fought by the opposition with every means at its disposal, not because the separatists did not wish to increase the number of recruits, but because they did not want to strengthen the army which Hungary had in common with Austria. Rudolph had for a long time opposed all attempts at increasing Hungarian autonomy in army matters ; he considered that the fighting value of the army would be seriously diminished by separatist encroachments. But during the last months he had been beset from all sides by so many disappointments that he might have considered the autonomist movement in Hungary a means of redressing his grievances, by becoming its head and severing connections with Austria.

It is otherwise difficult to explain why Count Pista Károlyi, so close a friend of Rudolph, should have been so outspoken in denouncing the Defence Bill in his Diet speech on January 25th. If some movement towards greater or full independence was afoot in Budapest the steadily mounting tension engendered by the Defence Bill would have been the right moment to strike, and had Rudolph been involved in such a conspiracy, now would have been the time to go to the Hungarian capital and take command.

He did not go. Like many highly strung people, he may have planned more than he could carry out. Now when the time had come to show his courage, to disavow so much he had stood for, to break his oath of allegiance as an officer to his father, he failed. Now the point of no return had been passed and death by his own hand, the idea he had so often toyed with, seemed the only way out of a dilemma. This may have been the problem discussed with Szeps during their last talk.

The idea of taking his own life had occupied his mind for some time, as he had, during those days, destroyed many of his personal papers, correspondence and other documents. Again this is no conclusive proof of his intention to die ; it could equally well be an attempt to remove evidence from Vienna before setting out for Budapest.

Early on Monday morning, January 28th, the journalist Frischauer came to give an account of the outcome of the French elections which had taken place on Sunday, as Rudolph had asked him to do. It was evident that an overwhelming majority of the deputies elected supported Boulanger. France seemed bound to experience another period of dictatorship. While Rudolph had no quarrel with Boulanger's anti-German sentiments — they would provide a tough problem for his enemy William of Germany — the general's dictatorial intentions might well

prove a temporary or permanent eclipse of French democratic Liberalism. The Crown Prince had stated on a
previous occasion to Frischauer that 'if I am chased out of
here I shall enter the services of a republic, probably
France'.[30] Now this avenue of escape too was closed to
him.

This may have been the reason for his excitement on
the morning of Monday, January 28th, 1889, after Frischauer had left. A little later he received Alexander of
Battenberg, formerly Prince of Bulgaria, who had now
relinquished his title to marry an opera singer, a Fräulein
Loisinger. He had assumed the name of Count Hartenau
and wished to serve as an Austrian officer, and he wanted
Rudolph to support his application for a commission. The
Crown Prince invited him to Mayerling, but Hartenau
declined. He was leaving Vienna that evening.[31]

After Alexander's visit, Rudolph wrote a few letters,
without dispatching them and some time between 10 and
11 rang for the footman on duty. Still showing signs of
excitement, he told the man : 'I am going to Mayerling
to-day. My carriage has been ordered for 12 o'clock. I
am only waiting for a letter and a telegram.' This seemed
strange, as an audience had been arranged for the Archbishop of Prague at 1 o'clock. The footman continued
his narrative : 'At eleven o'clock the expected letter
arrived. I took it . . . to the bedroom, and found the
Crown Prince there, standing at the window, looking
down . . . and quite lost in thought. He held his watch in
his hands, turning the regulator. He did not seem to have
noticed me. About half an hour later the expected telegram arrived. As I took it in, the Crown Prince was still
with his watch in his hands and again looking down. He
opened the telegram hastily, read it quickly, folded it again

and as I withdrew threw it on to the table, excitedly with a raised hand, saying as he did this, "Yes, it has to be".'[32]

REFERENCES

1. Berthold Frischauer, 'Kronprinzenlegenden, Aus meinen Erinnerungen an den verstorbenen Kronprinzen Rudolf', *Neue Freie Presse* (Vienna, August 21st, 1921).

2. Royal Archives, Windsor, Z 498 49.

3. Countess Marie Larisch, *née* Baroness Wallersee, niece of the late Empress Elisabeth of Austria and daughter of the Duke Ludwig of Bavaria, *My Past* (London, 1913), pp. 171 f.

4. Hoyos Memorandum (with Crown Prince Rudolph's papers), Staatsarchiv, Vienna.

5. Helene Vetsera, *Denkschrift* (Wien, n.d., reprinted Reichenberg, 1921), and partly in *Das Mayerling Original*, pp. 176-218. Later referred to as Vetsera Memorandum. A copy of the Reichenberg edition is in the Staatsarchiv, Vienna, with Crown Prince Rudolph's papers.

6. Royal Archives, Windsor. *Ibid.*

7. Italics in the original. This and the other quotations from Mary Vetsera's letters, Vetsera Memorandum.

8. Frischauer, *op. cit.*

9. Dnevnik V. N. Lamzdorfa, *Gosudarstvennoe Izdatelstvo* (Moscow and Leningrad, 1926), pp. 198 f.

9. Glaise-Horstenau, *op. cit.* p. 333.

11. Corti, *Elisabeth*, p. 410.

12. Dr. R. Kuppe, *Lueger und seine Zeit* (Wien, 1933), p. 196.

13. Lonyay, *op. cit.* p. 242.

14. *Das Mayerling Original*, p. 113.

15. *Briefe Kaiser Franz Josephs an Frau Katherina Schratt*, herausgegeben von Jean de Bourgoing (Wien, 1949), p. 138.

16. Lamzdorfa, *op. cit.* pp. 178 f.

17. Lamzdorfa, *op. cit.* pp. 178 f.

18. Letter from Monsignore Giusti, Assistant Director, Papal Archives, dated November 13th, 1956.

19. Walpurga Lady Paget, *Embassies of Other Days* (London, 1923), Vol. II, p. 465.

20. Paget, *op. cit.* p. 465.

21. Corti, *Franz Josef*, Vol. III, p. 116.

22. Frischauer, *op. cit.*

23. Glaise-Horstenau, *op. cit.* p. 334.

24. Paget, *op. cit.* p. 465.

The Road to Mayerling

25. Szeps-Zuckerkandl, *op. cit.* p. 120.
26. Larisch, *op. cit.* 208.
27. Hoyos Memorandum, Staatsarchiv, Vienna.
28. *Mayerling Original*, p. 110.
29. Szeps-Zuckerkandl, *op. cit.* p. 120.
30. Frischauer, *loc. cit.*
31. Corti, *Franz Josef*, Vol. III, p. 116.
32. Rudolph Püchel, 'Persönliche Erinnerungen an den 30. Januar 1889', in *Reichspost* of January 31st, 1926.

CHAPTER TWELVE

'Night's Candles are burnt out'

I

BEFORE Rudolph left his rooms at the Hofburg he told his messenger, Püchel : 'Expect me tomorrow afternoon. I shall be back by 5 o'clock, as I shall dine together with Her Imperial Highness with their Majesties.' [1]   He then went to say goodbye to Stephanie, and told her too that he would be back in Vienna on the following day for the big family dinner which the Emperor was to give, so that it was not necessary for her to come with him to Mayerling. Lastly he went to say farewell to little Elisabeth.

According to a police report his carriage, which he drove himself, was already several miles from the Palace by 11.50, and was heading south.   He continued his journey to the Zum grünen Baum, a well-known inn a dozen miles or so from Vienna.

While he was speeding on his way, Countess Larisch appeared at police headquarters and asked for an interview with the President of Police.   This was immediately granted, as she was the Empress's niece.   She told a strange story.   'Soon after 10 A.M. she had called for the 17-year-old Baroness Vetsera at her mother's address and taken her by *fiacre* to a shop in the Kohlmarkt [a thoroughfare in the central part of Vienna], to settle an account.   The Countess had entered the shop while the

Baroness remained in the car. After a while she sent an assistant to ask the Baroness to come into the shop, but Mary was no longer in the *fiacre*, and the coachman said that she had entered another *fiacre* and been driven away. The Countess had hurried out to see for herself what this report meant and had found a brief note in which the Baroness announced in a few words her intention of committing suicide.'[2] This cumbersome story, as recorded by the President of Police himself, continued that Countess Larisch did not take the idea of suicide seriously. She had, however, immediately contacted an uncle of Mary, who had expressed a suspicion that the Crown Prince might have something to do with it. In this way Countess Larisch, who knew well what was happening, tried to disclaim responsibility and to build up an alibi. The Police President remarked that both the Imperial Palace in Vienna and the hunting-lodge at Mayerling were outside his province.

He was well aware that Rudolph had intended to go to Mayerling. The nearest telegraph office had been 'activated', the staff had been reinforced to cope with the expected increased number of telegrams. In addition the police knew what domestic staff had been ordered to the lodge and were surprised that only a small number of mainly female servants would be there, hardly enough even for a brief stay.

It cannot be stated with any safety when the Crown Prince arrived at Mayerling ; nor what he did there during the first evening. Bratfisch, Rudolph's favourite coachman, stated many years later that he had waited with his carriage at the Rote Stadl near the inn Zum grünen Baum, and that Rudolph had arrived there in his carriage. Mary Vetsera had come a little later in a *fiacre* driven by Bratfisch's son-in-law, who had waited for her at the Kohlmarkt. From the Zum grünen Baum Bratfisch had driven both to Mayerling.[3]

Countess Larisch tells an unconvincing story in her memoirs, according to which Rudolph went to see her at 5 o'clock in the afternoon of the day on which he is supposed to have gone to Mayerling. She stated that it was two days after the reception at the German Embassy,[4] which could not have been the case. On the other hand, there *may* be a grain of truth in her story, as it was known to the police that the Crown Prince had been at her hotel on Sunday 27th, the day before going to Mayerling.[5] According to Marie Larisch, Rudolph told her that his life was in danger. He asked her urgently to keep a small steel box for him among her personal belongings and not to hand it over to anyone except to himself or to a person giving the right pass-word. The Emperor, he said, might at any moment give orders to have his personal belongings seized. When Larisch advised that he should confide in his father, Rudolph had replied that he would, by doing so, 'sign his own death warrant'.

This story is highly improbable ; the Crown Prince would have been wise enough not to confide in a spiteful woman, as Countess Larisch doubtless was. On the other hand, it is conceivable that she heard some time after her cousin's death that he had been involved in some fantastic political adventure, or he may really have come to see her and she construed one of his remarks into her fantastic tale.

At seven o'clock, on Monday the 28th, according to the police report, she came again to see the President of Police, this time accompanied by Alexander Baltazzi, Mary's uncle. Baltazzi stated that his sister had opened an iron box — this may be the real object which Marie Larisch used for her tale — which belonged to Mary and had found numerous photographs of the Crown Prince, but no letters in it. It also contained all her rings and some sort of Last Will and Testament. From these facts and the suicide note found by Marie Larisch, her mother concluded that she really intended committing suicide, although considering the girl's usual *joie de vivre* it was difficult to assume such a thing. The mother wanted to inform the Emperor, but she could not do so before being sure that Mary was with the Crown Prince.[6]

The police officer was not anxious to deal with this problem, so he reaffirmed that he had no jurisdiction as far as Rudolph was concerned and that Mary's reputation would certainly suffer if he had to set in motion the usual procedure when somebody was missing from home. He succeeded in avoiding the scandal which would doubtless have ensued, had Baltazzi insisted in making an official report. So there was at least a respite until Tuesday morning.

II

On Tuesday morning at 8.10 Hoyos and Prince Coburg arrived at Mayerling for the shooting. As they approached the lodge they saw that all the blinds were drawn and the gates closed, as though nobody were in residence. They went into the billiard room, where meals were usually served, and after a few minutes the Crown Prince appeared, still in his dressing-gown. Breakfast was served and Rudolph had a good appetite. He told a story about the difficulties which he had encountered on the icy roads on his way from Vienna, that the horses had slipped and that he had helped to push the carriage. He had not taken off his fur coat, and as he had perspired from the effort he had caught a cold. The story seemed a little odd to Hoyos, as to anyone knowing the district; there were several contradictions, but he naturally accepted it without asking questions.

During the meal Rudolph told them that on the previous night he had thought that he was going to be seriously ill — it turned out to be only a cold, but such a heavy one that he thought it better not to go shooting, particularly as the hillsides where the shooting was to take place were very steep. Hoyos and Coburg went without him and he remained at the lodge.

.   .   .   .   .

Sixteen miles away, in Vienna, Mary's mother, accompanied by her brother Alexander Baltazzi, went to see the President of Police, Herr Krauss, who had just received a letter from Countess Larisch asking him to be as discreet as possible in his enquiries, to let the past rest and to concentrate on the future. This rather confused letter was interpreted by Herr Krauss to mean that the Countess not only knew Rudolph's intentions but was acting according to his wishes. Consequently he asked Mary's mother directly if she thought that Marie Larisch had been instrumental in procuring Mary for Rudolph; Helene Vetsera denied this. She still had confidence in Countess Larisch. Nevertheless the police officer was almost convinced of Marie Larisch's complicity and decided to submit the matter to the Minister President, Count Taaffe, as soon as he succeeded in quietening his visitors sufficiently to promise that they would wait until the morrow before taking further action. All he advised was that Herr Baltazzi should go to Mayerling to find out whether his niece was there.

At lunch time Herr Krauss saw Count Taaffe. The Minister President fully agreed with the course taken by the police, except that he himself would have sent Countess Larisch directly to the Empress. He also agreed that for the moment no action was required.

. . . . .

Prince Coburg had been invited to attend the Emperor's dinner-party that Tuesday. Consequently he left his stand at 1.30 without saying farewell to Hoyos, who remained, although shooting was not very successful, and joined the Crown Prince for tea before going on to Vienna. Rudolph seemed in a good mood. He told Coburg that he had something to tell him, but appeared reluctant to speak. He rubbed his hands and gave the impression of being generally embarrassed. At last when it was time for the visitor to leave, Rudolph, reminded that he had something to say, only asked his brother-in-law to excuse him at the dinner which he was unable to attend because he did not feel well. The Crown Prince also had a telegram sent to Stephanie, in which he asked her to offer his father his apologies, that on account of a severe head cold he would not be present at the dinner, but would stay at Mayerling with Hoyos.[7] When the telegram arrived at the Hofburg Püchel was on duty and took it to Stephanie. She opened it in his presence and he noticed that she cried and said, half to herself, half to him, 'Oh God, what shall I do! I feel so strange!'[8]

. . . . .

At six o'clock Taaffe sent for the President of Police. The Minister President told Herr Krauss that an hour earlier Mary's mother had been to see him. He had been curt with her, as was his usual way, but he told Krauss to

235

send a police agent to Mayerling to see if Mary was there and to get a report as to whether Rudolph was at the Palace. Krauss told his superior that on the same evening a family dinner was to take place which Rudolph was expected to attend, so that Mary too was likely to return to Vienna.

Back in his office the President of Police gave orders immediately that a plain clothes man should go to Mayerling next morning to discover whether Mary was there. He also gave instructions to find whether the relations between the Crown Prince and Mizzi Kaspar 'had grown cold', and what Rudolph's movements had been during the last few days.

· · · · · · ·

When the Imperial family gathered for the dinner, Rudolph's place was empty. The Emperor gave orders to wait, as he was bound to come. Rather late, Prince Coburg appeared and gave the Crown Prince's apologies.[9] According to Stephanie's memoirs it was she who apologised for her husband's absence.[10] Archduke Albrecht suggested that Rudolph must indeed feel very ill, as he had not attended a meeting of the army council that afternoon. It was known how seriously he took these meetings and they had waited for a full hour before beginning without him. Now, when Rudolph's absence had been explained, the Emperor gave the order for dinner to be served.

· · · · · ·

After his return from the shoot Hoyos arrived punctually at seven o'clock at the lodge. Rudolph joined him after a few minutes and the two men dined alone. The Crown Prince was very talkative, told his guest that he had written a great deal. He seemed disappointed at the meagre result of the shoot and hoped for better results next day, when, so Hoyos understood, he also would take part. The Count used the opportunity of being alone with his host to thank him for several shooting invitations in the Vienna Woods. 'I know,' replied Rudolph, 'the Vienna Woods are very beautiful indeed.' He seemed to Hoyos very mild in his judgements, and in a tender mood. During their meal he 'exercised the entire spell of his personality'.

They talked of many things, such as the cooking at the lodge and the intelligence of various breeds of gun dogs. Only once did a more serious mood creep in. The Crown Prince showed the Count three telegrams which he said he had received from Count Pista Károlyi, and declared that they were the result of a bad conscience ; he had spoken against the new Defence Bill, opposition news-papers had printed his speech and also the news that he had immediately before received a letter from the Crown Prince. They did so in order to compromise the heir to the throne. Rudolph continued, 'the matter was dis-astrous, but really one could not be offended at their behaviour, on account of the peculiar nature of these gentlemen. First Károlyi spoke against the Defence Bill and then sent his congratulations when it was passed.'

Hoyos, not a politically minded man, accepted these remarks without asking questions. After the meal they smoked and at nine o'clock the Crown Prince withdrew, saying that his head cold required an early bed. Hoyos offered him some handkerchiefs, but he declined the offer saying he would have enough to last him till the next day. After shaking hands Hoyos left for his lodgings which were four or five hundred yards from the lodge. Breakfast had been fixed for eight o'clock next morning.

III

The matter was disastrous. So Rudolph had stated in his talk with Hoyos. There seemed to be no way out of his difficulties. We do not know whether, or how far, he had committed himself in the Hungarian affair, but he seems to have taken the matter very seriously. Telegrams had come in on Tuesday, probably also on Monday — and he had brought one with him. He showed three to Hoyos but he may have received more. Budapest, the Hungarian capital, was seething with unrest during the last stages of the Defence Bill, and the military had to be called out to maintain order while parliament voted. It is inconceivable that Rudolph would have been uninformed. Additional staff had been sent to the little telegraph office in near-by Alland and he had sent at least one telegram from there.

What had he to do with Hungarian events ? Had he promised to come to Budapest and to lead the rebels ? Had his nerves and courage failed him at the last moment ? Was Károlyi's telegram of congratulations just irony ? Was there no way back to normal life ? Whatever the answers to these questions Crown Prince Rudolph of Austria said 'no' to the last one. He had passed the point of no return — even if all these surmises were untrue and he had nothing to do with Hungary and her troubles, he could not go back. 'Yes, it had to be.' The solution to his problems, whatever they were, for which he had so eagerly waited all day, had not come.

Rudolph withdrew to his bedroom, where Mary Vetsera had been waiting. There was still a little time, a few hours in which they could enjoy life, although the sands were fast running out. The cellar of the lodge was good, there were some noble wines and champagne. Rudolph's old coachman, Bratfisch, was called into the bedroom. He knew how to sing and to whistle the sentimental Viennese songs which both Rudolph and Mary loved so much. He excelled himself that night.

At long last Bratfisch was told he could retire. He had not been told what was on Rudolph's and Mary's minds, but he had divined it. Now in the light of the flickering candles, the girl wrote her farewell letters. She had all the time been prepared to die for her lover, and now, when he saw no way out and demanded her supreme sacrifice to go with him into the unknown, she did not hesitate. All seemed so easy, so natural. It had become very still and nothing could be heard, except the crackling of the logs on the fire and the scratching of the pen. At dead of night Mary said good-bye to her mother : 'Dear Mother, Forgive me for what I have done. I could not resist my love. In agreement with him I would like to be buried beside him at Alland. I am happier in death than in life. Yours Mary.' To her sister she wrote : 'We are both going blissfully into the uncertain beyond. Think of me now and then. Be happy and marry only for love. I could not do it and since I could not resist love, I am going with him. . . . Do not weep for my sake. I am crossing the line merrily. It is so beautiful out here. . . . Again farewell.' She asked her sister to have a gardenia laid on her grave every year on January 13th and on the day of her death, and concluded : 'As the last wish of her dying daughter I ask Mama to care in future for the family of . . . [follows the name of her personal maid] so that she does not suffer for my sake'. Mary had loved her little brother dearly and so she promised him, 'I shall watch over you from — the other world, because I love you so much. Your faithful sister.'

Yet they did not feel as sentimental as these letters would indicate. To the Duke of Braganza, who would have liked so much to marry her, Mary wrote a flippant note, in which she bequeathed him a fur boa, advising him to hang it up over his bed. Rudolph added '*Servus Wasserer*'. (*Servus* was the greeting among Austrian officers, *Wasserer* the expression used in Vienna for a coachman's assistant, whose main duty was to provide water for the horses. The Duke of Braganza had been known by this nickname ever since he appeared at a shoot with a particularly loud red shawl.)

Rudolph had written his farewell letters while still in Vienna. There was one more to write and a brief note to the ever faithful Loschek. There remained only the question of how they were going to die. They discussed the alternative, poison or revolver, and decided in favour of the latter. Mary recorded their decision on an ash-tray. 'Rather revolver, a revolver is safer', she wrote.

The candles were burnt out, the cups were empty. Mary stretched herself on the bed ; she had not lied in her letters, she was not afraid. It seemed bliss to die by the hand of her well-beloved, although she cried a little. Nor did his hand tremble. A slight touch of the trigger and Mary Vetsera had ended her young life.

Now Rudolph should have followed, yet he hesitated. What his thoughts were in those hours, alone with the dead girl, none can ever know. Morning was approaching. In the East, where the last foothills of the Alps make room for the wide Hungarian plain, the first signs of dawn were appearing on the horizon. At about half-past six, after what must have seemed an eternity, he unlocked the door and told Loschek to have breakfast prepared and to call him in an hour's time. He was still wearing his dressing-gown, and, whistling softly, he went back to the bedroom and locked the door behind him.

Why had he paused ? It was too late to hope, too late even for a miracle to happen. Was it the weakness of the flesh refusing to face death ? Or had Mary's going sapped his resolve ? Now, after talking to Loschek and limiting his time, he had forced his own hand.

The last respite was over. He poured himself a glass of brandy, took a hand-mirror and placed it on the bedside table. He sat down on the bed — there was room enough. Mary seemed peaceful, as if she were asleep, although her eyes were still open. He placed a flower in her hands. Looking into the mirror he lifted his pistol and, finding the right spot, pulled the trigger. He died so quickly that his right forefinger remained in its crooked position when death came.

REFERENCES

1. Püchel, *op. cit.*
2. *Das Mayerling Original*, pp. 13-14.
3. *Neues Wiener Tagblatt*, Wochenausgabe, August 4th, 1928.
4. Larisch, *op. cit.* pp. 209 f.
5. *Das Mayerling Original*, p. 38.
6. *Das Mayerling Original*, pp. 24 f.
7. Lonyay, *op. cit.* p. 242.
8. Püchel, *op. cit.*
9. *Das Mayerling Original*, p. 46.
10. Lonyay, *op. cit.* p. 244.

Aftermath

(1) 'The Sight is Dismal'

At a quarter to eight next morning Hoyos was ready to walk to the Lodge, where he was to join the Crown Prince for breakfast at eight o'clock. It was a little too early to set out — his rooms were only a short distance away — and while he was waiting, Herr Zwerger, the Lodge warden, was announced. He reported that Loschek was alarmed; he had called the Crown Prince at 7.30 as ordered, but could get no answer. At first he had knocked softly, then more and more loudly, and finally had taken a wooden log and knocked the door with it. The two doors to the bedroom were locked on the inside.

Hoyos hurried to the scene, where Loschek confirmed Zwerger's account. He gave orders to break open one door, but when Loschek told him that Rudolph was not alone, that Mary Vetsera was with him, he hesitated. Prince Coburg now arrived, and as a relative gave his authority for forcing the door. No sound came from the bedroom, and it took some time to break the stout door. When at last one of the panels was knocked in, Loschek could see the Crown Prince and Mary lying, apparently lifeless, on the bed. He went into the room alone, but returned very soon to confirm what they all feared — that both were dead and beyond any help. The Crown Prince, he said, was half lying on the edge of the bed with a pool of blood in front of him ; death had probably been caused by poisoning with potassium cyanide, which, Loschek maintained, brought about haemorrhage. Hoyos and Coburg, upset and bewildered, decided that one of them should hurry to Vienna to inform the Court, while the other would remain at the Lodge. Coburg was almost in a state of collapse, so Hoyos hurried away in Bratfisch's waiting carriage and Loschek was told to wire for the Court physician, Dr. Widerhofer, but not to disclose to him the nature of the disaster. At the nearest railway station, Baden, Hoyos left the carriage, and informing the station-master that he was acting on the Emperor's orders, had him stop the next train on its way to Vienna. At eleven minutes past ten he arrived at the Burg. He went first to see the Crown Prince's Court Marshal, and after informing him of the disaster as briefly as possible both men went to see Elisabeth's Court Marshal and sent for the Emperor's Adjutant, Count Paar. Together they decided that the Empress should be informed first, and that she should break the news to her husband.

Elisabeth was having a lesson in Greek and was annoyed when her lady-in-waiting, Mademoiselle Ferenczy, announced the Court Marshal. Only when she had been informed of the serious nature of his report was he permitted to see the Empress. As gently and considerately as possible he told her of the tragedy. When Mademoiselle Ferenczy returned in a few minutes' time she found her weeping. Now the Emperor was announced, but had to wait until Elisabeth had dried her eyes. He came in, and for a few minutes they were alone.

When the Emperor returned to his room with the gentlemen of the two suites, Elisabeth went to see Frau Schratt. She was an actress whom the Empress had introduced to her husband to be his companion while she herself was on her frequent travels, and she was visiting their Majesties at the Hofburg that day. Elisabeth took her to Francis Joseph and left them while she went to break the news to her daughter Valerie. After a while the Emperor joined them, and Stephanie was sent for. She was at her singing lesson. According to her own testimonial, she immediately guessed that Rudolph was dead.

Mary's mother, the Baroness Helene Vetsera, was also in the Burg. It was the third day since her daughter had disappeared, and, weary of the prevarications of the police officers, she had decided to come herself to see the Empress. She was waiting in Mademoiselle Ferenczy's ante-room when Elisabeth returned after seeing Valerie, and turning to her eagerly she cried, 'I have lost my child. Please help me to find her'. The Empress could only reply : 'Baroness, gather all your courage. Your daughter is dead.' Helplessly Baroness Vetsera began to cry, 'My child, my dear, beautiful child. . . .' 'But,' continued the Empress, 'do you know that my Rudolph too is dead ?' The Baroness fell on her knees : 'My unhappy child, what has she done ? She has done this ?'[1] Curtly the Baroness was dismissed with the words, 'And now remember that Rudolph died of heart failure'.

In the first natural confusion, when Hoyos's report was the only one, and poison administered by Mary Vetsera was assumed to be the cause of Rudolph's death, it may have seemed the best way out of a terrible difficulty to say that he had died of heart failure if a bulletin was to be issued the same morning. But this was not done. The first official report was not published until next morning in the official Gazette. By this time the truth could have been ascertained and published. Not only was the Austrian public misled, but the telegrams to foreign courts too contained reports of heart failure.

Dr. Widerhofer had gone to Mayerling immediately on receipt of Loschek's telegram ; at Baden Bratfisch was waiting for him with his carriage. Even had there been no immediate train from Vienna he would still have reached the Lodge by lunch-time. It could have taken no more than a few moments to establish the cause of death. The doctor examining the body was bound by law to question the person who last saw him alive, and during their talk it is likely that Loschek would have spoken of his suspicions of cyanide poisoning. Dr. Widerhofer must have realised that Hoyos had given a distorted version of Rudolph's death. Why did he not send a telegram immediately to correct this mistake ? He need not have sent it *en clair* ; as Court Physician he must have had the Emperor's cipher. Had he considered even this unsafe, he could have gone to Vienna and reported in person, or he could have asked Coburg, who was still at the Lodge, to report the true facts to Francis Joseph. Nothing was done, and the distorted version was repeated when Hoyos had an audience with the Emperor at twelve o'clock. He must have given the same version to Stephanie when he saw her that evening. She told him 'that she had seen the disaster coming and that, although she could not absolve herself of all guilt, the catastrophe could not have been prevented'.

The Lord Chamberlain's office was informed soon after twelve o'clock that Rudolph was dead ; no cause of death was given. In accordance with Hapsburg family law a commission of Court officials went to the place of death to find if there was a will and to enclose the body in a coffin.[2] It took some time for the commission to assemble and when they reached Mayerling night had fallen.

At the Lodge they found Dr. Widerhofer and Prince Coburg waiting. Both bullets had been found. There was no doubt that in each case death had been instantaneous. Mary was hardly changed by death ; she held a rose in her stiff hands and a little handkerchief which showed that she had cried a little. Nor was Rudolph's face distorted, but his skull had been badly damaged by the shot. He looked peaceful — the bitter smile habitual during the last few months had vanished. But Court etiquette and convention had no respect for sentiment, and Mary's body was removed to a lumber room.

Several letters and a telegram were found by the commission, but, as was expected, there was no Will. This Rudolph had deposited in the Lord Chamberlain's office. Some of the officials were aware of this, but the letter of the law had to be obeyed. There was a letter from Rudolph to Szögyenyi, and a note to the faithful Loschek in which he asked him to arrange for the delivery of all the letters. He wished for a priest to pray by their bodies, and asked that they be buried together at near-by Heiligenkreuz. He thanked his faithful retainer for many years of devoted service. The other letters found were Mary's farewell messages. The telegram was to the Father Prior of the Abbey at Heiligenkreuz, asking him to come with some of his monks to pray for them.

When these findings had been recorded the youngest member of the commission, Slatin, who later wrote this account, was sent to Vienna to the Lord Chamberlain, so that a further report could be made to the Emperor and Empress. Widerhofer had now realised his earlier omission, and tried to repair it ; but the damage was done. It cannot have been late when Slatin arrived at the Burg, but

the Lord Chamberlain did not communicate his report
to Francis Joseph, and consequently the official bulletin
announcing heart failure as the cause of Rudolph's death
was not altered and was allowed to appear in the official
Gazette on Thursday morning. Nobody believed it.
Already other facts were becoming known.

At Mayerling the body was laid in its coffin and taken
to Vienna, where it arrived at 2 A.M. on Thursday morning.
It was taken to Rudolph's rooms at the Hofburg, while
Widerhofer remained to await the summons to the
Emperor, who was an early riser. Soon after six Francis
Joseph sent for him. The physician, unaware that his
report had not reached the Emperor, immediately stated
that he could give an assurance that Rudolph had not
suffered in the least, because the bullet had killed him
instantaneously. The Emperor grew excited. What was
this? There had been no bullet. Rudolph had been
poisoned. Only now did the Emperor learn the truth, as
Widerhofer related to him the full findings : Mary had
not poisoned Rudolph ; he had shot her, then followed
himself. Now Francis Joseph's 'grief knew no bounds.
. . . He fell on the floor and writhed in pain and despair,
no longer in a state of self-control.'[3]

A little later he went to pay his last respects to his son.
He took his sabre and gloves in accordance with regu-
lations and custom : correct even when overwhelmed
with sorrow, he bade farewell to a dead brother officer.
Rudolph's literary executor, Szögyenyi, was then sum-
moned ; the letter addressed to him had been handed
to the Emperor by Widerhofer. Szögyenyi asked the
Emperor to open and read the letter first, but this he
declined to do, and waited until Szögyenyi had himself
read it. The letter expressed Rudolph's regret at having

been unable to see Szögyenyi (who because of a case of measles in his family had had to keep away from people). He asked him to attend to his papers and enclosed the key of his desk, adding that he had no choice left but to die.

The farewell letters which Szögyenyi found had been written before Rudolph had left Vienna, with the possible exception of that to his mother. There were letters for Stephanie and for his sister Valerie, but none for his father. Only one of these letters, that to Stephanie, has been published in full ; of the others only more or less detailed summaries are available. To his wife Rudolph had written : 'You are relieved of my presence and vexation ; be happy in your own way. Be kind to the poor little one ; she is all that remains of me. Give all friends, particularly Bombelles . . . my last greetings. I approach death composedly ; it alone can save my good name. I embrace you tenderly, your loving Rudolph.'[4] Rudolph advised his sister Valerie, who was engaged at the time, to leave Austria on her father's death. What would happen in Austria-Hungary after Francis Joseph's day was unforeseeable. He added that he did not welcome death.[5]

In the letter to his mother Rudolph asked that he be buried at Heiligenkreuz, beside the 'pure angel who accompanied him into the other world'. Again he spoke of the necessity to die.

Next day a post mortem was carried out. The question of a Church burial had to be considered. It was a clear case of suicide and medical grounds for an assumption that Rudolph had been of unsound mind had to be established, if the ecclesiastical authorities were to permit the full burial service. The autopsy showed some anomalies in the formation of the skull. 'The premature cohesion of the fontanelles, the remarkable depth of the skull cavity and

*The removal of the Crown Prince's body from Mayerling
(after a contempory drawing)*

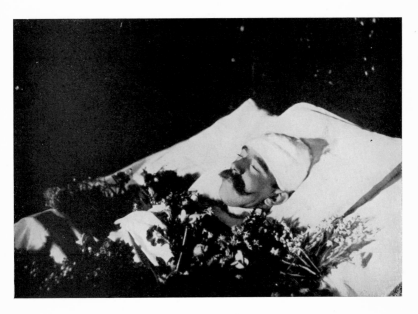

Crown Prince Rudolph lying in state

the so-called "fingerlike" impressions on the inner surface of the skull-bones, the evident subsidence of the brain passages, and the enlargement of the brain chamber are pathological circumstances which experience has proved appurtenant to abnormal mental conditions, and which therefore justify the supposition that the deed was committed in a state of mental derangement.'[6] This statement was sufficiently vague to justify a Christian burial without at the same time stigmatising a member of the Imperial House as a madman.

Permission for Church burial was not easily obtained in spite of the result of the post mortem. Apparently its findings were not unequivocal enough to dispel the doubts of many Cardinals, particularly the Cardinal Secretary of State, Rampolla. Despite the Pope's decision to grant a Church burial he maintained his opposition. Francis Joseph was so hurt by this that he exercised his veto on Rampolla's election as Pope in 1903, when he was considered the most likely candidate. The Emperor is supposed to have sent a telegram of two thousand words asking the Pope to grant the rites of the Church and to have threatened his abdication if his request was refused. No copy of this telegram is available, but its dispatch has never been repudiated, and it must therefore be assumed to exist.

The difficulty of the situation is also characterised by a report from the German Ambassador, Reuss, to the Foreign Ministry, dated February 5th, 1889. Reuss had been in conversation with the Papal Nuncio, Monsignore Galimberti, and wrote : 'The Papal Nuncio has told me of the serious embarrassment in which the Pope found himself when he had to give his agreement to a Church burial. Had this agreement been refused and were the suicide to be buried without religious rites, the Vienna population would have doubtless rioted. His Majesty the Emperor was therefore greatly worried until the post mortem had taken place and the assembled doctors and judicial officials had declared that madness was possible.

'The Emperor immediately sent Count Kálnoky to the Nuncio to show him the official communiqué. Herr Galimberti (*sic*) has immediately reported this to Rome by telegram and dispelled all scruples the Church may have had. Many queries have also reached the Nuncio here from Bishops as to what attitude they were to take ; he has stressed that mental derangement excused suicide also in the eyes of the Church. "My official conscience is clear", the Nuncio added, "I need *only* believe what I am told by the Minister of Foreign Affairs. But it is probably the first time in history that the Papal Nuncio attends the funeral of a murderer and suicide in *Pontificalibus*." ' [7]

When the Crown Prince lay in state in his bedroom, the Empress Elisabeth, his sisters and his widow came to bid him farewell ; Stephanie had brought little Elisabeth — 'all that remained of him' — to say farewell to her father. Five years old at the time, the little girl hardly knew what the many tears were about. In his last Will Rudolph had asked his father to become his daughter's guardian, and the Emperor assented.

Not all shed tears at the Palace. Slatin reports [8] that less than forty-eight hours after Rudolph's death, Taaffe, the Minister President, who as the Emperor's friend should have felt some grief at the death of the heir to the throne, was discussing funeral arrangements with the Lord Steward as serenely 'as if it had concerned the arrangement of a court ball'.

The Austrian people had been told by a communiqué

issued in the afternoon of January 30th and repeated in the official Gazette, the *Wiener Zeitung*, on the 31st, that 'His Imperial and Royal Highness, the Most Serene Crown Prince, Archduke Rudolph has died suddenly on the 30th between 7 and 8 A.M. through heart failure, in his hunting lodge at Mayerling near Baden'. Nobody believed it. The report could have been corrected had Widerhofer's findings been brought to the Emperor's knowledge earlier. The communiqué published on February 1st that 'yesterday's information had been based on the first observations', but that the examination by the Court Physicians had shown that he had died by his own hand, was disbelieved as well. The situation was not improved when again, a day later, the result of the post mortem was published. Public confidence had been forfeited.

By this time it had become known that a second body, that of a woman, had been found, and only a frank statement could have saved the situation. This the Emperor, on Count Taaffe's advice, refused, although a love affair in the eyes of the Viennese would have been far less derogatory than the possibility of madness which was admitted by the bulletin of February 2nd. It must have been a sad blow to Francis Joseph's pride to have to admit that his son may have been mad, but without the publication of the post-mortem findings nobody would have understood why Rudolph, a suicide, could be granted Christian burial.

People began to tell, and to believe, all kinds of wild stories. There were rumours that Rudolph had been murdered, either by a jealous husband or lover. There was also gossip about an American duel, in which the contestant drawing a black ball has to shoot himself within twenty-four hours. Police agents were sent into all parts of Vienna to find out what people considered the reason for the tragedy.

Had the Austrian newspapers been permitted to add their own comments to official bulletins many of the rumours would have been scotched early, but rarely in the history of human failure has so little imagination and human understanding been shown by any government. The police could not prevent foreign papers from publishing what news they liked, and the authorities, hard as they tried, could not entirely prevent foreign papers finding their way into Austria. There was some justification for the attempt to hinder the entry of foreign newspapers. 'It must be allowed that the Austrian Government, being unable to proceed save by costly diplomatic and legal processes, is justified in stopping the circulation of certain foreign journals which have not scrupled to rake up every fragment of scandal that could be collected about the Crown Prince's life. The relatives of the Crown Prince are at least entitled to as much protection against slander as private persons.' [9]

As a consequence of police action a black market in foreign newspapers developed, although many were seized by the police before they reached the public. On one single day, February 19th, 4790 copies of various newspapers from abroad were confiscated. This greatly inflated the value of those papers which did escape the police. A ten minutes' perusal cost up to 40 Kreuzers (about 8d.) ; another source gives a price of a quarter of a litre of wine. [10]

This difficulty in obtaining news and the high price demanded for it made people more gullible, and stories were believed, no matter how hare-brained they sounded. It would be wrong to blame the correspondents entirely for the nonsense printed. Journalists were prevented from getting authentic information and what they did obtain was sent out of the country only with great difficulty, owing to unofficial postal censorship. Even foreign diplomats were not immune. The British Ambassador stated in a letter to Lady Paget : 'I had a very hard day writing a long report to Her Majesty and to Lord Salisbury, and it would not have done to send either by post'.[11]

The funeral took place on February 5th. No foreign Princes were admitted except Stephanie's parents. The Kaiser wished to attend but was given to understand that he would not be welcome. Countess Larisch's father was in Vienna. He was given a hint and developed a sudden cold which prevented him from attending. Queen Victoria sent a wreath of immortelles with the inscription which she had chosen herself, 'A token of the closest friendship' (*Ein Zeichen innigster Freundschaft*). After the Church ceremony the body was carried to the Capuchin vaults, the resting-place of the Hapsburgs. Only the Emperor and Gisela, the elder daughter, followed the coffin, the Empress with her younger daughter stayed at home ; it would have been too much of an ordeal for Elisabeth's frayed nerves. On the last evening before the body was carried away to lie in state, she said to her daughter : 'It's not true, it can't be that Rudolph lies dead in there. I must go and see if it is true.'[12]

The vault doors were closed as the funeral cortège approached. The Lord Chamberlain knocked and from inside a voice asked, 'Who is there ?' 'His Imperial and Royal Highness, the most serene Crown Prince, Archduke Rudolph.' The reply came, 'We know him not'. Again the Chamberlain knocked. Again came the voice, 'Who is there ?' This time the reply was shorter, 'Archduke

Rudolph', but the response was the same, 'We know him not'. The Chamberlain knocked a third time. Once more he was asked, 'Who is there ?' This time his answer was still simpler, 'A poor sinner'. 'He may enter.' The burial service was read among the many coffins of earlier Hapsburgs. *Et lux perpetua luceat ei !*

The Emperor was much affected. 'I held myself well, but in the vaults it was impossible any more. There never was a funeral like today's', he told Elisabeth.[13]

Rudolph, by the decision of the Holy See, had had a Christian burial. Rome had spoken, but the matter was not closed. There were, in many parts of Austria, conflicts about the holding of requiem masses. In spite of the Pope's decision, many priests, even supported by some bishops, without the slightest spark of charity tried to vent their spite against the dead Liberal. Sheltering behind their consciences they refused to say Mass. Ambassador Reuss, after another talk with Monsignore Galimberti, reported : 'Here one awaits not without misgivings the impression which the Crown Prince's suicide will create among the bigoted rural population in the Alpine provinces. The clergy there in their majority take a very spiteful attitude. The requiem Masses are either not read at all or in a mutilated form, as for instance in the capital of the Southern Tyrol, Trient. In Meran it was entirely impossible to get the Churches opened and the local Loyal Sharp Shooters battalion had to hold its memorial service in the open. In many places the bells were not tolled, and the confiscation of many clerical [political Catholic] journals became necessary, *e.g.* of the *Innsbrucker Stimmen*. In Laibach the German Liberal majority of the population had to force the Bishop Missin to celebrate requiem Mass on the day of the funeral. During the day a threatening

crowd had assembled in front of the Bishop's palace so
that in the end he gave in and ordered a requiem, although
in a mutilated form. The Nuncio complained repeatedly
of the difficulties of his position between Rome and Vienna
in the face of local feudalistic intransigents, who made use
of Archbishop Schönborn [Archbishop of Prague since
1885], in whom he, Galimberti, recognised increasingly a
false friend and perfidious character, although in the face
of his mental inferiority he was more the servant of others
than his own master. In response to repeated questions of
Schönborn's, regarding participation by the bishops at the
memorial and mourning service, the Nuncio has given the
following clever ruling : Mental derangement had officially
been given as the cause of suicide. Science said that the
supposition was in favour of insanity of the suicide. The
Church had no reason to judge differently from science,
unless the contrary was proved in a special case. Count
Schönborn should, if he likes, prove it. Lacking such
proof, he, the Nuncio, was acting strictly in accordance
with Papal orders, in consequence of which he answered
all queries from the provinces with the order *Fate come a
Vienna* [do as in Vienna].'[14]

It was, of course, not religious qualms which caused
these members of the clergy to disobey the Pope's decisions. It was a cheap and mean method of political retalia-
tion when their opponent was dead. Political and not
conscientious reasons were the cause. Among Queen
Victoria's papers dealing with the tragedy of Mayerling was
found a cutting from the *Standard* of February 8th which
fully confirmed and augmented Reuss's report. 'The
Clericals believed that their time had come again. They disobey the Pope, who does not often assert his authority,
as well as the Civil authorities. They intrigue against the

Papal Nuncio, Monsignore Galimberti, because he is not an intransigent, or one of the "fighting party", and almost exulted in their organs at the death of the Liberal Crown Prince Rudolph, from whose reign they expected nothing.

'A number of the Clerical papers were confiscated for disrespectful articles on the late Prince ; and in some places where the Parish priests, regardless of the example set them by the Pope and the Archbishops . . . had refused to allow mourning services to be held or the bells to be tolled, the people themselves rang the bells and surrounded the priests' houses. Not less ungenerous than the conduct of the Clericals, who have at least some excuse for their attitude, was the bearing of the anti-Semites, whose organs have behaved as scandalously during the last eight days as those of the Clerical fanatics.' *The Times* of the same date confirmed that the want of respect was due to political reasons. 'Several of the anti-Semite journals have behaved with great indecorum in abstaining from all words of respect for the Crown Prince's memory.' On the previous day the paper had reported that stones had been thrown at the windows of the Episcopal Palace at Laibach because of the Bishop's refusal to have Requiem Mass read. When it is borne in mind that Taaffe himself was inclined towards the Catholic Conservatives, they must have exceeded all bounds of decency before he would consider it necessary to have their periodicals confiscated. Naturally Schönerer and Lueger and their friends could not resist showing their hatred of Rudolph. Many of these pretended to be good Austrian patriots, yet not one of them could have considered how his attitude must have hurt the Emperor in his grief. In a proclamation Francis Joseph had stated : 'The heaviest blow which could have hit a father's heart, the immeasurable loss of my dear only son, has filled with the deepest mourning myself, my house and my faithful peoples. Shaken to my very depth, I bow my head in humility before the unfathomable decision of Divine Providence. . . .'

Unmitigated indecent hostility beyond death combined with irresponsible rumours to deny the dead Crown Prince a true and rightful place in the history of his country. Although no one in high society was ready or willing to defend his honour, Rudolph was not forgotten by the humble people. They had loved him, and, years after his death, his portrait still hung in many houses — even where there was none of the Emperor. In the remote hilly districts of Dalmatia peasants refused to believe that he was dead and were sure that one day he would return.[15]

REFERENCES

1. According to the only complete record given in Corti, *Elisabeth*, pp. 416-20.

2. Dr. Heinrich Freiherr von Slatin, 'Die Wahrheit über Mayerling', *Neues Wiener Tagblatt*, August 15th, 1931.

3. Lamzdorfa, *op. cit.* p. 178.

4. Lonyay, *op. cit.* p. 248 (in an imperfect English translation) and a facsimile copy in Corti, *Franz Josef*, Vol. III, pp. 96 f.

5. Corti, *Elisabeth*, p. 422.

6. Quoted from the English edition of Mitis (London, n.d.), p. 152.

7. P.R.O., F.O. 553/LA, No. 57, also quoted in Albert E. J. Hollaender, 'Streiflichter auf die Kronprinzen-Tragödie von Mayerling', in *Festschrift für Heinrich Benedikt*, herausgegeben von Professor Hantsch (Wien, 1957, pp. 135-160. The word 'only' (*nur*) is underlined in the original.

8. Slatin, *op. cit.*

9. *The Times*, February 7th, 1889.

10. *Das Mayerling Original*, pp. 104 ff.

11. Paget, *op. cit.* p. 471.

12. Corti, *Elisabeth*, p. 425.

13. Corti, *Elisabeth*, p. 426.

14. P.R.O. *op. cit.*, also quoted by Hollaender, *op. cit.*

15. R. W. Seton-Watson, *The Southern Slav Question and the Habsburg Monarchy* (London, 1911), p. 115, footnote.

(2) 'Such Maimed Rites'

RUDOLPH had wished to be buried beside the 'pure angel' who had died with him. To the Austrian Court officials Mary Vetsera was not a pure angel, but an 'unknown female body, found at Mayerling'.[1] They wanted to deal with the body in their own way, but to do this they had first to receive the Baroness Vetsera's authority and then to get the poor woman out of their way. While she was still at the Burg on the morning of the 30th, when the Empress had told her that both their children were dead, her brother-in-law, Count Stockau, had been looking for her. He had been ordered by the Emperor to tell her what had happened at Mayerling (at this stage the verdict of poisoning was accepted) and to obtain from her instructions to fetch the corpse from the Lodge and bring it to Vienna.

Together they went to the Vetsera home, and had hardly arrived there when 'a high personality' (it was Count Paar, the Emperor's Adjutant-General) was announced and declared that he had had orders to inform them that Mary Vetsera had poisoned the Crown Prince and herself while they were breakfasting together ; that she had probably not wanted to return home after spending a few days with Rudolph. This was also the version which Taaffe was anxious to have accepted. The Baroness was left with the impression that this story would be officially published, and before having any opportunity of checking the truth of the statement she was 'emphatically advised' by the Adjutant to leave Vienna. Believing the story told to them to be the true one, her brother and brother-in-law supported the Adjutant in this, so that their sister would escape the public indignation which was sure to follow the announcement that her daughter had poisoned the heir to the throne. Baroness Vetsera left that night, bound for Venice.

She did not go all the way. Leaving the train *en route* she returned late next morning to her home in Vienna. Meanwhile her brother, Alexander Baltazzi, and her brother-in-law, Count Stockau, had learned that the story of the poisoning was untrue. Although the truth had by then been established, the first version believed, that of Mary having poisoned both herself and her lover, had been deliberately used to get the mother out of the way and to prevent her demanding her daughter's body for a decent burial. On the same morning the farewell letters had been found, and among them was one to Mary's mother, with the address in Rudolph's handwriting. By the Emperor's orders this letter was to be handed to the Baroness on condition that she would return it to Francis Joseph after reading it, and that she would appoint her brother-in-law, Count Stockau, as her attorney. She had no choice but to obey. Stockau now told her what he had learned that morning that no permission would be granted to have Mary's body buried in Vienna, but that she was to be buried at Heiligenkreuz. Further, no coffin was to be brought to the Lodge, nor would permission be given for a hearse to convey the body to the cemetery.

Late on that afternoon Stockau and Baltazzi went to Mayerling to obey the orders of the Court. By the time they arrived night had already fallen, and they had to wait outside the gate for half an hour until Rudolph's surgeon-in-ordinary, Auchenthaler, and Slatin, of the

Court Comptroller's office, arrived. At half-past seven the group was led into the Lodge, where they were taken to a door locked with the Imperial seal. The seal was removed and they entered. Inside, by the light of a flickering lantern, they found Mary's body, covered by a heap of old clothes. It was nearly forty hours since she had died, but she had received no attention. Her eyes were still open, and the blood which had oozed from the wound in her temple had congealed. In her stiff hands she still held the little handkerchief which she had used to wipe away her last tears.[2]

An official record was now made. It stated that a female body had been found within the boundaries of the village of Mayerling. The surgeon Auchenthaler diagnosed death by shooting — doubtless suicide. The wound in the left temple was described and a statement made that death must have been instantaneous, then the body was handed to Count Stockau and Alexander Baltazzi, who had recognised it as that of their niece, Baroness Mary Alexandra Vetsera.[3]

The official recording finished, the corpse was next washed by Auchenthaler and fully dressed, even to the outdoor clothes. Coat, hat, boa and veil, and shoes, were all carefully put on. An ordinary carriage was waiting at the Lodge gates — a hearse might have attracted attention. The girl's two uncles had then to link arms with the corpse and accompany it as a living person from the Lodge, carefully guiding it down the steps and along the approach to the carriage. Here it was placed in a half-sitting position and supported by the two men. A plain-clothes detective travelled with them, and Auchenthaler and Slatin followed in another carriage. In spite of the darkness and the late hour the authorities feared they might be

seen, and forbade them to take the main road. Along a
small side road they carried the sad load to the little village
of Heiligenkreuz. It was a rough night, with rain and
sleet and a howling wind. The icy road was almost im-
passable and the horses slipped constantly, so that the
coachmen had to stop the little procession to caulk their
shoes. Inside the carriage the body swayed from side to
side so that the two men had constantly to readjust its
position. The journey took more time than the police
had anticipated, and it was midnight when they arrived
at the cemetery, which lay about a mile outside the village.
Here a number of high-ranking police officers were waiting
with a crude coffin, hurriedly made by the Monastery's
carpenter. Into this the body was laid, put in a small shack
which served as mortuary, and guarded by detectives.

Slatin and Auchenthaler had gone directly to the
Monastery as the first carriage made its way to the
cemetery, and in the refectory had joined a number of
police officers and local representatives of the Ministry
of the Interior. Mary's uncles followed, after their
harrowing journey. The cellars of Heiligenkreuz were
well known, and the wine dispensed by the hospitable
monks soon loosened tongues and introduced a heartiness
which contrasted painfully with the grim mood of others.
Only with difficulty could one of the monks keep some
of the police officers in order.

Early next morning Auchenthaler and Slatin left for
Vienna to report on the success of their mission. Although
suicide had been officially recorded, a funeral with full
Church ceremonial took place early on the morning of
Friday, February 1st, and was conducted by the Prior of
Heiligenkreuz himself. Mary's two uncles and some
police officers were the only people present. It was a

stormy day with heavy rain, the soil frozen, and although the senior police officer had been at the cemetery to hurry the gravedigger, the funeral could only begin at nine o'clock and not at the early hour the police had demanded. Storm and rain made the ceremony so difficult that police officers had to assist in the actual interment. Although the weather was so bad and the road from the monastery buildings to the cemetery was deserted, the police still feared that somebody might see the little group consisting of the Prior, Herr Baltazzi and Count Stockau on their way to the cemetery.

On the evening of Mary's funeral Count Taaffe went to see Baroness Vetsera. He came by Francis Joseph's order and asked her in the name of the Emperor to leave Vienna for a time ; in no circumstances was she to have anything done to her daughter's grave at Heiligenkreuz, since, so the Minister President said, 'so many journalists were infesting the district'. Later the mother would be free to have her daughter's body removed to wherever she pleased.

Baroness Vetsera answered Count Taaffe that she was prepared to obey the Emperor and leave Vienna ; but she had no intention of disturbing her daughter's rest by exhumation and reinterment. Taaffe then asked her to keep the whole matter a secret, particularly from her servants. He was not satisfied with her promise and, as she was still in Vienna the next morning, he instructed the police to keep an eye on her.[4]

The government planned to spread the rumour in 'aristocratic circles' that Mary Vetsera was with Countess Larisch in her residence at Pardubice, and from there the news was to come that the young girl had committed suicide. It was futile to expect such a plan to succeed.

A Munich daily paper published on February 8th a report from its Vienna correspondent of events at Mayerling, a report not so far removed from the truth as many biographers have subsequently claimed. About Mary it stated, 'Her body was conveyed to the Cistercians at Heiligenkreuz and quietly buried there'. As the police had not succeeded in suppressing all foreign newspapers it is fair to assume that the Austrian people had by now a fair knowledge of the sad events.

When Mary's mother returned to Vienna in the middle of March the police were immediately informed. The official attitude had meanwhile changed. A representative was sent from the Minister President to the Baroness to inform her that the government would bear the cost if she had Mary's body exhumed from Heiligenkreuz and reburied elsewhere, but indignantly she refused to disturb her daughter's rest. The grave is still in the little cemetery in Heiligenkreuz, a simple grave, simply inscribed :

MARY

FREIIN V. VETSERA

geb. 19. März 1871
gest. 30. Jänner 1889

Wie eine Blume spriesst der Mensch auf
und wird gebrochen

(*Man cometh forth like a flower and is cut down*)

A plain-clothes detective was ordered to watch the cemetery at Heiligenkreuz and another to watch the Baroness. They reported that she and her daughter went every week to lay flowers — camellias — on the grave.[5]

By June the government considered the matter closed, but in Vienna society there was an outburst of gossip which blamed Mary for Rudolph's death. In defence of her daughter the Baroness had a pamphlet privately printed in which she tried to reconstruct the course of events which had led to Mary's untimely death. It was intended for private circulation, as only two hundred and fifty copies were printed. The police immediately confiscated the memorandum, and now very few original copies remain. Some were bought by newspapers — *The Times*, *le Temps*, and *l'Éclair*. Only *The Times* refrained from reprinting ; *le Temps* published a few extracts and *l'Éclair*, in 1891, printed nearly the whole. After 1918 two reprints were published, and parts are included in *Das Mayerling Original*.

It was through this memorandum that Mary Vetsera's farewell letters became known, and that she was brought to life again, a young girl, very much in love with Rudolph, who in her romantic infatuation saw more clearly than anyone else how unhappy he was. It eased his troubled mind not to cross into the unknown alone, and she went with him, happy, even in death, to be near him.

REFERENCES

1. Slatin, *op. cit.*
2. Vetsera Memorandum.
3. Vetsera Memorandum and Slatin, *op. cit.*
4. Vetsera Memorandum.
5. *Das Mayerling Original*, pp. 173 f.

(3) 'Something is Rotten in the State'

I

EARLY in March 1889 Francis Joseph wrote to his friend, Frau Schratt : 'Yesterday the gentlemen of Rudolph's former suite and Widerhofer were in audience to thank me for the honours I granted them. The latter was also with me in the afternoon for an hour and we discussed again all the sad events and tried to find some correlation between them and searched for reasons. It is of no use and serves no purpose, but one cannot think of anything else and the discussion is a certain consolation.'[1]

The Emperor and Dr. Widerhofer were not alone in their search for reasons. All the world was searching and, although most people were satisfied with the wildest and most incredible rumours, foreign governments and serious people wanted to know the truth, why Rudolph had thrown away such a promising future. Queen Victoria had ciphered to Sir Augustus Paget on February 1st, 'Pray give all details you can gather however distressing they may be'.[2] This was not mere curiosity, because on February 4th she asked Prince Philipp Coburg, her relative, to tell her the real reasons for Rudolph's death, adding 'I want to be able to contradict the rumours' (. . . *Möchte ich solchen Gerüchten wiedersprechen* [sic] *können*).[3]

The diplomats accredited to the Vienna Court did all they could to satisfy their sovereigns' wishes. Queen Victoria was not the only one who wanted to know everything. The diplomats had few reliable sources of information ; Szögyenyi was the most important — it had become known that Rudolph had appointed him his executor. As he was a diplomat himself his language was guarded, and yet the various reports based on his statements form a decisive part of our information about the possible reasons for Rudolph's death. The Nuncio, Cardinal Galimberti, also came in for much attention, as the rumour that the Crown Prince had applied to the Holy See for an annulment of his marriage was widely believed, and that the tragedy had been precipitated by the subsequent quarrel with the Emperor. Reuss, the German Ambassador, was at an advantage. As the representative of a closely allied Monarch he had access to Francis Joseph himself. There is little outside diplomatic dispatches which can be seriously considered. Marie Larisch's autobiography was a clumsy attempt to whitewash herself, and books written on the Mayerling Tragedy, with only a few notable exceptions, can be disregarded, as they are not based on fact.

The historian's usual way of supplementing diplomatic reports by memoirs fails in this particular case ; they are either reticent or palpably untrue. The archives too fail. The official papers concerning the death of the Crown Prince were not deposited in the former Imperial (now State) Archives in Vienna, but handed by the Emperor to his Minister President, Taaffe, who kept them at his castle Ellischau in Bohemia, where they are supposed to have been destroyed in a fire. Only the memoranda written by Count Hoyos were kept and are now available. Not even the full post-mortem report is to be found, nor any of the farewell letters, except the note to Stephanie, which she herself published. Rudolph himself had apparently destroyed a large proportion of his papers before he set out for Mayerling. Szögyenyi, in a talk with Reuss on April 8th, stated Rudolph 'had done away with all letters addressed to him', as he could not find a single letter from himself, nor from the Kaiser. The Crown Prince seemed only to have kept letters from his parents, his sister Gisela, a letter from the German Emperor Frederick III, and a few letters from King Ludwig II of Bavaria.[4] This was not quite correct. The letter mentioned was not from Emperor Frederick III, but from his widow. It cannot have been without interest, because it was removed from the Archives a little after Rudolph's death by Francis Joseph's order.

While Rudolph, according to Szögyenyi's statement, 'had done away with all letters addressed to him', quite a number must have remained which his executor considered dangerous. Stephanie in her memoirs stated that 'Count Szögyenyi, in accordance with the terms of the Prince's will, opened the drawers of his writing-table in my presence and burned the contents'.[5] This information is confirmed by Major Fritsche, an officer of Rudolph's suite. In a letter to Mitis he stated that on February 1st, by Stephanie's orders, he handed Szögyenyi a document case which belonged to Rudolph and which was always kept locked and taken with him on all his journeys, as well as a letter from the Crown Prince. Szögyenyi read the letter aloud in Major Fritsche's presence. As far as the officer could recollect some forty years later, it said, 'I must quit this life, I ask you to go through my papers and to burn everything which you think necessary'.[6] The letter also contained the key to the case, which the diplomat opened immediately. He looked through its contents and burned some of the papers, returning the rest into the bag which he took to the Hofburg. There a few days later he burned some more. Szögyenyi told Prince Kantakuzene that Francis Joseph had handed to him the letter from

Rudolph.[7] This contradicts Major Fritsche's statement
that he gave Szögyenyi the letter in obedience to Stephanie's
orders. There is, however, no reason to doubt the truth
of his statement that Szögyenyi burnt many of Rudolph's
documents, a statement which agrees with Stephanie's
own observations.

II

In the face of so many rumours the first question to be
established is whether Rudolph's death was due to murder
or to suicide. The stubbornly recurring assertion that it
was murder is only supported by one serious document, a
report by Reuss of a talk with Cardinal Galimberti of
February 9th. In view of its unique importance this
report is given *in extenso* and in a translation as near the
German original as possible.

'Secret. By Royal Messenger. As I had already the
honour of pointing out to-day in another report, the
official version is maintained, that Crown Prince Rudolph
committed suicide by shooting, and thereby minor details
which are in general known to all the world are suppressed.

'I must refer to this matter again, because very serious
people doubt it [the official version] and again and again
refer to the rumour that the Crown Prince, as well as the
young lady who was found on his bed, were murdered.

'The following circumstances speak in favour of it.
After the statement of heart failure had become untenable,
suicide was alleged in order to avoid admitting the fact
of the presence of a female corpse. Indeed not only out
of consideration for the Crown Princess and out of regard
for public morals, but also because it was feared the Church
could make difficulties regarding the funeral. The proof

that the murdered man had lived in concubinage would have made Church ceremonies difficult, if not impossible. If the murder had been admitted, public opinion would have demanded the discovery of the perpetrator and his punishment ; to do this would have necessitated an exact juridical investigation of the circumstances whereby the whole scarcely moral facts would have come to light. In order to avoid this the Emperor had decided to admit suicide, which perhaps is much worse and more humiliating ; but suicide could be explained by insanity.

'Herr Galimberti, who probably has good sources, shares these views : he has nevertheless immediately accepted the official version in order to save both the Pope as well the Court here great difficulties. He even sticks to this version *vis-à-vis* everybody.

'Under the seal of secrecy he has, however, told me the following. The gun-shot wound of the Crown Prince did not go from right to left, as had been declared officially, and would have been natural for suicide, but from left behind the ear towards the top of the head, where the bullet came out again. Also other wounds had been found on the body. The destruction of the upper skull was indeed so explained that the revolver had been held quite close to the head and that the escaping gun powder gases had wrought this destruction ; this effect however is doubtful. The revolver which was found next to the bed had not belonged to the Crown Prince ; all six shots had been fired.

'The shotgun wound of the young girl was not found in the temple as has been maintained so far but on top of the head. She too is said to have shown other wounds.

'These details had been given to the Nuncio by the Grand Duke of Tuscany and also by other people.

'That many circumstances speak in favour of pre-meditated suicide cannot be brought into line with all this. Nor that the Crown Prince had announced his death in advance by letters which had demonstrably been written while still in Vienna, and it is indeed not likely had a struggle preceded his death that he should have had sufficient time to write to Herr von Szögyenyi and to send him his keys which he has shown me on the morning of February 1st. To be sure I have not seen the letter.

'I may add that I know now for sure that Count Hoyos and the Prince Coburg had seen *the two bodies* [underlined in the original] immediately after breaking down the door and that the Count really believed that it was strychnine poisoning in which case also haemorrhage is supposed to take place, and that he hurried to Vienna to report without convincing himself in greater detail. Both Majesties have learned this version and believed it until next morning. Therefore the attempt had been made to ascribe death to heart failure. . . .'[8]

In this report two different statements must be distin-guished, Reuss's summary of public opinion and Galimberti's information. It is remarkable that the Nuncio should have had information which fitted so well with the popular belief. While the importance of this report cannot be denied, most of the underlying facts cannot stand close scrutiny. In the first place, if the Catholic Church, as the Protestant Reuss asserted, had been so strict as to condemn any adulterer as living in concubinage and to refuse him a Christian burial, quite a number of members of the Imperial house would have been buried as heathens. Reuss's argument is very weak. Just as weak is the next that the Emperor would have refrained from seeing that his son's murderer was punished, because a prosecution in court might have exhibited some 'scarcely moral facts'. To judge by what is known of Francis Joseph's character he would have preferred to admit his son's fornications than his tendency to insanity.

Galimberti's assertions would have to be taken more seriously were it not for two circumstances : he mentioned both the number of bullets used and that the story of the alleged murder was confirmed by the Grand Duke of Tuscany. With regard to the number of bullets the Cardinal's knowledge cannot have been very accurate or well founded. The Court Official Slatin told in his account [9] that, shortly after the tragedy while he was at Mayerling making an inventory, Galimberti came along and told him that he had to pray in the room where Rudolph had died. Later there was a conversation between the Nuncio and Slatin which was made rather difficult by the fact that the Cardinal did not speak German and Slatin spoke no Italian. Neither apparently thought of conversing in French and they were thus forced to use some sort of dog-Latin ; Slatin gave the following account of their talk : 'As I soon realised the main purpose of his visit was not prayer, but investigation, particularly whether Baroness Vetsera had in fact been at Mayerling. This was then rather well known, but had not yet been admitted. Consequently one of his questions which had stuck in my mind because of its originality, was "Quam multi globuli", how many bullets had there been in the revolver. I had never handled the revolver and could consequently answer without qualms "Nescio" [I do not know]. Otherwise I would have been certainly trapped by the jovial, but wily prince of the Church.' [10]

This rather strange way of fishing for information does

not suggest much knowledge of the facts, and while he may have acquired better information later, it is legitimate to doubt its authenticity. This doubt is reinforced by his mention of the Grand Duke of Tuscany as a source. According to the Grand Duke's son, later Herr Wölfling (he renounced his rights as a member of the Imperial house), the Grand Duke had told him at the time that Rudolph had been beaten to death with a champagne bottle.[11] Apparently therefore this source is not reliable. Generally, Galimberti, while well liked as a moderate and mild Nuncio, was also fond of gossip and Reuss seems to have been taken in by his talk.

There is only one point in Galimberti's account which gives food for thought, and which was accordingly stressed in Dr. Hollaender's study : the gunshot wound. The undeniable fact that Rudolph's cranium had been largely destroyed by the shot would not by itself be surprising, had not the right half been destroyed, where, according to the post-mortem findings, the bullet entered the skull. The well-known Court Painter Angeli told Count Monts, Reuss's chargé d'affaires, that 'the whole right temple was smashed'.[12] Anybody who has ever fired a shot knows that the exit wound is much bigger than that made by the entry of the bullet. If the shot, as Galimberti asserted, had been fired from the left the destruction wrought by it would be consistent with the actual facts and the Cardinal's statement in this point seems much more probable than the official version.

It is the great merit of Dr. Hollaender's study that he has drawn attention to the only point where Galimberti's statement is relevant. In his discussion of the Mayerling tragedy, murder as the cause of death, so far the subject of backstairs gossip, has been raised to the level of historical research, but more evidence would be required before murder can be considered a serious possibility.

III

Whether he committed suicide or not, Rudolph had been fully determined to end his life before he set out for Mayerling. If he was murdered, it can only have happened within that brief margin of time between his last instructions to Loschek and the time when he was found dead. Hoyos's account of events is fully corroborated by Prince Coburg's letter to Queen Victoria. This view was also shared by the Prince of Wales who, basing his judgement on a report from Austria, emphatically contradicted Lord Salisbury, who believed the murder story, and who had expressed this belief to the Queen. The Prince of Wales wrote to his mother from Marlborough House on February 12th : '. . . you tell me that Ld Salisbury is positive that poor Rudolph and that unfortunate young lady were murdered — all I can say is that everything points to suicide — I have seen an Austrian gentleman who has just come from Vienna — & who is a personal friend of the Emperor & Empress and knew poor Rudolph since [his ? — word illegible] childhood who in the long conversation I had with him entirely corroborated all Sir A. Paget wrote to you — even giving more details — It seems poor Rudolph has had suicide on the brain for some time past — he wrote letters saying he was going to die — & the poor young lady wrote the same to her family — He shot her first — then decked her out with flowers — & then blew his brains out — & he had only half an hour for all this — He wrote to his Mother, wife, youngest sister 2 cousins &

some personal friends but not to his Father & I am afraid
that some of his letters were quite incoherent — Nobody
knew that the young lady was with him but his valet.
The latter seems to have had orders from the Emperor not
to leave him alone — but he peremptorily ordered him
away — agst the poor Man's wishes before the deed was
done — My friend told me that there was some unknown
reason why he committed suicide & he does not believe
that it was on account of the young lady. It has been
ascertained that on January 13th. he seduced her & committed the last fatal act on 30th! There are details I could
tell you — which I cannot write — which clearly shew
complete aberration of the mind for some time past —
the whole story is like a bad dream & I can think of
nothing else — . . .' [13]

It is the suicide which has to be explained, the reasons
found and the motives laid bare which drove the heir to
the throne of one of the Great Powers to such an untimely
death. One reason, frequently quoted, that Rudolph quar-
relled with his father over the question of his divorce, is
not fully convincing. It is asserted that Rudolph applied
to the Pope for an annulment of his marriage, and that the
Pope informed the Emperor of the request. No such
application can be found in the Vatican Archives [14] and
this is also confirmed by Galimberti. Sir Augustus Paget
reported to the Queen about the rumour: 'Sir A. Paget
has not been able to ascertain any confirmation of this
[story], of which the Nuncio at all events, he is enabled to
say, knows nothing'. [15]

Szögyenyi was even more categorical in the denial
which he gave to Sir Augustus. 'It may further interest
Her Majesty to know that Monsieur de Szögyenyi whom
I saw yesterday gave me the most unqualified contradiction

to the report that the late Crown Prince had ever applied to the Pope respecting a divorce from the Archduchess Stephanie, and stated equally positively that there had never been any altercation between the Emperor & his Imp. Highness.'[16]

Reuss also discussed this possibility with Galimberti, who seemed to have been more expansive with the German Ambassador than with Sir Augustus. Reuss reported : 'Herr Galimberti did not in the least credit the rumour which was hawked around frequently during the last few weeks that the late Crown Prince had considered a divorce and written to the Pope of it. Nothing went through his hands which was connected with it. He opinioned it was not impossible that the Pope, if such a letter existed, had sent it to Brussels and that the Emperor was informed from that end. I have no reason to believe this rumour, even if the Crown Prince was very unhappy in his married life.'[17] The story of the quarrel is contained — if we restrict our investigation to serious reports and leave out conjecture and backstair talk — in Berta Zuckerkandl's memoirs and Lamsdorff's journal. Frau Zuckerkandl's story has been dealt with in Chapter XI. Lamsdorff's account requires more attention : 'Labanov writes that when a few days before the catastrophe Franz Josef categorically refused the Archduke his consent to his divorce, the Prince did not mention suicide, but only said : "After this I know what I have left to do", while His Majesty apparently answered, "Do what you like, but I shall never agree to your divorce"'.[18] This is not very convincing; moreover in the same passage there is a report that Herr von Szögyenyi had stated to Kantakuzene that 'people have spoken about a violent scene which took place between the Emperor and his son. But even if we assume that this was so, this would not have appeared in the eyes of M. Szögyenyi a sufficient reason for the desperate resolution of the Crown Prince. He (S.) does not attach any more significance to the stories of an unhappy marriage, of the divorce for which the Archduke was pressing, etc. etc. . . . In his view the truth must be sought elsewhere.' [19]

Had a scene between father and son taken place shortly before Rudolph's death the Emperor could not have spoken to Reuss as he did shortly after the tragedy. 'The Emperor then spoke to me of the death of his son, whose cause was even to-day quite unfathomable to him. . . . It was now maintained that the Crown Prince had been very excited. The Emperor had noticed nothing of it. "He was such a clever man, had such a good head, was such a faithful and good son. I have never had any complaint about him. And now . . ." [Three dots in the original.] The decision to die was, as was shown by the letters, premeditated. The Emperor seems entirely incapable of getting over it that he had left his father without any farewell, not even a written one. . . .' [20] To the Bavarian Minister the Emperor was even briefer, but no less to the point : 'He was always a dear good son and only gave me joy'.[20]

It has been stated repeatedly in this biography that Francis Joseph was not imaginative ; neither was he deceitful, and both statements quoted have the ring of sincerity. The story of the quarrel between father and son which is supposed to have precipitated the suicide, while supported by more credible evidence than the murder story, must also be considered unlikely.

There is one argument in favour of the assumption of a quarrel with the Emperor — Rudolph left no farewell

letter to his father. This might have been due to a more
or less heated altercation. The Crown Prince could have
discussed his intention to separate from Stephanie without
sending a formal application to the Pope. The Emperor
would have objected strongly. But this is not necessarily
the cause. It may well have been that Rudolph saw in the
omission of a farewell letter to his father a means of
recording his protest either against the many humiliations
he had caused him by his lack of imagination, or it may
have been a demonstration against the Emperor's policy,
or both. A discussion, no matter how heated, can hardly
be considered a reason for Rudolph's suicide. He knew
his father well enough to realise that divorce would be
unacceptable to him and that, if he was ever to be given
permission, he would have to repeat his request for it many
times. Again, as in the murder story, the evidence is,
although somewhat stronger, yet not convincing enough
to lead to the assumption that his desire for a divorce from
Stephanie, foiled by his father's stubborn refusal, had driven
Rudolph to Mayerling.

The Prince of Wales had stated in his letter to the
Queen that Rudolph was out of his mind when he committed suicide. It is, on account of the abridged report on
the post-mortem, impossible to state positively that he was
of unsound mind. Neither is there any witness who would
give any indication that madness had become apparent.
Prince Coburg in his letter to Queen Victoria stated that
it was possible 'that his fall from his horse on November
19th had brought his brains into disorder, at least he complained frequently of headache and stomach trouble, but
it was not the only reason for his mental disorder'.[21]
Szögyenyi in his many talks with the Ambassadors did not
once refer to a positive sign of insanity, but only to the

possibility indicated in the post-mortem, as, for instance, when he said to Reuss 'that the suicide as well as the previous eccentricities of the Prince and the consequent total exhaustion lead back to the abnormal skull found at the autopsy'.[22] In his talks with Sir Augustus Paget and Prince Kantakuzene, on the other hand, he made no mention of the post-mortem findings. Thus insanity too is ruled out as an immediate cause while no more conclusive evidence is available. How far was the argument of insanity used, not only to explain Rudolph's suicide, but also to discredit his Liberal views ?

IV

All ambassadors tried to get information from Szögyeny, but he was not always consistent in his explanations. In his talk with Reuss he had admitted that some pathological state of the brain, unnoticed while Rudolph was alive, must have been the cause of his death, but in his talk with Sir Augustus he confessed that he could not think of any reason. 'Monsieur de Szögyenyi . . . added in the most earnest and truthful tone "Dieu seul sait quel ait pu être le motif de cette funeste décision ; sur ma parole d'honneur personne ne sait rien qui puisse l'expliquer".' (God only knows what could have been the motive of this mournful decision ; on my word of honour, nobody knows anything that could explain it.) [23] Yet he suggested an explanation in his talk with Prince Kantakuzene : 'He has always considered that he knew the Prince better than anybody else, but now this does not help him at all ; he finds no solution. "There are many", he suddenly exclaims, "serious statesmen, who ascribe this misfortune exclusively to political causes. In their opinion the Crown Prince had so compromised himself by his more and more openly manifested enmity to the current policy of the Viennese cabinet and its allies, his position in regard to the Emperor William II and Germany had so deteriorated, and a return had become so impossible, that he could not fail to become aware that he was becoming a source of serious difficulties and even dangers for his country, if he was going to continue on this path.'" [24]

In this talk for the first time there is an indication of an acceptable motive for Rudolph's suicide — politics. Politics had always been of vital importance to him. Murder or suicide — the Crown Prince had arrived at his decision before going to Mayerling, and it is unthinkable that political affairs were not a decisive factor.

There are a number of serious, though not conclusive, grounds which lead to the assumption that Rudolph was involved in a Hungarian conspiracy occasioned by the Defence Bill, and that he died because his 'resolution is sicklied o'er with the pale cast of thought'. All his farewell letters indicate that he felt compelled to die. To Stephanie he had written: 'I approach death calmly, it alone can save my good name'.[25] To Szögyenyi, 'I must die', and the same to his sister Valerie, whom he also advised to leave Austria.[26] This necessity to die is also expressed in the letter to his mother, where he also mentioned that he was not worthy to be his father's son.[27]

In this context the remark made to Hoyos on his last evening at Mayerling, when Rudolph showed three telegrams, 'The matter is disastrous', must be mentioned. Count Pista Károlyi, to whom it referred, went to Vienna on January 30th to see the Crown Prince. By the time he left Budapest, it was not yet known that he was dead, but Károlyi was told the sad news when the train stopped at Poszony (now Bratislava), whereupon he immediately returned to Budapest. This matter seemed important enough for a special secret file labelled : 'Count Pista Károlyi's journey to Crown Prince Archduke Rudolph with reference to the Defence Bill in the Hungarian Parliament', to be kept at the Ministry of the Imperial House. In 1899 this file was removed and never replaced, although for a long time it was listed with the secret documents.[28] As is well known, all telegrams sent or received by members of the Imperial House were checked by the Post Minister.[29] Thus copies of the telegrams which the Crown Prince received shortly before he died may well have been kept in this secret file.

Could not documents concerning some Hungarian plan have been among those which either Rudolph or Szögyenyi burned ? It is noteworthy that in his talk with Prince Kantakuzene, Szögyenyi had said 'that he did not see what greater misfortune than the death of the Archduke Rudolph could have befallen the Monarchy. Its consequences, particularly in Hungary, would be deeper and more dangerous than was imagined. The Hungarians had been wholeheartedly devoted to the Crown Prince : they had accepted and loved warmly the Emperor and the Empress, but of the other members of the House of Austria they knew only that they were disposed against Hungary.'[30] As a civil servant Szögyenyi was hardly likely to have been a member of the conspiracy, but he may have known of its existence. That Rudolph's last thoughts must have concerned Hungary is shown by the fact that his farewell letter to Szögyenyi, who spoke German as fluently as Hungarian, was written in the Magyar tongue.[31] The country referred to in this letter — 'all good fortune to our adored Fatherland'—was consequently Hungary, not Austria-Hungary.

It cannot be denied that Rudolph behaved strangely before leaving the Hofburg for Mayerling on that fateful Monday. He had been absent-minded when an expected letter had arrived for him, and had behaved even more strangely when he got the telegram which drew from him the exclamation, 'It has to be!' According to a report by the German Military Attaché Deines, 'Rudolph said to his Chief of Staff that he could stand it no longer in town, that he had a severe headache and he positively ran down the stairs to get to the carriage . . . '.[32] All this would point to alarming or disquieting information in the telegram, and it would be strange indeed if the contents of the telegram had not been ascertained after Rudolph's death. Yet it is neither published, nor is it available in the Archives. The assumption that this and the later telegrams must have had some bearing on the suicide, and have been of a character which precluded the disclosure of their contents, seems justified. There was nothing of political importance under discussion at the time except the Hungarian Defence Bill, and the conclusion that Rudolph was somehow involved in the unrest it engendered seems evident.

Whether or not we accept this — and it must be admitted that the evidence while strong is not conclusive — the basic fact remains. Rudolph had been for long utterly dissatisfied with political conditions, the policy pursued by his father and the government. The hopelessness of the situation had in earlier years required all the optimism he could muster. The urgency of the frustrating, torturing political problems had increased, and his tormented nerves, together with his diminished health, may well have made obstacles appear even more formidable than they were. To escape the inevitable compulsion of having to watch helplessly Austria's future being systematically undermined he may have agreed to become King of Hungary. Now lacking the strength, morally and physically, to go on, he died. It seems possible, even probable, that he had added to the troubles which beset him by becoming involved in a Hungarian conspiracy ; but this is not decisive. Even could the theory of murder be proved it would still be true that Rudolph was killed by despair.

     •   •   •   •   •

Mary made his decision easier. They had talked together frequently of dying. The thought of death had been with Rudolph often since his childhood, and Mary had divined his innermost thoughts as no one else had done. M. Gabriel Dubray, her French tutor, recalled how a little before her death she had discussed with him the question of suicide, and had stoutly defended everyone's right to end his own life [33]; and her mother remembered how a few weeks before the end Mary had persuaded her singing master to study with her two songs, whose words he considered very melancholy for so young a girl. But she felt that they expressed her feelings so well :

> What drew you so powerfully to me ?
> A tear that told me
> How your soul in its innermost secrecy
> Suffers untold torment.

and

> Love stronger yet than death
> Will cut with force the evil's snare —
> Love stronger yet than death
> Will in the deepest sorrow of its heart
> Attain the friend's eternal bliss.

     •   •   •   •   •

While Rudolph was not mad, he was aware of the streak of insanity in his mother's family, and he probably feared that he too might become a victim. He had seen the Emperor Frederick III on his sick-bed after so many years of waiting, passing like a shadow without trace. Would madness do to him what cancer had done to Frederick ? Could he expect to have enough strength, enough time, to resuscitate what had always been his faith — Liberalism?

With Frederick Liberalism had died in Germany and reaction reigned. In Austria Taaffe would be overcome not by Liberalism, but by the new barbarism of Schönerer and Lueger. Queen Victoria wrote of Rudolph soon after his death : 'The poor dear Crown Prince was singularly gifted and accomplished, and with large liberal views & was looked upon as one likely to withstand the 2 wicked Bismarcks' tyranny and dangerous views'.[34] She was right ; he was singularly gifted, could see so clearly what was to be done, but lacked the strength and singleness of purpose to surmount the difficulties which surrounded him on all sides.

During the Revolution of 1848 Liberalism had still been weak in Central Europe ; it was defeated and suppressed. In the 'seventies it was essential to economic progress ; it had to be tolerated but only until it had served its purpose. Its appeal had increased, and it became a danger to the reactionary forces who wanted economic, but not political, progress. By the middle 'eighties it had served its purpose and was extirpated by all means fair and foul like a canker-ous growth in the body politic. As the Counter Reforma-tion tried to exterminate Protestantism in Central Europe, and forced Protestants to become Catholics, so now Liberals were hounded both in Germany and in Austria.

Rudolph was aware of this, but with his highly bred body and highly strung mind he had neither the equanimity nor the strength to rally the scattered forces of Liberalism which still remained. With him died all hope for Austria as a liberal universal power, and the idea of a progressive Central Europe has been submerged for more than half a century.

REFERENCES

1. *Letters to Frau Schratt*, p. 135. It is not without interest that only part of this letter was kept by Frau Schratt ; the first part, which also apparently dealt with Rudolph's death, was probably destroyed by her. This is the only one of her letters from the Emperor found to be incomplete.

2. Royal Archives, Windsor, Z 498 23.

3. Royal Archives, Windsor, Z 498 38.

4. P.R.O., *op. cit.* No. 149 and Hollaender, *op. cit.*

5. Lonyay, *op. cit.* p. 259.

6. Letter from Major Fritsche to Oskar Freiherr von Mitis, with Rudolph's papers in the Staatsarchiv, Vienna.

7. Lamzdorfa, *op. cit.* pp. 178 f.

8. P.R.O., *op. cit.* No. 68, also quoted in Hollaender, *op. cit.*

9. Slatin, *op. cit.*

10. Slatin, *op. cit.*

11. Leopold Wölfling, *Habsburger unter sich* (Leipzig, 1921), pp. 80 ff.

12. *Monts Erinnerungen*, p. 108.

13. Royal Archives, Windsor, Z 498 56.

14. Letter from Monsignore Giusti, Assistant Director, Papal Archives, dated Nov. 13th, 1956.

15. Royal Archives, Windsor, Z 498 57.

16. Letter to Sir Henry Ponsonby of February 19th, 1889, Royal Archives, Windsor, Z 498 61.

17. P.R.O., *op. cit.* No. 57, also Hollaender, *op. cit.*

18. Lamzdorfa, *op. cit.* p. 178.

19. Lamzdorfa, *op. cit.* pp. 178 f.

20. Viktor Bibl, *op. cit.* pp. 79 f.

21. Royal Archives, Windsor, Z 498 52.

22. Bibl, *op. cit.* p. 81.

23. Letter from Sir A. Paget to Queen Victoria, February 14th, 1889, Royal Archives, Windsor.

24. Lamzdorfa, *op. cit.* pp. 178 ff.

25. Lonyay, *op. cit.* p. 248, and Corti, *Franz Josef*, Vol. III, p. 97.

26. Bibl, *op. cit.* p. 81.
27. Corti, *Elisabeth*, p. 422.
28. Mitis, *op. cit.* p. 242.
29. Mitis, *op. cit.* p. 416.
30. Lamzdorfa, *op. cit.* pp. 178 f.
31. *The Times*, February 6th, 1889.
32. Quoted in Hollaender, *op. cit.*
33. *Letters to Frau Schratt*, p. 138.
34. Letter to Lord Salisbury of February 3rd, 1889, Salisbury Archives, Oxford. Quoted in Hollaender, *op. cit.*

INDEX

Index

Index

52 f., 128-30, 156, 206 ; visits
Spain, 53 ; makes first Will, 53 ;
and Count Taaffe, 54, 65 f., 78,
121, 123, 125, 176 ; chooses bride,
60 ; visits Brussels, 60, 64 ; engagement, 60, 62 f., 64 ; Rudolph
and Stephanie compared, 61 ; relations with Stephanie, 61, 65, 67 f.,
73, 77 f., 83 f., 85, 89-95, 157,
174 f., 214, 220 f. ; loneliness, 64 f.,
94 f., 103 ; wedding, 68-71 ;
honeymoon at Laxenburg, 71 f. ;
belief in Austria's Balkan mission,
75-9, 89, 142-5, 146, 148 f.,
150 f., 154, 161, 191 ; later
writings, 78-80, 81, 88 f., 134 f.,
139 f., 148 f., 184, 186 ; first
political memorandum (1881), 78-
84 ; foreign policy, 81, 119-21,
131, 137, 141-52, 153, 157 f., 158 f.,
160 f., 165, 193 f., 219 f. ; lacks
responsible position, 85 ; shooting
and nature observation, 86-8, 186 ;
relations with Szeps, 89, 113-20,
122-4, 145, 162, 171 f., 180, 195,
200 f., 215 f., 224 f. ; first Balkan
tour, 89, 141-5 ; increasing representative duties, 90, 138 ; delight
at prospect of heir, 90 f. ; birth
of daughter, 91, 136 ; transferred
from Prague to Vienna, 91, 136 ;
ancestry, 96-9 ; relations with
Ludwig II of Bavaria, 100-6 ;
Ludwig's death and funeral, 106 f.,
157 ; serious illness, 106, 157 ;
police supervision, 115 f., 117 f.,
175, 230, 236 ; persecution, 117,
126, 128-30 ; alleged plan to
crown him King of Hungary, 126-
128, 282 ; relations with Hungary,
126-8, 133, 137, 154, 279-82 ;
opens Vienna Electricity Exhibition, 134 f. ; moves into the Hofburg, 136 ; and anti-Monarchical
movement in Austria, 138-9 ; *The
Austro - Hungarian Monarchy in
Word and Picture*, 139-41 ; awarded
honorary Ph.D., 140 f. ; and
Balkan railways, 142 f. ; relations
with Baron Hirsch, 142 f., 195,
201 ; second Balkan tour, 147 ; at
meeting of Emperor and Tsar,
Kremsier, 147 ; second political
memorandum (1886), 152-5, 165,

191 ; mishap at shooting party,
156 ; censures Archduke John
Salvator, 158 ; Reuss reports on
him to Bismarck, 159 f. ; meets
Clemenceau, 160 f. ; visits Berlin
for Emperor's 90th birthday, 166 ;
Duke Ludwig in Bavaria reports
on him to Bismarck, 167 ; William
II offends in Potsdam speech,
168 f. ; signs of frustration, 172,
174-6, 176 f., 181 f., 193, 214, 282 ;
relations with Mizzi Kaspar, 175,
218, 224, 236 ; signs of moral
decadence, 177 f., 185 f. ; takes
morphia, 179 f., 188 ; shows signs
of neurosis, 180 f., 283 ; and
Emperor William I's death, 183 f. ;
and funeral, 185 ; attacked by
Schönerer, 188 ; and his sister
Valerie's marriage, 190 ; visits
Bosnia and Hercegovina, 190-2 ;
visit of Prince of Wales, 194-7,
205 f. ; visit of William II, 195-7 ;
widespread newspaper attacks, 197-
203, 219 ; meets Mary Vetsera,
205 f., 208, 210 f. ; and Marie
Larisch, 209 ; relations with Mary
Vetsera, 214, 217 f., 238-41, 282 ;
death of his grandfather, 218 ;
proposed visit to Berlin and Russia,
219 ; alleged wish for divorce,
220 f., 266, 274-7 ; arrangements
for shoot at Mayerling, 221, 224 ;
and Hungarian Defence Bill, 221,
225 f., 237, 238, 279 f. ; dines with
Sir Augustus and Lady Paget,
221 f. ; and William II's birthday
party at German Embassy, 222-5 ;
and French elections, 226 f. ; visit
of Alexander of Battenberg, 227 ;
leaves for Mayerling, 230 f., 231 ;
reported visit to Countess Larisch,
232 ; entertains Count Hoyos and
Prince Coburg at Mayerling,
233 f., 235, 236 f. ; does not attend
family dinner-party, 235, 236 ;
shows Count Hoyos telegrams
from Budapest, 237 ; death, 240-
246 ; farewell letters, 240, 246-8 ;
Emperor and Empress informed of
his death, 243-7 ; official announcement of death, 244 f., 247, 250 f. ;
wish to be buried beside Mary
Vetsera, 246, 258 ; body removed

Index

THE END

PRINTED BY R. & R. CLARK, LTD., EDINBURGH